D0914192

Superheroes and Critical Animal Studies

Critical Animal Studies and Theory

Series Editors: Anthony J. Nocella II and Scott C. Hurley

This book series is a project of the Institute for Critical Animal Studies, www.criticalanimalstudies.org.

This series addresses human relations with other animals in the context of socio-political relations and economic systems of power. It sees liberation not as a single-issue phenomenon, but rather as inseparably related to human rights, peace and justice, and environmental issues and movements. Rather than emphasizing abstract theory, the series links theory with practice and emphasizes the immense importance of animal advocacy for a humane, democratic, peaceful, and sustainable world. Taking an interdisciplinary approach to questions of social change, moral progress, and ecological sustainability, the *Critical Animal Studies and Theory* series connects with disciplines such as feminism, globalization, economics, science, history, education, critical race theory, environmental studies, media studies, ecopedagogy, art, literature, disability, gender, political science, sociology, religion, anthropology, philosophy, and cultural studies. The series will serve as a foundational project for one of the fastest growing and most exciting new fields of scholarship, Critical Animal Studies. Rooted in critical theory as well as the animal advocacy movement, the series argues for an interdisciplinary approach to understanding our relationships with nonhuman animals. Rejecting the notion that nonhuman animals do not have a voice, the series stresses that nonhuman animals do have agency, and, thus argues for an animal standpoint. In keeping with the principles of Critical Animal Studies, the series encourages progressive and committed scholarship and views exploitation of nonhuman animals, such as animal research and studies, as interrelated with other oppressions such as class, gender, and racism. Against apolitical scholarship, the series encourages engaged critical praxis, promotes liberation of all animals and challenges all systems of domination.

Titles in Series

Animals and War: Confronting Animal Studies and Theory edited by Anthony J. Nocella II, Colin Salter, and Judy K. C. Bentley

Screening the Nonhuman: Representations of Animal Others in the Media edited by Amber E. George and J. L. Schatz

Weaving Nature, Animals and Disability for Eco-ability: The Intersectionality of Critical Animal, Disability, and Environmental Studies edited by Anthony J. Nocella, Amber E. George and J. L. Schatz

Superheroes and Critical Animal Studies: The Heroic Beasts of Total Liberation edited by J. L. Schatz and Sean Parson.

Superheroes and Critical Animal Studies

The Heroic Beasts of Total Liberation

Edited by
J. L. Schatz and Sean Parson

Foreword by
Vas Stanescu

LEXINGTON BOOKS
Lanham • Boulder • New York • London

Published by Lexington Books
An imprint of The Rowman & Littlefield Publishing Group, Inc.
4501 Forbes Boulevard, Suite 200, Lanham, Maryland 20706
www.rowman.com

Unit A, Whitacre Mews, 26-34 Stannary Street, London SE11 4AB

Copyright © 2018 by Lexington Books

All rights reserved. No part of this book may be reproduced in any form or by any electronic or mechanical means, including information storage and retrieval systems, without written permission from the publisher, except by a reviewer who may quote passages in a review.

British Library Cataloguing in Publication Information Available

Library of Congress Cataloging-in-Publication Data

Names: Schatz, J. L., editor. | Parson, Sean, editor.
Title: Superheroes and critical animal studies : the heroic beasts of total
   liberation / edited by J.L. Schatz and Sean Parson.
Description: Lanham, Maryland : Lexington Books, [2017] | Includes
   bibliographical references and index.
Identifiers: LCCN 2017046395 (print) | LCCN 2017046223 (ebook) | ISBN
   9781498549271 (Electronic) | ISBN 9781498549264 (cloth : alk. paper)
Subjects: LCSH: Comic books, strips, etc—Moral and ethical aspects. |
   Animals in literature. | Superheroes in literature. | Humanism in
   literature. | Animal rights.
Classification: LCC PN6712 (print) | LCC PN6712 .S84 2017 (ebook) | DDC
   741.5/384—dc23
LC record available at https://lccn.loc.gov/2017046395

♾ ™ The paper used in this publication meets the minimum requirements of American National Standard for Information Sciences—Permanence of Paper for Printed Library Materials, ANSI/NISO Z39.48-1992.

Printed in the United States of America

We dedicate this book to the human and nonhuman victims of the agriculture, medical, and entertainment industry as well as the activists and artists who have dedicated their lives to exposing and stopping these injustices.

Contents

Foreword

Vas Stanescu

What, one might ask, do superheroes have to do with critical animal studies? On the one hand, animal studies and the mistreatment of nonhuman animals are viewed as a deeply serious and important issue. On the other hand, superheroes, generally speaking, are not according to contemporary cultural biases. Are we to conclude that these authors and editors, therefore, do not understand the importance of what is routinely being done to nonhuman animals? That they are unaware of the abuse nonhuman animals suffer? I would say, instead, perhaps people have failed to understand the cultural importance of superheroes. *Spiderman Homecoming* just recently opened; its box office for the opening weekend was over 117 million dollars from the over four thousand locations that it played (Kelley 2017). And how many movies have we now had, just about Spider-Man alone? To say that comics have become mainstream would be an understatement; comic culture is rapidly simply becoming "culture," as can be witnessed in Sean Parson's chapter within this book.

The truth is that the human relationship to animals and the nonhuman world runs deep and that our critique of this dysfunctional and violent relationship must run just as deep. I remember in my own childhood rooting for "Poison Ivy" (an "eco-terrorist") in *Batman* comics and "Cheetah" (another "eco-terrorist") in *Wonder Woman*. I remember, much later, reading *Animal Man*—an explicitly animal rights–themed comic—in college and the profound influence that text had on me. The movie *Okja* was recently released on Netflix. It is purportedly a "sci-fi" based movie, and yet its critique of "humane farming" and meat production could not be clearer. What would the effects of a movie which took Poison Ivy or Cheetah as explicit heroes look like? How would a film remake of *Animal Man* help to shape our culture? If comic culture is rapidly simply becoming "culture," how can we understand comics to include animal rights ideas and themes?

I would say that these questions matter because at their core what comics represent are our own myths to ourselves: Superman, Batman, Wonder Woman, the X-Men—these are mythic characters. Their battles become our battles; their message becomes our own message. Right now young (and not so young) children might leave a movie imagining battling criminals on the street. Could they imagine stopping people who abuse animals? Could they imagine growing up to become "crime fighters" against gigantic agri-business corporations? What do we want our cultural myths to become? What—exactly—are the lessons that comics teach us about ourselves? This very question is the subject of the chapter by J. L. Schatz within this collection.

While in graduate school, I had the opportunity to talk to Scott Bukatman, one of the most well-known academics on comics and graphic novels, about his own research on superheroes. He said that what he found most interesting is that while comic book superheroes are traditionally seen as perfect images of traditional masculinity—strong, brave, and muscular—at the same time, there was always a second, hidden message in their appeal. For example, he highlighted the enjoyment of getting to wear fabulous costumes in bright colors. Are the young people (and, in particular, the young men) reading the comic always imagining themselves in the ideas of stereotypical masculinity? Or, are they—perhaps secretly—also imagining themselves getting to wear some fantastic outfits? His point is that while comics, on the surface, would seem to uphold traditional norms (and, in part, they certainly do); at the same time they always possess a "subversive" element as well (personal conversation).

So, too, I would say that a similar kind of "hidden" message permeates all of comics. On the surface Superman, Batman, Spider-Man, Wonder Woman and the rest are paragons of "Law and Order." They support the State. Superman flies around dressed in, in essence, a literal American flag. And, yet, at the same time, they are all "outlaws." They all call into question: Is there a call for justice, for action that goes beyond the usual boundaries of the legal? Superheroes may—by and large—fight criminals, but in order to do so they must go "outside of the law." They must become—themselves—"outlaws." The question that superheroes raise is not the question of the police versus the criminal but the tension between an "outlaw" and a criminal, assuming the reader identifies with the heroes and not the villains of these stories.

Such are, I think, important questions we must begin to ask in terms of nonhuman animals. By law, all nonhuman animals are property. A chicken has the same rights as a chair, a shoe, a piece of fabric. The pots and pans that people use to cook animals have—in many cases—the same legal rights as the animals being cooked in them. The coop that holds a chicken has—by and large—the same rights as the chickens inside of them. In fact, under federal law all birds, all rodents, all reptiles, all fish are not even—legally speaking—"animals." Incredibly, the vast majority of animals who live our world are not, yet, legally "animals" at all.

In such a world, to believe that a chicken is different than a chicken coop is to inherently be an "outlaw." Even if no law is ever broken, it is to try to believe in a call to morality, or justice, that exist beyond the usual boundaries of the legal. In other words, it is—at its core—a call to become an "outlaw" in order to be able to battle the actual "criminals" who run factory farms, make fur, or produce leather. Even if the first category may still be beyond the scope of the law and the second still fully legal. And, increasingly—because of laws such as the Animal Enterprise Terrorism Act and industry funded Ag-Gag laws—to take any action at all in favor of animals—filming a farm, engaging in whistling blowing, even hosting a website—is becoming reclassified as a crime. One of the first edited volumes in Critical Animal Studies (CAS) about Animal Liberation Front was entitled *Terrorists or Freedom Fighters?* Perhaps, instead, in view of this edited volume, we could rephrase the question *Terrorists or Superheroes?*

It has long been my belief that animal rights and liberation is an argument without a response. All of the rational arguments have been settled years ago. As far as I've been able to tell the arguments first raised by Peter Singer, Tom Regan, Carol Adams and many others in the 1970s and 1980s have remained just as unanswered today as they were when they were first raised decades ago (Best 2004). Admittedly, there are intermittent updates that have to be re-debated ("humane meat," "in vitro meat" etc.). However, by and large, we are not winning the battle for animals, not because we are not "winning" the arguments; we are not winning the battle because we have yet to "win" the culture. But to "win" the culture, we have to first to understand it, and then—as is the ultimate goal for everything that CAS studies—to start to actually *change* it. As comic culture is increasingly simply becoming "culture," I can think of no better place to start then here, on the questions that this timely and important edited volume have started to raise.

WORKS CITED

Adams, Carol J. 2015. *The Sexual Politics of Meat: A Feminist-Vegetarian Critical Theory.* New York: Bloomsbury Academic.

Best, Steven, and Anthony J. Nocella. 2004. *Terrorists or Freedom Fighters?: Reflections on the Liberation of Animals.* New York: Lantern Books. 2004.

Kelley, Seth. 2017. "Box Office: 'Spider-Man: Homecoming' Slings to Massive $117 Million Domestic Opening" Variety. July 9, 2017. http://variety.com/2017/film/box-office/spider-man-homecoming-box-office-opening-weekend-2-1202490552/

Regan, Tom. 2004. *The Case for Animal Rights*. Berkeley, CL: University of California Press.

Singer, Peter. 1997. *Animal Liberation*. New York: Avon Books.

Introduction

Saving the Planet through Total Liberation

The Need for Superheroes in Critical Animal Studies

J. L. Schatz and Sean Parson

THE PURPOSE AND INTENT OF OUR PROJECT

This collection of chapters is unlike other anthologies within either comic studies or Critical Animal Studies (CAS). While many works theorize about the importance of superheroes and comics within popular culture, and a growing number of books critically explore the intersection of human and nonhuman oppression, none have looked to put these two growing fields in dialogue with each other. Adding to that, this work, in the spirit of CAS, is not interested in just academic analysis but in translating that theory into action (Nocella II et al. 2014). This approach to bringing praxis into academia is not new. Rather this book builds upon the principles that came from the Institute of Critical Animal Studies (ICAS) that was founded in 2006, which itself was an outgrowth of the Center for Animal Liberation Affairs that was created five years earlier (George and Schatz 2016, xii). At the same time, this collection is also unlike many other works in CAS, most of which only focus on the real-world consequences of nonhuman exploitation and human injustice (Salter et al. 2015; Nocella 2014). Instead, this book theorizes popular culture through the lens of the superhero in order to examine the way representations tangibly shape speciesist institutions. While different chapters outline the ways superheroes and comics can either entrench or help dismantle forms of human supremacy, what they all have in common is the belief that representations matter. Ultimately, this book brings together the benefits of both fields in order to outline novel ways to alter the discursive landscape beyond just the page or the silver screen.

To be clear, CAS is not ignorant of the importance of media. For at least the past five years the annual ICAS conferences in both North America and Australia have included panels focusing on the media. Even as recently as 2017, Amber George wrote, "the analysis of nonhuman representations in cartoon media gives context to the wider social structures, cultural practices, and power hierarchies as they relate to gender, disability, and LGBTQIA+ identity" (132). However, while even presentations on anime have found their way into ICAS conferences and have been recognized for their contribution, presentations on superheroes are conspicuously absent, even though, as a genre, superheroes are dominating the Hollywood box office numbers. This is not unique to CAS as a field because, even as comic studies have gained traction within the academy, educational institutions and journals have had a tendency to favor more "serious minded" graphic novels while continually passing over the genre of superheroes (Hatfield, Heer, and Worcester 2013, xi). This focus on literature-type graphic novels has change in recent years as a range of innovative and provocative superhero collections have come out exploring a diversity of important topics from race (Nama 2011; Gateward and Jennings 2015; Howard and Jackson 2013) and gender (Cocca 2016; Gray and Kaklamanidou 2011; Madrid 2016) to disability (Alaniz 2014; Foss, Gray, and Whalen 2016) and queerness (Fawaz 2016). Nevertheless, the growth in superhero studies, while impressive in its scope, has often failed to question the human/animal dichotomy, and how it intersects with other forms of oppression as anything other than a prop to talk about human-centered values. Until such speciesism is ungrounded, total liberation will be impossible since it is a foundational element that ties together the webs of oppression (Best 2006).

The omission of superheroes from CAS scholarship is curious for at least four reasons. First, given how "super heroes such as Captain America came to be lasting symbols of patriotic America values," one would imagine there would be at least a handful of presenters or publications that would link superheroes with conversations on imperialism within CAS (Mercier 2008, 28). Second, beyond the ability to use comics to explore US imperialism, the comic industry has regularly focused on nonhuman animal politics in super-hero series like *Animal Man*, *We3*, and *Teenage Mutant Ninja Turtles*, among countless others. This wide range of nonhuman superhero comics provides plenty of ground for analysis. Third, given that ICAS was designed to promote engagement outside of the academy alongside younger scholars, one would imagine utilizing something as popular as superheroes would be valuable in reaching out to a wider range of activists. With the US box office alone bringing in over $4.76 billion in 2016, the superhero genre has quite a large appeal—presumably among a good chunk of graduate students (Trumbore 2017). Fourth, given the demand of ICAS to appeal toward individuals beyond the ivory tower, one would guess that the so-called non-serious-minded academics with something important to say about superheroes would have found their way into this global organization. ICAS acknowledges the importance of representations as evidenced by the publication of a previous book devoted exclusively to the topic discussed within this very series (George and Schatz 2016). Ultimately, it is odd that no one has yet found it as an ideal platform to talk about representations of justice—for both humans and nonhumans alike.

Of course, the failure of comic studies in general, and superhero studies in particular, to seriously take up the question of CAS is troubling as well. However, this too should largely be unsurprising because of how often nonhuman animals exist only as an absent referent or a metaphor for human subjugation, if they're even mentioned at all (Adams 1998). This is one of the many reasons why bridging the gap between these two fields is essential. For starters,

> [so] long as this humanist and speciesist structure of subjectivization remains intact, and as long as it is institutionally taken for granted that it is all right to systematically exploit and kill nonhuman animals simply because of their species, then the humanist discourse of species will always be available for use by some humans against other humans as well, to countenance violence against the social other of whatever species—or gender, or race, or class, or sexual difference. That point has been made graphically in texts like Carol Adams's *The Sexual Politics of Meat*, which, despite its problems, demonstrates that the humanist discourse of species not only makes possible the systematic killing of many billions of animals a year for food, product testing, and research but also provides a ready-made symbolic economy that overdetermines the representation of women, by transcoding the edible bodies of animals and the sexualized bodies of women within an overarching "logic of domination"—all compressed in what Derrida's recent work calls "carnophallogocentrism." (Wolfe 2003, 7–8)

This project seeks to unsettle the anthropocentrism that is currently at the heart of superhero studies by centralizing intersectional analysis to take seriously the interaction between human and nonhuman oppression. While many chapters will take up the warrants for the above claim further, the demand for thinking through CAS can quite literally mean the fate of the planet along with the billions of creatures that are being systemically oppressed for a handful of people to profit. Given this, there is likely no better genre than superheroes to talk about total liberation, because at this point it will likely take a hero to save the world from the many environmental disasters that industrial animal agricultural alone has caused (Nibert 2013).

Put simply, both CAS and superhero studies have much that could benefit from one another given their often-overlapping themes and general outsider status from the academy. By following in the footsteps of ICAS, which was able "to demonstrate how with very little money ... a new social movement can emerge," scholars interested in theorizing superheroes can tap into the potential of activists to give their theorization real meaning (Schatz, George, and Nocella II 2017, xx). There is no reason why activists wouldn't be readily drawn to such scholarship if oriented toward practice given the continual superhero motifs of protagonists struggling to save the planet, fight oppression, and promote justice.

> In fact, the question of what a superhero is has become central to our culture's understanding of itself and our future. The superhero genre has ... served as a useful metaphorical way of discussing immigration, Americanization, urbanization, American identity, changing conceptions of race and gender, individualism, capitalism, modernism, and so many other central cultural concerns. (Rosenberg and Coogan 2013, xvii–xviii)

Of course, chief among these "other central cultural concerns" is that of the nonhuman and educational modes of praxis designed to change the way readers tangibly interact with the world. Consumption is never neutral. It is always a political act whether it be the food we eat, the clothes we wear, the cleaners we use, or the comics we read.

Unfortunately, there are those who would contend that humans are obviously more intelligent than other animals and therefore logically deserve greater moral consideration. In response, it is worth remembering that there is no more self-serving understanding of who is deserving of moral consideration than exclusively basing it on the individual privileges one already possesses based upon one's species, race, sex, gender, or nationality. To decide that opposable thumbs or logocentric rationality is more valuable than night-vision or flight is fundamentally arbitrary, and to create such a hierarchy ultimately reproduces an interlocking system of inequality (Nocella II et al. 2014). This is in addition to the fact that concepts of species, race, sexuality, and so on have been constantly redefined ontologically throughout history as a result of a managerial violence that hierarchically orders all living things (McWhorter 2010, 76–81; 91–93). More pointedly, even if one conceded that nonhuman animals have a lesser sentience, to draw the line there would leave many mentally disabled children to die—as some utilitarian thinkers like Peter Singer would have it (2009). To this end, the very human self-awareness that is often taken as the pinnacle of evolution has almost exclusively been used to increasingly drive advanced methods of violence ranging from nuclear proliferation to factory farms to enslavement, and beyond. "When taking a wider view of history ... it becomes clear that the human heritage ... has occurred on the back of seemingly endless acts of violence, destruction, killing and genocide" (Kochi and Ordan 2008). In short, if human intelligence was so superior to other animals, it would stop us from continuing to be a substantially larger threat to the planet than any other species in the history of the planet. And, any form of intelligence that ultimately hastens the extinction of its own species along with the world around them should not, at minimum, be the only the only one deserving of moral consideration, and more honestly also shouldn't be considered the highest form of sentience around.

Others might object to this project saying that if we, as editors, really cared about nonhuman animals or human liberation, we should do something other than spend nearly two years working on a book about superheroes for an academic press. For starters, there is nothing mutually exclusive with our time examining superheroes and participation in other forms of activism and action that such critics would desire. Secondly, the very purpose of this collection is not merely to theorize how superhero representations function but how they can be used to actively undermine dominant institutions while providing strength to new ones. To this end it is worth recalling the words of Henry Giroux:

> Under the present circumstances, it is time to remind ourselves that academe may be one of the few public spheres available that can provide the educational conditions for students, faculty, administrators, and community members to embrace pedagogy as a space of dialogue and unmitigated questioning, imagine different futures, become border-crossers, and embrace a language of critique and possibility that makes visible the urgency of a politics necessary to address important social issues and contribute to the quality of public life and the common good. (2011)

In relation to the violence nonhumans face, "activists must ... stick relentlessly to exposing cruelty ... and seeking out the audiences who are most likely to respond[, namely] ... high schools and colleges" (Marcus 2005, 123–124). Given the popularity of superheroes as a genre, it is precisely collections like this one that can inspire a new generation of activists to put on a mask and fight for total liberation.

In addition, CAS as a field calls upon a multiplicity of approaches to be combined simultaneously in order to attack hegemonic institutions of human supremacy from multiple fronts at once (Nocella II et al. 2014). Therefore, no single site should be forfeited just out of a fear of academic co-optation so long as one's end goal remains firmly situated toward total liberation. Sadly, "despite recent decades of growing animal advocacy and environmental struggles, we are nevertheless losing ground in the battle to preserve species, ecosystems, and wilderness. Increasingly, calls for ... compromise ... can be seen as treacherous and grotesquely inadequate" (Best 2009). Discourse and representations matter in how we approach these struggles. A space for theorizing it is essential. Absent this, "there will be practically no spaces left for dissent, dialogue, civic courage, and a spirit of thoughtfulness and critical engagement. Knowledge is about more than the truth; it is also a weapon of change. The language of a radical politics needs more than hope and outrage; it needs institutional spaces to produce ideas, values, and social relations" (Giroux 2011). "Politics as usual just won't cut it anymore. We will always lose if we play by their rules rather than invent new forms of struggle, new social movements, and new sensibilities" (Best 2009). The struggle to create spaces for liberation and organizing requires theorists to imagine not just more effective grassroots politics, more complex and nuanced criticisms of capitalism and the state, but also an engagement with the cultural institutions of society. Capitalism, the state, speciesism, and all other forms of oppression have cultural foundations that buttress and intersect with their material foundations. Dismantling and weakening these cultural aspects to the system of domination is essential in the struggle for a better world. Organizations such as ICAS, and book series such as this one, seek to do precisely that by linking various activists and theorists together to foster new communities, which would otherwise be isolated from each other, in order to produce concrete forms of change.

OVERVIEW OF BOOK AND CHAPTER OUTLINE

The book emerged from the conversations and friendship that developed following the ICAS conference in Binghamton, New York in 2015. While both of us had been working in CAS, regularly published in the same edited books, and had been involved in ICAS for years, that was the first time we had met. It was also during that time Joe-Lessen Schatz and Amber George were completing their edited book *Screening the Non-human Representations of Animal Other in the Media* (2016), the first major book that linked critical animal studies to cultural and media studies. As scholars, activists, educators, parents (in Joe's case) and nerds, the two of us decided over Facebook conversations and discussions on comics to focus our edited book on a topic that both of us have loved since our childhood—superhero comics.

To realize our project's goal, we have divided this book into four sections. The first section is focused on theorizing the nonhuman superhero. In this section, the compiled authors look to theorize the ways in which the superhero genre engages with the nonhuman world through myth and cultural currency. They do this by decentering the human narratives of comics and by exploring political agency during growing ecological and political crises. In the second section, the chapters explore critical and creative ways in which comics and superhero narratives in film and television can be used to bolster a CAS pedagogy both in the classroom and at home to undermine the speciesist logic of contemporary society. The chapters in the third section focus on analyzing and deconstructing animal liberationist heroes, both human and nonhumans by providing a lens to critically reflect on political agency, process of social changes, and the tensions of ethical action. In the final section, the authors use CAS theories in conjunction with analysis of film and television to explore the messages and themes embedded within many popular representations. Through an intersectional approach, the authors unpack the ways in which superhero films either undermine or reinforce speciesist, racist, and heteropatriarchal systems of oppression. Ultimately, together all four sections aim to provide the reader with ways to use an increasingly popular genre in order to meaningfully impact the planet, alongside specific examples of how this can be done. Our hope is that it will inspire successive work in the fields of both CAS and comic studies to better problematize what it means to be human in the first place.

In more detail, in chapter 1, John Lupinacci presents how comics, most notably Grant Morrison's *Animal Man* and Matt Miner's *Liberator*, can serve as pedagogical materials for teaching about the animal and earth liberation front by inspiring and engaging in utopian and dystopian (im)possibilities of posthuman identities. Drawing from CAS, anarchist pedagogies, and an ecocritical educational framework Lupinacci illustrates how comics can be used to teach in support of imagining and enacting resistance to modernist subjectivities. His orientation toward teaching superheroes in the classroom serves as the very model by which radical praxis can come about by teaching through popular culture.

In chapter 2, Kent Worchester looks to the late 1980s small press series *The Puma Blues* in order to present an illustrative reading of how graphic novels concerning the ecology can get read. The series itself deploys an unusual variety of storytelling elements and many of its pages are devoid of people or dialogue, emphasizing instead flora and fauna. Much of the book's second half represents an effort to situate animals and plants at the center of the narrative. This chapter focuses on two questions. First, what are some of the ways in which *Puma Blues* utilizes the formal properties of comics to convey their message of ecological awareness? Second, what kinds of assumptions and implications are baked into the creators' unrelenting eco-pessimism? In answering these questions Kent Worchester not only theorizes the nonhuman but also explores questions of ecological pessimism and apocalyptic narratives in comics.

Continuing the discussion on nonhuman superheros, in chapter 3, José Alaniz examines this obscure titular Marvel character from a CAS perspective, tracing his narrative form his debut through subsequent appearances

in *Marvel Team-Up* and *The Incredible Hulk*. In the chapter, Alaniz traces
how Woodgod escapes humanity's tyranny and strives to establish his own
alternative community of animal-people. Alaniz argues that Woodgod's late
1970s/early 1980s mash-up of animal liberation and superheroics anticipates
Grant Morrison's subsequent *Animal Man,* even as it demonstrates the limits
of exploring radical politics in a commercial medium popularly associated
with children's entertainment.

In chapter 4, J.L. Schatz argues that unless children are taught an awareness of CAS while consuming popular culture, no matter how liberatory the
message is within any particular piece, the everyday reality of suffering for
nonhuman animals will not change. Fortunately, when CAS is accompanied
in connection with superheroes it can become a powerful enough force to
help bring an end to practices like factory farms—in effect, saving the world.
After providing a critique of various film and comic figures, he goes on to
outline ways these texts can be read against their hegemonic appeal in order
to teach children and young adults to foster a more critical awareness about
the world.

Chapters 5 through 7 explore different aspects of animal liberationist
heroes, starting with Márcio dos Santos Rodrigues and Matheus da Cruz
e Zica's chapter on the seminal Grant Morrison series *Animal Man*. The
authors propose a discussion about the relations of comics with environmental issues, considering them a way of expressing concerns and perceptions
on themes dear to the social world—in this case, the complex relationship
between humans and other animals. The authors turn to the series *Animal
Man*, a work that openly criticizes animal testing and championed activism
in defense of animals. The authors seek to understand in what extent the work
of Morrison can be understood as a political act, to subscribe it in a terrain
of dispute and negotiation that reproduces on a cultural level paradoxes and
dilemmas around animals rights.

Allison Dushane, in chapter 6 looks to another Grant Morrison series,
We3. She reads the miniseries *We3* by Morrison and Quitely as a text that
offers a critique of the anthropomorphic conceptions of rights that tend to
arise from cultural representations of animals. Her reading unfolds as a conversation between the panels of *We3*, Cary Wolfe's work on the "question
of the animal" and Jean Baudrillard's essay "The Animals: Territory and
Metamorphosis" (1994). In particular, Dushane argues that the comic series
evokes sympathy for the animals and that the series can also be read as a self-
reflexive critique of this sympathetic response and a manifesto on the ways
in which animals have been appropriated by culture to serve human interests.

Chantelle Gray van Heerden continues the discussion of animal liberation and superheroes in chapter 7 by looking at the 2015 Hungarian film
White God. This movie narrates the story of a mix-breed dog, called Hagen,

in such a way that human subjectivity and animal subjectivity are ontologically equiponderated. She argues that the movie's denial of the primacy of human subjectivity can thus be viewed as a movement toward ahuman theory; a silencing of the human which effectuates an "opening to the expressive potential of the other" (MacCormack 2014, 3). The central argument of this chapter is grounded in Gilles Deleuze and Félix Guattari's notion of becoming-animal. Rather than focusing on semantic and identity representations, becoming-animal denotes a reciprocal becoming. While this concept allows us to think through the nature of our relationship to and with nonhuman animals, she argues for a deeper understanding through which to reconceptualize negotiated and non-negotiated processes of human and non/human subjectivities.

The last section of the book starts with chapter 8, in which Jeffrey Pannekoek and Karin Anderson claim that, while Buffy has been critically acclaimed for its gender politics, the series did not successfully address issues of either race or animality. Using, Carol Adams' analysis of the conflation of femininity and animality to show that, while the series works to elevate the feminine, it ultimately displaces animality onto racial minorities and fails to be appropriately intersectional. The authors support this interpretation primarily by looking at the relationship between Buffy and Sineya, the First Slayer, who is African, prelingual, and presented as brute.

The last two chapters in the book provide critical readings of Donna Haraway's work on both cyborgs and interspecies relationships while deconstructing popular films. In chapter 9, Matthew Evans examines the relationship between bats and Batman through Haraway's theoretical frameworks of companion species and cyborgs. Batman functions as a cyborg, while bats serve as companion species in Christopher Nolan's *Dark Knight* trilogy. Bats help Bruce Wayne transform into Batman and advance his superhero abilities. Both characters use their voice to contribute to a communal identity of the general will within Gotham, but the power of capitalism ultimately undermines their efforts.

Sean Parson's chapter concludes the book with a reading of Rocket Raccoon from the 2014 film *Guardians of the Galaxy*. In this chapter, he explores the complicated identity relationship between Rockets' "human" and "animal" traits to explore the ways that *Guardians of the Galaxy* constructs these traits and mediates their interactions. Using the work of ecofeminist scholars such as Val Plumwood, cyborg theorists such as Donna Haraway, and the body of critical animal studies, this chapter argues that the cyborg queerness of Rocket Raccoon blurs the lines between human and nonhuman as well as between artificial and natural. This queering should make Rocket both a monstrous creature to be feared and a unique character that blurs the lines between many of the traits that CAS wish to blur. However, unlike CAS, the film does not undermine or complicate the speciesist logic of western philosophy but actively reinforces it through Rocket. He argues that we do not view Rocket as a queer figure because the character embraces toxic masculinity as a form of psychological defense mechanism to protect from accusations of queerness.

Taken together this collection as a whole works to connect various strands of intersectional modes of rhetorical analysis in order to demonstrate how CAS can breakdown the power anthropocentric institutions often perpetuate in their production of popular culture. Providing analysis of comics and films through the lens of CAS enables readers to not only understand how the consumption of media is never neutral but also how the trope of the superhero can serve as the symbolic power necessary to influence us to take action to change our world. More than anything, media is meant to move and influence how people feel and help communities to relate to and understand each other. With so many messages of heroism being tied to saving the environment, fighting for justice, and liberating nonhumans it is imperative that scholars, activists, and casual consumers of media take these opportunities to realize there is a hero in all of us. As the talking superhero dog, Butterball, says, in Disney's 2013 *Super Buddies* film, "Superhero rule number one, you don't have to have superpowers to be a superhero." And, while this is a good message, if consumers fail to recognize how the farm that the film opens with means the death of those nonhumans held in captivity there, we have lost a critical opportunity for praxis. However, if the messages of such characters can be understand and reread in ways that challenge institutions such as agribusiness and vivisection then a new tomorrow can be possible and we can really be the types of superheroes that popular culture should be inspiring us to be.

WORKS CITED

Adams, Carol. 1998. *The Sexual Politics of Meat: A Feminist-Vegetarian Critical Theory.* New York: Continuum Publishing Company.

Alaniz, José. 2014. *Death, Disability, and the Superhero: The Silver Age and beyond.* Jackson: University Press of Mississippi.

Baudrillard, Jean. 1994. *Simulacra and Simulation.* The Body, in Theory. Ann Arbor: University of Michigan Press.

Best, Steven. 2006. "Rethinking Revolution: Animal Liberation, Human Liberation, and the Future of the Left." *The International Journal of Inclusive Democracy* 2(3). http://www.inclusivedemocracy.org/journal/vol2/vol2_no3_Best_rethinking_revolution.html

Best, Steven. 2009. "The Rise of Critical Animal Studies: Putting Theory into Action and Animal Liberation into Higher Education." *The Journal for Critical Animal Studies* 7(1): 9–52.

Cocca, Carolyn. 2016. *Superwomen: Gender, Power, and Representation*. New York: Bloomsbury Academic, an imprint of Bloomsbury Publishing Inc.

Fawaz, Ramzi. 2016. *The New Mutants: Superheroes and the Radical Imagination of American Comics*. Postmillennial Pop. New York; London: New York University Press.

Foss, Chris, Jonathan W. Gray, and Zach Whalen, eds. 2016. *Disability in Comic Books and Graphic Narratives*. New York: Palgrave Macmillan.

Gateward, Frances K., and John Jennings, eds. 2015. *The Blacker the Ink: Constructions of Black Identity in Comics and Sequential Art*. New Brunswick, NJ: Rutgers University Press.

George, Amber. 2016. "Would Bugs Bunny Have Diabetes?: The Realistic Consequences of Cartoons for Non/Human Animals." In *Screening the Nonhuman: Representations of Animal Others in the Media*, edited by Amber George and J. L. Schatz, 59–72. Lanham, MD: Lexington Books.

George, Amber E., and J. L. Schatz, eds. 2016. *Screening the Nonhuman: Representations of Animal Others in the Media*. Critical Animal Studies and Theory. Lanham, MD: Lexington Books.

Giroux, Henry. 2011. "Occupy Colleges Now: Students as the New Public Intellectuals." *Truth-Out*. November 21. http://www.truth-out.org/news/item/5046:occupy-colleges-now--students-as-the-new-public-intellectuals

Gray, Richard J., and Betty Kaklamanidou, eds. 2011. *The 21st Century Superhero: Essays on Gender, Genre and Globalization in Film*. Jefferson, NC: McFarland.

Hatfield, Charles, Jeet Heer, and Kent Worcester. 2013. *The Superhero Reader*. Jackson, MS: University Press of Mississippi.

Howard, Sheena C., and Ronald L. Jackson, eds. 2013. *Black Comics: Politics of Race and Representation*. London; New York: Bloomsbury Academic, an imprint of Bloomsbury Publishing Plc.

Kochi, Tarik and Noam Ordan. 2008. "An argument for the global suicide of humanity." *Borderlands* 7(3). http://www.borderlands.net.au/vol7no3_2008/kochiordan_argument.htm

MacCormack, Patricia. 2014. *The Animal Catalyst*. London, New York: Bloomsbury.

Madrid, Mike. 2016. *The Supergirls: Fashion, Feminism, Fantasy, and the History of Comic Book Heroines*. Revised & Updated edition. Ashland, ON: Exterminating Angel Press.

Marcus, Erik. *Meat Market: Animals, Ethics, and Money*. Boston, MA: Brio Press.

Mercier, Sebastian. 2008. "'Truth Justice and the American Way:' The Intersection of American Youth Culture and Superhero Narratives." *Iowa Historical Review* 1(2): 21–59. http://ir.uiowa.edu/cgi/viewcontent.cgi?article=1010&context=iowa-historical-review

McWhorter, Ladelle. 2010. "Enemy of the Species." In *Queer Ecologies: Sex, Nature, Politics, Desire*, edited by Catriona Mortimer-Sandilands and Bruce Erickson. Bloomington, IN: University of Indiana Press.

Nama, Adilifu. 2011. *Super Black: American Pop Culture and Black Superheroes*. 1st ed. Austin: University of Texas Press.

Nibert, David Alan. 2013. *Animal Oppression and Human Violence: Domesecration, Capitalism, and Global Conflict.* Critical Perspectives on Animals: Theory, Culture, Science, and Law. New York: Columbia University Press.

Nocella II, Anthony J. et al., ed. 2014. *Defining Critical Animal Studies: An Intersectional Social Justice Approach for Liberation.* Counterpoints: Studies in the Postmodern Theory of Education, v. 448. New York: Peter Lang.

Nocella II, Anthony J., Amber E. George, and J. L. Schatz, eds. 2017. *The Intersectionality of Critical Animal, Disability, and Environmental Studies: Toward Eco-Ability, Justice, and Liberation.* Critical Animal Studies and Theory. Lanham: Lexington Books.

Nocella, Anthony J., Richard J. White, and Erika Cudworth, eds. 2015. *Anarchism and Animal Liberation: Essays on Complementary Elements of Total Liberation.* Jefferson, NC: McFarland & Company, Inc., Publishers.

Rosenberg, Robin and Peter Coogan. 2013. *What is a Superhero?* Oxford, UK: Oxford University Press.

Salter, Colin, Anthony J Nocella, Judy K. C Bentley, and Colman McCarthy. 2015. *Animals and War: Confronting the Military-Animal Industrial Complex.*

Singer, Peter. 2009. *Animal Liberation: The Definitive Classic of the Animal Movement.* Updated ed., 1st Ecco pbk. ed., 1st Harper Perennial ed. New York: Ecco Book/Harper Perennial.

Trumbore, Dave. 2017. "Superhero Cinemath: Who Won the Battle of the Box Office in 2016?" *The Collider.* January 5. http://collider.com/superhero-movies-box-office-winner-2016/#best-opening-weekend

Wolfe, Cary. 2003. *Animal Rites: American Culture, the Discourse of Species, and Posthumanist Theory.* Chicago, IL: University of Chicago Press.

Part I

Chapter 1

Critical Animal Studies and Comics in the Classroom

Liberation and Everyday Superheroes

John Lupinacci

The more I address anthropocentrism—or what may be better understood as the belief that human beings are superior to all other living beings—in my teaching and scholar-activism, the more I am confronted by the tendency of many in higher education to dismiss the importance of taking very seriously a critique of human supremacy. When met with such dismissal, I've found texts like films, art, and comics to be pivotal for teaching in accordance with a Critical Animal Studies (CAS) framework and winning over skeptics. While I admire, value, and am a firm supporter of a shared commitment to activism responding to the undeniable atrocities of many social injustices, none of these atrocities occur in isolation from the undergirding assumption that all that is nonhuman is less in worth and objectified as a resource for human purpose (Kahn 2010a; Lupinacci 2015; Martusewicz, Edmundson, and Lupinacci 2015; Nocella II et al. 2014). Thus, I find it paramount to work with other scholar-activist educators in support of those suffering while simultaneously challenging and confronting the systemic roots of oppression on all of our respective fronts. As a scholar-activist educator committed to CAS, I work from the position that I have a responsibility, as a privileged member of an unjust society, to support the oppressed in whatever capacity I can toward justice and the abolishment of the systemic ways suffering is perpetuated. In all efforts, I take the position that together our common goal is to break the will of the oppressor no matter who or what is suffering unjustly. In this chapter, I'll share how as an educator that one way of taking action is working to teach about the multitude of ways that direct actions aimed at total liberation can be taken—which include the radical work of groups like the Animal Liberation Front (ALF) and the Earth Liberation Front (ELF). Specifically, how these kinds of activist organizations call for questioning how it is we identify as human beings in relationship to addressing social suffering and environmental degradation—or to our commitment to alleviating and eliminating injustice for all living beings from the ills of authoritarianism masquerading as democracy.

In this chapter, I share a few examples of how I use comics in the college classroom to teach about the complexity, and the ethical dimensions, of the kind of activism that stems from actions taken when folks love something so much that they are willing to sacrifice freedom, and even their lives, in defense of animals and any multitude of diverse living beings on the planet. In the following paragraphs, I start with sharing a bit of the backstory and context for using comics in my teaching beginning with *Animal Man* (2001–2003) in teacher education, and then describe how and why I choose to bring radical comics, like *Liberator* (2014), into the graduate classroom to help teach about CAS. The chapter ends with how *Animal Man* and *Liberator* offer potential departures for students from learning about activism through comics, the artwork and storytelling that inspires radical possibilities for education in support of interspecies equity.

COMICS IN THE CULTURAL STUDIES CLASSROOM: TEACHING ABOUT ETHICS, EDUCATION, AND RADICAL ACTIVISM

Cultural studies in education as a scholarly tradition draws from a wide range of academic disciplines (Barker 2012). When it's enacted with rigor and responsibility it offers a strong framework for grounding scholarly activist research endeavors that offer the potential for intergenerationally engaging members of any community in direct actions aimed at disrupting the hegemony of everyday life on campus, in neighborhoods, at schools, and in classrooms. The primary focus of the pedagogical examples in this chapter center on how I work to include sequential art in the curriculum. Furthermore, I offer a glimpse of how comics can be a way to engage students in learning about the critical and ethical perspectives informing radical activism—and illustrate, quite literally for students, the everyday nature of interruptive efforts taken by direct-action activists.

In the graduate level course Environment, Culture, and Education, I seek to engage students in addressing the following: (1) How they, as scholar-activists in cultural studies, both teach and learn from and with *all* members of the community. Further, how they as critical scholar-activists examine the direct actions of anarchic networks—like the ALF and ELF—and contribute to how they engage as researchers, scholars, educators, policy-makers, and activists within higher education, PreK-12 schools, and other educational contexts in the community as accomplices to human, Earth, and animal liberation; (2) How critical theory in connection with a CAS framework contributes to how they prepare to work within community contexts to serve a diverse population inclusive of all participants—which includes the more-than-human members of the community; and (3) How their activist-scholarship and teaching engages members of the community in considering questions such as:

- How is knowledge constructed in the academy, our classrooms, and in mainstream Western industrial culture? How do current dominant forms of teaching and learning inform views of "legitimate" knowledge? How do such knowledges get constructed and viewed, and how are they then often enacted as research and what possibilities are there to resist dominant authoritarian education?
- What critical foundational knowledge is necessary for activists, scholars, and educators in the twenty-first century to face the complexities of teaching/learning relationships in a variety of community contexts, and be responsive to the particular needs of marginalized, exploited, and endangered communities?
- What is the relationship between cultural studies and knowledge, research, and teaching within and outside of the academy? How do our epistemologies have an impact on social justice and environmental degradation? In other words, how do we learn how to *be* in the world?
- What skills and knowledge are required to successfully engage in direct action as a public pedagogy as activist-scholar educators who enact cultural studies as research and teaching in action within and among the community?

The course draws from and builds upon ecofeminism (Warren 1990, 2000; Plumwood 1993, 2002; Code 2007), ecopedagogy (Kahn 2010a), and ecojustice frameworks (Martusewicz, Edmundson, and Lupinacci 2015; Lupinacci and Happel 2015) as students explore how they as scholar-activist educators might contribute to learning to recognize, resist, and rethink how we relate to each other and the more-than-human world (Lupinacci and Happel-Parkins 2016). This particular course engages students in the art and practice of designing and implementing public pedagogies that represent and value what I refer to in the course as "resistance wisdom"—the everyday ecological knowledge supporting life, communicated and understood through relationships of belonging. Further, the course engages students in recognizing, resisting, and rethinking dominant discourses of human supremacy, patriarchy, racism, classism, ableism, individualism, consumerism, and other forms of discursive domination in Western industrial culture.

Focusing on an example from the Environment, Culture, and Education course, in the next section I share insight into how comics play a central role in learning with and from sequential art to connect content in classes to learning experiences that extend far beyond the traditional classroom. These learning experiences help students connect, empathize, and more thoroughly understand the reasoning for direct action activism. I assert the position that the cultural assumptions undergirding problematic ways of thinking and acting, like anthropocentrism as a foundation of Western industrial culture, are in fact cultural. Thus, sites of such change are possible through critical classrooms. Given this premise, the examples I share offer a reflective glimpse at how teaching using comics might offer students the opportunity to dispel myths about Western industrial culture—and in particular about activism—and for them to contribute to an ongoing intergenerational narrative shared and preserved in activist cultures.

BACKGROUND: EXPERIMENTING WITH COMICS IN THE CLASSROOM

I have often taught using more mainstream comics and graphic novels like Marvel's *Civil War* to introduce the role of federal policy, a police state, and surveillance (Miller and McNiven 2007). I have also done so with the graphic novel *Persepolis* by Marjane Satrapi in order to teach about childhood in diverse political contexts (2007). And I have found the use of Bill Ayers and Ryan Alexander-Tanner's *To Teach: A Journey, in Comics* to be especially helpful as an introduction to the social reproduction of industrial culture in US public schools (2010). Following some experimentation with those texts in the curriculum, I had a strong experience with positive feedback from graduate students when I used Sacco's *Palestine* (2001) and Seth Tobocman's *You Don't Have to Fuck People Over to Survive* (2009) in a course on globalization, identity, and education. An anecdotal example of the kind of informal feedback came from a student who received feedback for a critique of capitalism that hinged on the assumption that all economics were exploitive and it was human nature to compete in order to survive. The class had spent two weeks reading about economic theories of development and then reading Marxist (Harvey 2011). I followed that up with anarchist critiques of capitalism (Shannon and Nocella II 2012).

After meeting with one student and discussing the paper, the student seemed discouraged that the paper seemed to contradict his espoused political beliefs. However, when we later read Tobocman for class something seemed to click for this student (2009). He rushed up after class and described how clear the possibility of having a thriving community that did not require the marketization of resources and exploitation of each other now made sense. For this student, it took him seeing it unfold in the graphic story. The student's revised paper was markedly better and we talked about how helpful it can be to storyboard a paper or idea out and develop the structure and theory along with the story. While anecdotal, this kind of learning moment provided the opportunity for a learner to connect and engage with the ideas in a way that sunk in and made sense for him. One might argue that it allowed for the learner to relate to the concepts being taught in the course and to grapple with the content through the sequential art of the story and characters.

However, most important to this chapter is how I came into learning more about the Animal and Earth Front through *Animal Man*, which I found useful while teaching about the ethical dimensions of Grant Morrison's work considering animals—and other more-than-human beings—as equivocal in worth to humans. When I learned about the short series *Liberator*, I was excited to bring it together with Grant Morrison's *Animal Man* (Minor, Aranda, and Pereyra 2014; Minor and Earth Crisis 2014a, 2014b). I had been using *Animal Man* for some time and it was great for bringing up questions about the ALF and for providing visual representation of animal rescue. Morrison's writing introduced and reinforced theoretical concepts like post structuralism, anti-human supremacy, interconnectedness, and a rationale for action in defense of animal torture (DeLeon 2009; Parson 2017; Parson 2018). However, I was excited to bring Minor's *Liberator* series together with *Animal Man* in class with the goal of having the inspiring art and story of these comics connect students more closely with critically reflecting on the realities of the lives of political activists and the reasoning for such direct actions.

FOUNDATIONS FOR COMICS IN THE CULTURAL STUDIES CLASSROOM: TOWARD PEDAGOGIES OF SOLIDARITY

After setting up the foundational basis for students to consider interspecies equity, I then commit a couple weeks of class meetings to examining how social justice and environmental sustainability are deeply entangled within Western industrial cultural assumptions that everything is to be commodified, colonized, and dominated. As a human being in Western industrial culture, this sort of day-to-day systemic violence is predicated on the dominant assumption that such an understanding of the world is culturally constructed and dependent upon the notion of a human-being as an individual separate and superior to all other beings. In education courses, it is not uncommon for students to come to class with a strong interest in the potential role schools might play in alleviating social suffering. However, what many college students don't often recognize coming into the field of education is how much of a role schools have played, and continue to play, in creating and maintaining inequality. This is why I teach the relationship between authoritarianism, patriarchy, capitalism, and the North American prison industrial complex (Davis and Barasmian 1999; Alexander 2012). I do this in connection with neoliberalism and the animal industrial complex (Harvey 2007; Lupinacci and Happel 2014; Nosky 1989; Adams 1997; Twine 2012). This is done by explaining the interconnection between cases of increased environmental degradation and the school-to-prison pipeline (Nocella II, Ducre, and Lupinacci 2017). Given that students may or may not be aware of the interconnectedness of multiple systems of oppression, I introduce the "10 Principles of Critical Animal Studies" developed by Steven Best, Anthony J. Nocella II, Richard Kahn, Carol Gigliotti, and Lisa Kremmerer in 2007 (Nocella II et al. 2014, xxvii–xxviii).

To this end, I emphasize how for CAS educators critical praxis "advances a holistic understanding of the commonality of oppressions, such that speciesism, sexism, racism, ableism, statism, classism, militarism and other hierarchical ideologies and institutions are viewed as parts of a larger, interlocking, global system of domination" (Nocella II et al 2014, xxvii). Furthermore, the ninth principle of CAS calls for a form of praxis that "openly supports and examines controversial radical politics and strategies used in all kinds of social justice movements, such as those that involve economic sabotage from boycotts to direct action toward the goal of peace" (Nocella II et al. 2014, xxviii). Given these guidelines for CAS scholar-activists, together with critical pedagogies of solidarity, there is no apolitical way to engage in education or activism. In this chapter, and in my teaching, it is my argument that there is a key role CAS scholar-activists ought to play to support educational spaces that work toward bringing this diverse work together in solidarity, through what I have been calling pedagogies of solidarity (Lupinacci 2015; Lupinacci and Happel-Parkins 2016).

The concept of pedagogies of solidarity emerges from and is akin to Freire's pedagogies of the oppressed and freedom as well as other critical and ethical contributions to a diversity of approaches to the cultural aspects of education (1993, 2003). Richard Kahn, growing the work of Freire and critical pedagogy, advocates for solidarity between activism and critical education and conceptualizes what he calls an ecopedagogy (2010a, 2010b). An ecopedagogy movement in education applies the basic principles of critical pedagogy to the interrelated nature of social and ecological issues. Kahn, explaining ecopedagogy, illuminates how such pedagogical projects in the movement recognize "ecological ideas such as the intrinsic value of all species, the need to care for and live in harmony with the planet, as well as the emancipatory potential contained in human aesthetic experiences of nature" (Kahn 2010a, 19). In this sense, pedagogies of solidarity refer to educational projects—like the pedagogical efforts described by Kahn as ecopedagogy—that resist claims of a single solution for stopping injustice and remain open to what emerges from groups of beings that care enough about freedom and one another to take actions toward ensuring it for all members of the community. Such pedagogical projects facilitate the potential of education to empower local members of any community to not only respond and reframe the worlds they live in but also to contribute to the collective battle to break the will of their oppressors. Specifically, the phrase "pedagogies of solidarity" intentionally draws attention on the multitude of pedagogical possibilities and the value of the diverse experimentation of teaching and learning toward diverse, decentralized, sovereign communities for all beings.

As an anarchist and CAS educator navigating the authoritarian constraints of neoliberalized—and human-centered—institutions of higher education, the following section offers a glimpse into how I use the comics Grant Morrison's *Animal Man* and Matt Minor's *Liberator*. While in these examples I am not sharing formal education research on the comics as an intervention in the classroom, I introduced them into my class in effort to educate, organize, and support direct action through pedagogical projects that call attention to particular relationships and practices common in Western industrial culture. Such CAS pedagogical projects take place in a variety of locally situated learning initiatives that organize in support of living systems. These local and diverse pedagogies operate concurrently, sometimes separately, and in conversation with each other. Through critical pedagogies of solidarity these projects stem from the recognition that there are powerful phenomena occurring within schools and in our society that are profoundly abusive and are violently reproducing relationships that make racism, sexism, classism, and speciesism to name a few that seem inevitable and inescapable. However, CAS scholar-activism and the radical actions of activists working toward total liberation remind and encourage us to imagine possibilities beyond current constraints of culturally constructed regimes of cruelty—and most of all to take informed action however we can, wherever we are, in whatever capacity we can offer.

ANIMAL MAN: STUMBLING INTO BUDDY BARKER

For almost a decade now in some way or another, I have brought to class with me Buddy Baker—and by author association the author of the comic, Grant Morrison. Sometimes while teaching ethics and social justice to high school students, diversity and democracy to pre-service teachers, and most recently in a critical graduate cultural studies program where it seemed like a logical fit. Buddy Baker is a superhero (Animal Man), and while there are a few versions and variations of the comic *Animal Man*, the Grant Morrison era (1988–1990) is where I first developed my admiration for what the sequential art and story of this comic brought to my own learning and especially to the critical teaching in my classroom. In my late teenage years, I had become increasingly interested in all kinds of organized activist responses to animal suffering in connection with a growing concern and disgust I had for the so-called development of an ongoing and unstoppable suburban sprawl. One day while sitting at a local coffee shop I was listening to two people (actually eavesdropping) talking about Edward Abbey's the *Monkey Wrench Gang* (1975). I was immediately interested because I had just a few years prior been gifted a copy of Abbey's *Desert Solitaire* from a group of environmental activists I had met outside of Grateful Dead concert (1968). With my interest peaked, I listened in more intently and pre-internet book buying was planning to search for the *Monkey Wrench Gang* at the library when the conversation transitioned into a discussion between the two of them about *Animal Man*. I remember vividly their conversation which ended up being a convincing argument for me to head directly to the local comic shop and dig into the 'A' section of the D.C. comics where I thumbed through and landed on Grant Morrison's Volume 1 Issue #17 "Consequences" (1989). I was immediately captivated by the iconic cover art of Brain Bolland. The cover is of Buddy Barker in his Animal Man attire holding up a monkey whose eyes had been stitched shut. I bought the issue so began my self-indulgence with Buddy Barker and really with Grant Morrison, Chas Truog, and Doug Hazlewood as teachers putting words and illustrations to some of the themes I was myself interested in. Flash forward to a little over a decade later, I had since collected all of the *Animal Man* series and while I found an affinity for Buddy Barker I had really mostly enjoyed the run written by Grant Morrison. Now a few years into my adjunct gigs lecturing at a local university, while teaching at a nearby high school, I had yet to think about brining *Animal Man* into my teaching. I was attending a conference for the American Educational Studies Association (AESA) in Pittsburgh and at a session titled "Ecology, Space, and Possible Action," I listened to a paper presentations by Abraham Deleon "From the Comic Book to the Classroom: Animal Man and the Case for Critical Animal Studies" (2009). DeLeon, spoke of the connections between Grant Morrison's *Animal Man* and the theoretical concepts covered in the series. When I returned home, I ordered the trade paperback volumes and got to work planning for how I could use *Animal Man* in the course, "Schools in a Diverse, Democratic, and Sustainable Society," I was teaching for pre-service teachers.

I include this context because it is something I share intentionally with students in my "Environment, Culture, and Education" course. In doing so,

I introduce them to Buddy Barker and do a read aloud of some of the first issues to give a context for how Buddy Barker and I teach the class about "the Red." Or, I go over the "morphogenetic field" that Buddy Barker returned from a hunting trip mysteriously connected to this life-web that connects every animal on the planet. In class, I introduce Buddy Barker and "the Red" following teaching about Gregory Bateson's concept of an ecology of mind (1972). I also draw connections with Lorraine Code's ecological intelligence, in relationship to learning about interdependency and interconnectedness (2007). After a class period where students and I use Buddy Barker, and Animal Man, for discussing interconnectedness, dependency, and ethics, I read aloud Morrison's "Consequences"—which is a reprint of Issue #17 from 1989—from the end of the Kindle Edition of *Animal Man Book 2: Origin of the Species* (2013). I use the Kindle edition so that I can display the sequential artwork using a classroom projector. I have collected a handful of hard copies of the single issues over the years that are not in mint condition and so I distribute them during this intense read aloud for students to hold, follow along, and thumb through. I have found that having the artwork in your hands is powerful—especially in the actual format it was originally released and while the story is being read aloud. There is something aesthetically engaging about this pedagogical practice that seems to help get past the stereotypes the students have of animal rights and environmental activism. Of course, this practice isn't always practical and certainly has some drawbacks. For example, in recent years a few copies have gone missing. I would get bummed out because there are very limited copies of these issues. However, then I think to myself that it must have inspired someone enough for them to want to take it home and keep it. After the reading aloud in class on how Buddy Barker as Animal Man teams up with a group of activists to break into a University of California laboratory to free monkeys, we discuss the tension for Buddy that arises in the story when one of the activists sets fire to the facility. The class has a discussion exploring Buddy's concern for the ethical dilemmas he finds himself, and others, in as a result of their actions and political affinities. Using Buddy Barker and the comic as a catalyst for discussion, I facilitate the class sharing our first and primary experiences with caring deeply about and empathizing with the suffering of another life. Following this class meeting, I assign Morrison's *Animal Man Book 3: Deus Ex Machina* (2003) along with Rosebraugh's *Burning Rage of A Dying Planet: Speaking for the Earth Liberation Front* (2004), Pickering's *The Earth Liberation Front 1997–2002* (2007), and Colling and Nocella II's *Love and Liberation: An Animal Liberation Front Story* (2012). I ask students to consider how these four texts relate to one another and to their own identities forming as scholar-activists, critically and ethically aware of interspecies equity, social justice, and sustainability.

When we return from a week of reading *Animal Man* and about the ALF and ELF, I focus the course discussion on what Colling and Nocella II refer to as "teaching for liberation through storytelling" (2012, 19). Here I draw from Kahn's ecopedagogy which presents the strong case for how storytelling—or sharing narratives—about radical activism can in fact be pedagogical and a form of activism (2010). In the past, I have shown the Hennelly film *Bold Native* (2010) and then discussed it in class in relationship to these texts also exploring the ethical dilemmas while raising awareness, dispelling myths about the ALF and ELF and following it up with reading Lovitz's *Muzzling a Movement* (2010). However, more recently I've found that Matt Minor's *Liberator* comic book series is an excellent text following these readings and actually a powerful answer to some of the shortcomings of Animal Man—like the heteronormative, male-centeredness, blond hair, and blue eyes of Buddy Barker further representing the whiteness in both comics and the mainstream animal rights and environmental movements.

CONCLUDING WITH *LIBERATOR*: INSPIRED BY JEANETTE AND GUERRERO

Already both a comic reader and an activist-educator, I am always looking for texts that might potentially engage students through illustrations, story, and politics. I stumbled across *Liberator* while digging through potential texts to bring to the classroom while teaching about the Occupy movement. I had found Black Mask Studios' *Occupy Comics* series and since then have been a regular reader. While reading about some of the Black Mask Studio projects I came across a promo for Matt Minor's *Liberator* series that had artwork that grabbed my attention similarly as did Bollard's cover of *Animal Man* a decade earlier. The promotion on the back of *Occupy Comics* #2 was a riveting illustration of a broken chain with a hooded and masked woman in all black clothing kneeling down in front of overturned cages holding a white rabbit with three other white rabbits uncaged and nearby. This picture can be found on the cover of Issue #2 in the *Liberator* series, but the ad version also had two tag lines that further caught my eye, the first read: "Real heroes don't wear capes ... they wear ski-masks." The second read: "30% of Liberator profits will be donated to animal rescue efforts." These tag lines in combination with the art work were more than enough to convince me that I needed to make sure to follow the series closely. Sparing all the details, the series did not disappoint and in fact did play a prominent role in my classroom. Following the introduction to the ALF and ELF through *Animal Man* and the readings mentioned in the previous section, I have students read through the four-issue series of *Liberator*. Matt Minor (writer), Javier Sanchez Aranda (illustrator), and Joaquin Pereyra (color) deliver a stunningly realistic fictional account of two complex protagonists—Jeanette and Guerrero—who both bring unique dimensions to the story that make the series accessible and enjoyable to all sorts of readers.

Through Jeanette and Guerrero, readers in my class get to think critically and ethically about the individual decision to take action against animal cruelty. Furthermore, Minor develops the main characters in complex ways that makes it easy for readers to examine the political and ethical dimensions, and dilemmas, of how they both engage and identify as activists. Minor, Aranda, and Pereyra utilize great writing and brilliantly vivid illustration to depict many of the real-life tensions surrounding direct action to liberate animals and stop environmental degradation. Major themes surrounding these tensions that emerge from students reading this series together and having the comics in their hands in class include gender roles, the role of police, mainstream animal rights organizations, and trust and security culture.

Unlike in *Animal Man* where Buddy Barker has a superpower that connects him to nonhuman animals, students can recognize themselves in the day-to-day behaviors and relationships of Jeanette and Guerrero. These characters experience a life influenced by gender roles which are visible to students through the ways that Guerrero processes and works through often conflicting masculinities and vulnerabilities. Jeanette defies the submissive passivity traditionally ascribed to females in this medium as the two of them work through complicated friendship and relationship expectations. Throughout the story, the reader is exposed to a variety of forms of activism ranging from information sharing, organizing and protesting at rallies, and then planning and carrying out actions to liberate animals from dog fighting, lab experimentation, and mink farming. Along the way, and inextricable from the tensions and complications of the relationship between Jeanette and Guerrero, the story exposes to readers different perspectives taken regarding destruction of property and the actions of setting fire to a fur store, or the facilities from which they are liberating dogs, rabbits, or minks. It is repeatedly brought up in the character dialogues that Jeanette and Guerrero are both up against a society with the dominant belief that animals are property. This belief is accompanied by the right to use the animals as objects in the pursuit of the capital accumulation of wealth.

While they both know they are breaking laws, the story unpacks how they struggle with blurred lines of what constitutes harm and suffering. Readers are also exposed to the police actions taken against protestors. For example, in one instance at a protest the story exposes excessive force used by police and how the characters deescalate the situation to avoid more conflict and arrest. Students also took notice of how trust and security culture play into the dynamics of their relationships. At one part of the story, Jeanette questions Guerrero's attention to the anonymity of their actions and his erratic and destructive behaviors as they are working to carry out their plans. This sparked questions from students about surveillance and security culture. Inseparable from Jeanette's reflectivity and analysis of Guerrero's erratic and destructive macho behaviors, the storyline drives home the importance of anonymity, trust, and the effectiveness of infiltrators and informants in activism groups.

Throughout all of these themes, the readers are exposed to the diversity of nonviolent tactics that propose a need for rethinking how we often define violence. It is more than clear in the story that for both Guerrero and Jeanette, the goal for these anti-heroes is to put pressure on and stop humans from abusing animals. However, the characters differ in their ethics and beliefs regarding the destruction of property and this conflict exposes how differing motives can interfere with how things play out in the heat of the operations. Both characters remain strongly principled in that they do not directly harm humans. However, this gets complicated and tested throughout the story and inevitably exposes some big differences between the two animal activists. In sum, this series depicts a very real possibility for anyone interested in learning more about participation in decentralized and direct action movements. Jeanette and Guerrero don't have any superpowers but they do have conviction and passion for animal liberation, which makes for some very real discussions inspired by fictional characters much closer to the readers than Buddy Barker. I have only been able to use it in class once—though I have plans to include more of Minor's work and bring the miniseries *Liberator: Earth Crisis* (2014) and *Critical Hit* (2014) in future classes.

Concluding reading *Liberator* in class, we discuss how Minor himself is in fact enacting a form of activism and that writing and teaching through his comics runs parallel to his principles as an activist. Minor's work with dog rescues in New York aligns with these principles (Waterfield 2013). In the *Liberator* series at one point the anti-heroes compare themselves to comic book superheroes. I find this powerful in the classroom because the students are reading about everyday people who relate their efforts to those of superheroes. This draws students into the lives of Jeanette and Guerrero and presents a self-reflective opportunity for the reader to ask, 'What's stopping me from taking action?' Jeanette and Guerrero fight those abusing animals and the Earth without magic, extraterrestrial powers, radioactive strength, or titanium robotic suits.

Following the reading of *Liberator,* the students are asked to revisit the readings they have done in the previous weeks regarding the ALF and ELF and focus on Lovitz's *Muzzling a Movement: The Effects of Anti-Terrorism Law, Money & Politics on Animal Activism* (2010). I ask the students to consider Jeanette and Guerrero and analyze the final action that took place at a mink farm and apply what they learned from Lovitz in the analysis. The students write analytical essays centered on the policy and law influencing how the actions taken by Jeanette and Guerrero are likely to be interpreted through dominant views in the US. In class, the students bring their essays and discuss their work among each other and have a discussion around imagining and collaboratively drafting policy that do not support animal exploitation and uphold and extend human rights to other species.

Ultimately, I end this chapter in the same manner I end the discussion following my class' reading of *Liberator* and pose the following questions: What's stopping us from defending what we love from the abuse endured by any living being subjected to the torture of today's Western industrial society? Furthermore, what are the stories we need to keep quiet and how do we tell stories to also inspire and educate others about our potential to take action in defense of all that suffer unjustly? If such topics are not central to how we educate ourselves and one another then how can it be empowering or liberatory for any of our human, and more-than-human kin?

WORKS CITED

Adams, Carol J. 1997. "Mad Cow" Disease and the Animal Industrial Complex: An Ecofeminist Analysis. *Organization & Environment,* 10(1): 26–51.

Alexander, Michelle. 2012. *The New Jim Crow: Mass Incarceration in the Age of Colorblindness.* New York: The New Press.

Ayers, Bill, and Ryan Alexander-Tanner. 2010. *To Teach: The Journey, in Comics.* New York: Teachers College Press.

Barker, Chris. 2012. *Cultural Studies: Theory and Practice* (4th edition). Thousand Oaks: SAGE Publication Ltd.

Bateson, Gregory. 1972. *Steps to an Ecology of Mind: Collected Essays in Anthropology, Psychiatry, Evolution, and Epistemology.* Chicago: University of Chicago Press.

Best, Steven. 2009. The Rise of Critical Animal Studies: Putting Theory into Action and Animal Liberation into Higher Education. *Journal for Critical Animal Studies* 7(1): 9–52.

Code, Lorraine. 2007. *Ecological Thinking: The Politics of Epistemic Location. Studies in Feminist Philosophy.* New York: Oxford University Press.

Colling, Sarat, and Anthony J. Nocella II. 2012. *Love and Liberation: An Animal Liberation Front Story.* Williamston, MA: Piraeus Books.

Davis, Angela Yvonne, and David Barsamian. 1999. *The Prison Industrial Complex.* Chico: AK Press.

DeLeon, Abraham. 2009. *From the Comic Book to the Classroom: Animal Man and the Case for Critical Animal Studies.* Paper presented at AESA Annual Meeting in Pittsburgh.

DeLeon, Abraham. 2010. The Lure of the Animal: The Theoretical Question of the Nonhuman Animal. *Critical Education*, 1(2): 1–26.

Freire, Paulo. 1993. *Pedagogy of the Oppressed* (M. B. Ramos, Trans. Revised 20th Anniversary ed.). New York: The Continuum Publishing Company.

Freire, Paulo. 1998. *Pedagogy of Freedom: Ethics, Democracy, and Civic Courage* (P. Clarke, Trans.). Lanham: Roman & Littlefield Publishers Inc.

Harvey, David. 2007. *A Brief History of Neoliberalism.* New York: Oxford University Press.

Harvey, David. 2011. *The Enigma of Capital: And the Crises of Capitalism.* New York: Oxford University Press.

Hennelly, Denis. 2010. *Bold Native.* [DVD] Los Angeles: Open Road Films.

Kahn, Richard. 2010a. *Critical Pedagogy, Ecoliteracy and Planetary Crisis: The Ecopedagogy Movement.* New York: Peter Lang.

Kahn, Richard. 2010b. Love Hurts: Ecopedagogy Between Avatars and Elegies. *Teacher Education Quarterly* 37(4): 55–70.

Lovitz, Dara. 2010. *Muzzling a Movement: The Effects of Anti-Terrorism Law, Money & Politics on Animal Activism* Brooklyn: Lantern Books.

Lupinacci, John. 2015. "Recognizing Human Supremacy: Interrupt, Inspire and Expose." In *Anarchism and Animal Liberation: Essays on Complementary Elements of Total Liberation,* edited by Anthony J. Nocella II, Richard. J., White, and Erika Cudworth, 179–193. Jefferson: McFarland & Company, Inc. Publishers,

Lupinacci, John, and Alison Happel. 2015. "Recognize, Resist, and Reconstitute: An Ecojustice Response to Neoliberalism. In *Schools Against the Neoliberal Rule* (Volume 1), edited by Mark Abendroth, and Bradley Porfilio, 269–287. Charlotte: Information Age Press.

Lupinacci, John, and Alison Happel-Parkins. 2016. "Recognize, Resist, & Reconstitute: An Eco-critical Conceptual Framework. In *The Social & Cultural Foundations of Education: A Reader,* edited by Joshua Diem, 34–56. San Diego: Cognella.

Martusewicz, Rebecca, Jeff Edmundson, and John Lupinacci. 2015. *EcoJustice Education: Toward Diverse, Democratic, and Sustainable Communities* (2nd Edition). New York: Routledge.

Miller, Mark and Steve McNiven. 2007. *Civil War: A Marvel Comics Event.* New York: Marvel Comics.

Morrison, Grant, Chas Truog, and Doug Hazlewood. 1989. "Consequences." *Animal Man* 1(17). DC Comics.

Morrison, Grant. 2001. *Animal Man Book 1: Animal Man.* Burbank: Vertigo.

Morrison, Grant. 2002. *Animal Man Book 2: Origin of the Species.* Burbank: Vertigo.

Morrison, Grant. 2003. *Animal Man Book 3: Deus Ex Machina.* Burbank: Vertigo.

Minor, Matt, Aranda, Javier Sanchez, and Joaquin Pereyra. 2014. *Liberator Vol.1: Rage Ignition.* Los Angeles: Black Mask Studios LLC.

Minor, Matt. *Critical Hit: Issue 1.* 2014. Los Angeles: Black Mask Studios LLC.

Minor, Matt, and Earth Crisis. 2014a. *Liberator/Earth Crisis: Issue 1.* Los Angeles: Black Mask Studios LLC.

Minor, Matt and Earth Crisis. 2014b. *Liberator/Earth Crisis: Issue 2.* Los Angeles: Black Mask Studios LLC.

Nocella II, Anthony. J., John Sorensen, Kim Socha, and Atsuko Matsuoka. 2014. *Defining Critical Animal Studies: An Intersectional Social Justice Approach for Liberation.* New York: Peter Lang Publishing.

Nocella II, Anthony J., Richard White, and Erika Cudworth. 2015. *Anarchism and Animal Liberation: Essays on Complementary Elements of Total Liberation.* Jefferson: McFarland & Company, Inc. Publishers.

Nocella II, Anthony J., K. Animashaun Ducre, and John Lupinacci. 2017. *Addressing Environmental Justice and Dismantling the School-To-Prison Pipeline: Poisoning and Incarcerating Youth.* New York: Palgrave.

Noske, Barabara. 1989. *Human and Other Animals.* London: Pluto Press.

Parson, Sean. 2017/2018. "Our Heroes Need to Wear Ski-Masks: The Animal Man, and the Animal Liberationist Hero in Comics." In *Education for Total Liberation: Critical Animal Pedagogy and Teaching Against Speciesism,* edited by Carolyn Drew, Amber E. George, John Lupinacci, Anthony J. Nocella II, Ian Purdy, and J.L. Schatz. New York: Peter Lang.

Pickering, Leslie James. 2007. *The Earth Liberation Front 1997-2002.* Portland: Arissa Media Group.

Plumwood, Val. 1993. *Feminism and the Mastery of Nature.* London: Routledge.

Plumwood, Val. 2002. *Environmental Culture: The Ecological Crisis of Reason.* New York: Routledge.

Rosebraugh, Craig. 2004. *Burning Rage of a Dying Planet: Speaking for the Earth Liberation Front.* New York: Lantern Books.

Sacco, Joe. 2001. *Palestine.* Seattle: Fantagraphics Books.

Satrapi, Marjane. 2007. *The Complete Persepolis.* New York: Pantheon Books.

Shannon, Derek, Anthony J. Nocella II, and John Asimakopoulos. 2012. *The Accumulation of Freedom: Writings on Anarchist Economics.* Oakland: AK Press.

Tobocman, Seth. 2009. *You Don't Have to Fuck People Over to Survive.* Chico, CA: AK Press.

Twine, Richard. 2010. *Animals as Biotechnology: Ethics, Sustainability and Critical Animal Studies.* New York: Routledge.

Twine, Richard. 2012. Revealing the 'Animal-Industrial Complex'—A Concept & Method for Critical Animal Studies? *Journal for Critical Animal Studies* 10(1): 12–39.

Warren, Karen. 1990. The Power and the Promise of Ecological Feminism. *Environmental Ethics* 12(2):125–146.

Warren, Karen. 2000. *Ecofeminist Philosophy: A Western Perspective on What it is and Why it Matters.* Lanham: Rowman & Littlefield Publishers, Inc.

Waterfield, Andrew. 2017. "Interviews: Matt Minor (Liberator)." *Punknews.org.* Accessed May 23, 2017. https://www.punknews.org/article/51835/interviews-matt-minor-liberator

Chapter 2

Ecological Pessimism and
The Puma Blues

Kent Worcester

INTRODUCTION

The year 1986 was a banner year for North American comics. It was the year that the first volume of Art Spiegelman's *Maus* was published, that the first issues of the limited-series *Watchmen* appeared, and that *The Dark Knight Returns* trade paperback was released. It was the year in which over a dozen new independent comic publishers were launched, including Dark Horse, Gladstone, Malibu, and Slave Labor. And in June 1986 the first issue of the dystopian series *The Puma Blues* was published. This eccentric and formally inventive title was never "a big seller by any stretch of the imagination," but from the outset the series was distinguished by its single-minded focus on animals, habitat, and the Anthropocene (Bissette 2015, 534). While numerous comic books and graphic novels have invoked the threat of social and environmental catastrophe, few have exhumed humanity's relationship to the rest of nature with such relentless determination as Stephen Murphy and Michael Zulli's ambitious yet downbeat project, *The Puma Blues*.

Twenty-three issues of *The Puma Blues* appeared between 1986 and 1989, along with a self-published minicomic that came out in 1990. Written by Stephen Murphy and illustrated by Michael Zulli, the series suffered a fitful publishing history. Issues 1 to 17 were published by Dave Sim's Aardvark One; issues 18 to 20 were self-published; and issues 21 to 23 were published by Mirage Studios. The complete series, along with a four-page graphic story by Alan Moore, a new forty-page conclusion, and essays by Stephen R. Bissette and Dave Sim, was collected in 2015 by Dover Publishing. While this "avant-garde comic saga" was once "the most elusive entry in the comic book renaissance of the 1980s," the hardcover collection has brought a new level of attention to Murphy and Zulli's idiosyncratic project (Groves 2015).

In a review for the online magazine *A.V. Club*, Tim O'Neil admitted that "it seems almost lazy to call the work *sui generis*, but nothing really serves to adequately summarize such a surpassingly odd but also supremely affecting work" (O'Neil 2016). One comics blogger deemed it "essential reading … [a] beautiful definitive collection" (Chamberlain 2015). Another called the book "haunting, chilling, beguiling, and intensely imposing" (Wiacek 2015). And *Rolling Stone* magazine characterized *The Puma Blues* as one of the "50 Best Non-Superhero Graphic Novels" ever published (2014).

While *The Puma Blues* was not the first comic book series to take up environmental themes, it remains exceptional in terms of its attentiveness to issues of biodiversity and its stark assessment of the sources and consequences of multiple and overlapping ecological crises. Rather than offering a conventional hero-centric narrative, the book's main ambition is to cast an eerie light on a once verdant planet transformed by human activity. But while the book starts out as a near-future cautionary tale, it soon takes a surreal turn and "eventually grows to encompass pseudo-autobiography, New Age mysticism, conspiracy literature, UFO-logy, and natural history" (O'Neil 2016). The series' experimental and sometimes nonlinear plotting, attentive imagery, and crepuscular politics make for an unsettling reading experience. Now that the series has been collected into a single volume, *The Puma Blues* can be adduced to show how comics as a medium can offer underappreciated advantages when it comes to confronting global real-world topics. This chapter thus points to *The Puma Blues* as an important case study in the development of serious-minded comics. But the chapter also explores the strengths and weaknesses of the eco-pessimist perspective that pervades Murphy and Zulli's gloomy project and that lends the work to its powerful yet self-defeating take on contemporary environmental politics.

Understanding how contemporary environmental politics is represented within comics is crucial in learning new ways to shape activism concerning the ecology. This has become all the more important as eco-pessimism has become more mainstream with evermore people questioning what they can do in response. My analysis helps to flesh out other alternatives in order to foster a better form of awareness surrounding ecological politics and activism given contemporary popular culture.

UNDERSTANDING THE ANTHROPOCENE

The term "Anthropocene" was not in general circulation when Stephen Murphy and Michael Zulli were working on *The Puma Blues*. It was initially coined in the mid-1920s by "the Soviet geologist Aleksei Pavlov, who used it to refer to a new geological period in which humanity was the main driver of planetary geological change" (Foster 2016). It was later revived "by two earth system scientists, Paul Crutzen and Eugene Stoermer, in a short article in 2000 for the newsletter of the International Geosphere-Biosphere program" (Royle 2016). Although Murphy and Zulli were presumably unaware of the term when they started working on this project in the mid-1980s, their series is very much about the idea that the planet that "has entered a new geological epoch defined by human activity," which is the textbook definition of the Anthropocene (Royle 2016). For most of our species' existence, runs the argument, Homo sapiens have benefited from the mostly temperate conditions of the Holocene. As a consequence of developments like the Industrial Revolution, the splitting of the atom, and rapid population growth, human drive and ingenuity has inadvertently triggered a post-Holocene with a Homo sapien-dominated ecosphere. According to Crutzen and Stoermer, humanity will "remain a major geological force for many millennia, maybe millions of years, to come" (Royle 2016).

The concept of the Anthropocene has been the subject of vigorous debate among biologists and social theorists. While some Marxist political economists, such as Ian Angus (2016) and John Bellamy Foster (2016), have embraced the term, others have decried "the narrative of an entire species ascending to biospheric supremacy" (Malm 2015). The Swedish geographer Andreas Malm argues there is a "great ideological divide" between those who recognize the "myriad ways in which capital accumulation, in general, and its neoliberal variant, in particular, pour fuel on the fire now consuming the earth system," and those who point out, with environmental writer Paul Kingsworth, that "climate change isn't something that a small group of baddies has foisted on us," and that "we are all implicated" (Malm 2015). Malm places Angus, Foster, and Naomi Klein in the first category, but suggests that many academics who write on this topic are closer to Kingsworth's position. The English journalist John Gray has usefully framed this debate in terms of two radically different perspectives—"a confrontation between capitalism and the planet" versus "a clash between the expanding demands of humankind and a finite world" (Malm 2015).

The Puma Blues speaks to this second perspective. It sides with the version of eco-politics that assumes humanity writ large, propelled by innate traits like greed, laziness, and shortsightedness, bears primary responsibility for the state of the global ecosystem. This version of eco-pessimism reflects and speaks to the widespread fear and anxiety that exists even within activist circles that change is nearly impossible and that the problems of climate change and habitat destruction means that some form of societal and ecological collapse inevitably looms on the horizon. Implicitly rejecting a class struggle perspective on environmental crisis, *The Puma Blues* reproduces the "flattening" of moral guilt and responsibility that has been vigorously critiqued by a number of radical theorists (Moore 2015; Moore 2016).

The Puma Blues is notable not so much for its messaging than for the way it tells its story, however. Rather than delivering a straightforward political argument the book provides an immersive para-literary experience, one that depends as much or more on the visuals than on any of the characters' pronouncements or conversations. Even readers who might abjure the book's spirit of pessimism could be taken aback by its imaginative world-building and the heartfelt realism of Michael Zulli's pencils. Whatever the specific merits of the eco-pessimist perspective, *The Puma Blues* exemplifies the extent to which comics are an unusually democratic medium that offers few barriers to entry. It demonstrates the medium's versatility, its capacity to depict, as well as move between, just about any landscape or time period without confusing the reader or going over budget. And it showcases the permeability of comics, the way in which the comics page can house all kinds of information, from data and dialogue to the pictorial and the bibliographic. At a time when the audience for thematically mature graphic literature continues to grow, *The Puma Blues* provides a compelling case study of how comics can address complex topics in ways that are distinct from other media.

VARIETIES OF ENVIRONMENTAL DISCOURSE

Animals and the environment have been part of the mise-en-scene of comic book narratology if only by implication or incidental acknowledgment from the medium's outset. With the rise of environmental-minded activism and discourse, however, pop culture storytellers began to make direct use of ecological themes and tropes (Sturgeon 2008, 6). Numerous EC Comics titles in the 1950s, such as *Two-Fisted Tales* #33 (1953) and *Weird Science* #5 (1951), featured the grim specter of nuclear fallout, and planetary devastation. Meanwhile Marvel and DC superhero titles in the late 1960s and 1970s sometimes took note of the rising tide of environmental consciousness—for example, *Justice League of America* #79 (1970). DC's *Swamp Thing*, both in its original incarnation (1972–1976) and especially under Alan Moore's tutelage (1984–1987), incorporated a variety of ecological tropes that drew explicit connections between the perils facing Swamp Thing, a tragically misunderstood "swamp monster," and the ongoing threats to his beloved bayou. DC's *Animal Man* series—particularly when Grant Morrison was penning the title (1988–1990)—pushed even further in foregrounding animal and green issues, including hunting, vegetarianism, and the fishing industry. In 1991 Marvel published twelve issues of *Captain Planet and the Planeteers*, based on the animated television show. Green and pro-animal themes can also be found in the editorial cartoons of Steve Bell, Ron Cobb, Richard Willson, and in recent works of long-form graphic literature, including *Capitalism and Climate Change* (2015), *Climate Changed* (2014), *Concrete: Think Like a Mountain* (2006), *Nausicaa of the Valley of the Wind* (2012), *Pride of Baghdad* (2008), *Ruins* (2015), and *We3* (2014).

Stories that are explicitly concerned with environmental and animal issues often nestle into one of four categories. The first category, eco-optimism, constructs a vision of the future in which technology and nature exist in mutually beneficial harmony. This approach acknowledges problems like pollution, overcrowding, and species depletion, but suggests that with the application of good will, scientific knowledge, and wise leaders, a brighter future is possible. An early example of eco-optimism is the comic strip *Mark Trail*, which was launched in 1946. Patrick McDonnell's *Mutts*, introduced in 1994, offers a better-known example of a daily newspaper strip that exudes ecological awareness and empathy for nonhuman animals. McDonnell's prize-winning strip is not as upbeat as *Mark Trail*, but it can be cautiously hopeful. Another example is provided by the first generation of Star Trek-themed comic strips (1969–1973) and comic books (1967–1978), which presented environmental problems such as pollution as curios from a benighted past (Wein et al. 2005). There is little sense in the future-embracing world of Star Trek that there might be trade-offs between space exploration and complex ecosystems. Futuristic technology would dissolve or render moot any potential conflict between human aspirations and the natural world. Scott McCloud's comic book series *Zot!* (1984–1990) offers another pop art–influenced example of futurist optimism (McCloud 2008).

The second category is the post-apocalyptic story. Late twentieth-century popular culture is often remembered for its apocalyptic imagery and content, from *Mad Max* (1979) and *Road Warrior* (1982) to the *Terminator* (1984, 1991, 2003, 2009, 2015) movies. A profusion of mainstream and indy comic books, including titles spun off from these popular film franchises, rebelled against the sunny optimism of Silver Age cartooning and presented dyspeptic stories about hard-bitten anti-heroes who wander across urban wastelands and irradiated landscapes. Whether set in ruined cities or outer space, stories that take place in post-apocalyptic environments present a stern warning—suggesting that unless drastic steps are taken (to curb nuclear weapons proliferation, cull toxins from the ecosphere, and so on) these bitter fantasies could soon become our collective reality. As a practical matter, however, post-apocalyptic stories are more often thrilling than terrifying. Examples in comics include *Tank Girl* (1988 onwards), *V for Vendetta* (1982–1988), *Judge Dread* (1977 onwards), and *Xenozoic Tales* (1987–1996). This allows for a certain optimism to still exist even as it outlines the potential apocalypse awaiting humanity should they not be careful.

A third approach is one that imagines a world in which the worst features of the present—crowded cities, food shortages, authoritarianism, ecological decay, and so on—are projected onto the future. Rather than assuming a rupture between a normal present and an apocalyptic future, these kinds of stories are organized around concepts like entropy, devolution, and decay. The *Robocop* (1987, 1990, 1993) movies, and comics, represent a vivid example of near-future storytelling that rules out the apocalypse but at the same time precludes any form of ecological or societal rejuvenation. In these kinds of stories, the well-off and well-connected are often able to seal themselves off from the larger disrepair that surrounds them, but only at the cost of losing their humanity, as is the case in *Blade Runner* (1982) and *Elysium* (2013). In post-apocalyptic narratives, the line dividing the present from the future is geographic rather than chronological. A good example in mainstream comics of this kind of degraded presentism is offered by the Batman mythos, which draws a sharp contrast between Gotham's downtrodden masses and the city's pampered elite. If the Superman storyverse provides the paradigmatic example of glossy eco-optimism, then the Batman storyverse represents the quintessential case of funeral entropy in comic book storytelling.

Stories that present the eco-pessimistic view represent a fourth and final approach to the narratological challenge raised by ecological crisis and the rise of the post-sixties green and animal rights movements. In these stories, ecological catastrophe is foregrounded and problematized, rather than taken as a given, which is typically the case in post-apocalyptic and eternal-present tales. In an effort to contextualize and dramatize environmental issues, storytellers in this tradition practically dare the audience to acknowledge what is at stake in the story and the world at large. These kinds of narratives often investigate specific problems, from internal war and public sector breakdown to the degradation of ecosystems. By digging into the roots of crisis, eco-pessimistic stories raise important questions about trajectory, causality, as well as individual and social responsibility. At the same time, they offer little or no hope that the problems presented in the story will be overcome. Instead of treating ecological collapse as a backdrop on which to stage individual and small group dramas, eco-pessimistic stories push the reader or viewer to confront painful truths that many humans instinctively shy away from.

The Puma Blues exemplifies this fourth category of ecologically aware pop culture. From a tonal perspective it is neither optimistic nor post-apocalyptic, nor does it assume an unchanging future. It places ecological decrepitude at the center of the narrative, and assumes a continued downward spiral, providing the reader little in the way of hope or solace. As Stephen Murphy told one interviewer, "It was only too easy extrapolating today's horrors along their collective one-way path towards even more horrific future events. Gavia can only watch, frozen in pain, shuffling forward through his functional depression, isolated, alienated, deeply in love with a beautiful but dying world" (Dueben 2016). Murphy's disenchanted contribution to the eco-pessimistic subgenre might perhaps rouse some readers, spurring them to join the green and animal rights movements. But it seems more likely that his pessimistic realism invites passivity and demoralization. The stark logic of the eco-pessimistic narrative—what the historian Henri Forcillon once referred to as "a perpetual calendar of human anxiety"—can generate anger but it can also foster a sense of hopelessness (Kermode 1980, 11).

STORYLINE AND ARTWORK

The appeal of *The Puma Blues* is rooted in its richly detailed artwork and unconventional storytelling strategies. Its larger contribution to eco-political discourse crucially depends on the ability of the story and artwork to leave an impression on its readers. The series opens on a conventional note: a government agent collecting information about a small slice of remaining wilderness in the northeast United States that has been seriously harmed by industrial pollution, radioactive fallout, and the indiscriminate use of toxic chemicals. The agent's name is Gavia Immer, which also happens to be the Latin name for the Common Loon (Dueben 2016). The reader learns that, in this near-future alternative reality, the Bronx has been obliterated by white supremacists who detonated a nuclear weapon in 1995 during a botched effort to kidnap the president of the United States. Immer's job is to collect pH samples from a local reservoir, which is regularly limed to mitigate the impact of acid rain, as well as to keep an eye on the strange mutated animals that have resulted from the nuclear radiation.

In this world, these mutated animals are known as "animutes," or "bio-mutes," and the reservoir includes a colony of flying manta rays that the authorities want to keep under surveillance. Much of the time Immer works alone, although at one point a trespasser turns up to give him some company, and some of the animals seem to be keeping an eye on him. He stays in touch with his superiors via video conferencing, which he also uses on occasion to communicate with his mother. His father has passed away but left him a series of personalized videotapes that he watches most nights in his cabin. He shares with his dad a desperate need to understand the root causes of ecological crisis and to determine whether the blame lies with powerful special interests or humanity writ large.

As the story unfolds, the focus shifts from the Gavia Immer to the natural environment itself, particularly focusing on the fish, birds, insects, and mammals that have managed to survive into the Anthropocene. By the middle of the series many of Michael Zulli's pages are entirely devoid of people, dialogue, or conventional storytelling. Instead there is a far greater emphasis placed on flora and fauna rather than plot mechanics and human melodrama. Much of the book's second half represents an effort to dethrone Homo sapiens and to place animals and plants at the center of the narrative. With issue number twenty-one, however, the story abruptly leaps two years ahead. By this point Immer is no longer working for the US government and, as he embarks on a cross-country journey, it becomes evident that the environmental damage that haunts the main character is by no means confined to the northeast United States.

As the years pass, Immer sinks into a melancholic stupor as he waits for death in a remote corner of Alaska. "I remained in my cabin for longer and longer stretches of time," he tells the reader. "Months, entire seasons, then as long as an entire year, taking sole springtime trips to the city for the foods I couldn't grow, the painkillers I needed, the books that lent me sorrow, joy, and comfort" (Murphy and Zulli 2015, 501). At the close of the story a series of nuclear explosions—"So much for turning the other cheek"—illuminate the horizon, even as Immer's own body begins breaking down (Murphy and Zulli 2015, 518). "Oh, can you ... forgive us?" he forlornly asks the agitated puma that has been apparently stalking him since the series' very first issue (Murphy and Zulli 2015, 519). As Immer slips into a self-medicated coma, the "camera" pulls back and we see the solar system, the Milky Way, and then the universe itself that is contained in the iris of the eye of an alien fetus. It's a suitably trippy ending to an offbeat work of environmentally minded graphic literature.

Stephen Murphy and Michael Zulli expended an enormous amount of time and energy on this project, yet for many years it was uncertain whether the series would be completed, let alone collected in a single volume. As the comics artist Steven Bissette reports, "it was a turbulent run, taking a toll on Steve and Michael in the way such projects can and will" (Murphy and Zulli 2015, 530). Over the years, Murphy supported himself through his work on the *Teenage Mutant Ninja Turtles Adventures* series that was published by Archie Comics in the 1990s, which also canvassed environmental concerns, as well as his work on the *Teenage Mutant Ninja Turtles* comic strip (1990–1997), and the *TMNT* (1987–1996) animated series. In addition, in 2006 Murphy created *Umbra* (2006), a detective series for Image Comics, which Dover plans to reprint. Michael Zulli has also remained active in the comics industry. He drew seven issues of the legendary *Sandman* series (1989–1996) for Vertigo/DC and has illustrated numerous other Vertigo titles, such as *Shade* (1997), *Winter's Edge* (1998), and *Witchcraft* (1994; 1998). Zulli's pages are often thick with black ink, unconventional panel arrangements, and lush naturalistic details, and they offer a compelling accompaniment to Murphy's mordant prose. An artist less attuned to the natural world would have represented a poor fit with a writer whose main interest has to do with mourning habitat depletion and rising cancer rates, rather than propelling the reader through a familiar storytelling apparatus.

Zulli's pencils and inks may be the single most irresistible aspect of the entire series. Some of the figure work in the early pages is a little clumsy, but the artwork tightens as the series progresses. The main character is rendered in a way that makes him look like the late David Bowie in his Thin White Duke phase. Some of the incidental characters are very much of their time, with padded shoulders and New Wave hairstyles. This is a touch jarring given that the series is set not in the 1980s but at the end of the 1990s and the early years of the twenty-first century. Yet when the story takes Gavia Immer out of his nature preserve comfort zone, Zulli's pages nicely capture man-made environments, such as television studios, government offices, and urban landscapes. By far the strongest feature of Zulli's artwork, however, are the numerous scenes set in and about the New England wildlife refuge and, later on, the Alaskan wilderness. At times his artwork is almost forensic in its treatment of heron, mallards, deer, owls, snakes, frogs, and the eponymous puma. No doubt, the visual elegance of the wildlife and foliage depicted in these pages are intended to remind the reader of what's at stake when it comes to the health of the global environment. Murphy drops several informative charts into the narrative that show, for example, trend lines between 1800 and 2000 in terms of skin cancers, leukemia, ocean dumping, and nuclear waste. These empirical respites complement Zulli's vivid artwork, adding a factual component behind the work's fiction.

The sensitivity of Michael Zulli's linework is ably expressed in a wordless chapter titled "In the Empire of the Senses," which was originally a stand-alone issue (#5), and which remains one of the book's strongest sections. In the context of the larger story this is the first time that the narrative is turned over to what most comics writers would treat as incidental background information. The chapter is set late at night and provides a glimpse of how owls, racoons, flying manta rays, and the lone puma fend for themselves under the light of a full moon. The only sound effects are those generated by the puma ("tsip" and "snuf snuf") as she prowls the shoreline. Murphy's authorial decision to concentrate on mute animals rather than people is rewarded by Zulli's deft pencils, which alternate between naturalistic realism and stylized imagery. Toward the end of the chapter the narrative focuses on the puma's hunt for food, as she tracks and then dines on ungulate flesh on a rock ledge. The panel in which the puma charges into the water offers a blur of motion lines and teeth, while the successive panels in which the animal carries her meal back to her waterside perch are filled with blood splatter and inky shadows. The chapter exudes a you-are-there quality that is all-too-rare in North

American comics, which as Scott McCloud pointed out tend to emphasize "getting there" over "being there" (1993, 81).

THE ECO-POLITICS OF DESPAIR

In an interview with the comics journalist Alex Dueben, Stephen Murphy acknowledged that while he "would love to believe that there's a sliver of hope," the "signs, statistics, and facts" indicate that "we're in the midst of a sixth planet-wide extinction event, one that's going to wipe out a high percentage of species—an event currently underway—and that a large portion of humanity will die off as well" (Dueben 2016). The events depicted in *The Puma Blues* offer scant encouragement about the state of the planet. Gavia Immer is just about the only character in the book who even seems to notice let alone care about ecological issues. The exception is his conspiracy-minded deceased father, whose paranoid videotapes seem to suggest that alien lifeforms are either monitoring or manipulating the crisis for their own mysterious ends. "Where does rebellion begin?" his father asks in one tape, "Why is there rebellion? Does it point to the inevitability of change? To its necessity? Is it born of the widening gap of believability between the public and its governing institutions? Is it because the old systems eventually yield hell in the form of a world without meaning? Of meaning without relative worth? (Murphy and Zulli 2015, 222–223)."

But neither the tapes nor the events depicted in the book provide any substantive indications of rebellion—apart, that is, from Immer's decision to voluntarily extricate himself from the wider social world. He bears witness, perhaps, but fails to act (Murphy and Zulli 2015, 508). Rather than pointing toward concrete steps that people could take to reverse the damage, Immer's father shifts from vague talk of rebellion to enigmatic and mystical notions of alien hegemony. "It strikes me," says his father, "that in denuclearizing the very heavens we have made the planet a prison. A new prison with an as-yet little understood system of laws. But if so, who has been appointed warden? And by whom" (Murphy and Zulli 2015, 224–225)?

The accompanying imagery shifts from depictions of Strategic Defense Initiative satellites to pictures of alien spacecraft hovering above Earth, implying that our new overlords are intergalactic rather than terrestrial in origin. The book's conclusion suggests that his father has misjudged the aliens, which are in fact watchful rather than malevolent. This effectively places the blame on the shoulders of humanity writ large rather than specific economic forces and/or social structures. Murphy's script makes it clear that it would be a mistake to offload the responsibility for the planet's deteriorating condition on extraterrestrial or metaphysical forces, but he expresses little interest in issues of political ecology or political economy. From Murphy's perspective, humanity is a "bad seed." Population growth, industrialization, and capitalism simply gave an already fatally self-involved species the tools to destroy its surroundings. "In the history books that now shall never be written," the book's narrator intones, "it would have shown that the decimation of your planet was due to your endless hunger for more" (Murphy and Zulli 2015, 508).

A thoroughgoing disdain for humanity permeates *The Puma Blues*, which at one point segues from Immer's pensive musings to the detached face of a broadcast journalist as she recites on-air stories about the disappearance of fur seals, fin whales, and humpback whales without losing her advertiser-friendly smile. Murphy also has a bit of fun with the reader as he juxtaposes the "seafood crash of ninety-two," and the collapse of the ozone layer, with a sexed-up ad for a new kind of super-strong sunscreen (Murphy and Zulli 2015, 378). "The phantoms"—or the four riders of the apocalypse—"only sneer at my sermon and ride forward," Immer thinks to himself, as he pushes deeper into the Alaskan tundra, "with the pain of knowing the cost of tomorrow" (Murphy and Zulli 2015, 463). Toward the end of the story, when Gavia Immer has ventured into an Alaskan town for supplies, he becomes entangled with a group of armed teenagers who torture the defenseless for the sport of it. "Who the fuck are you, man?" asks one of the sadistic thugs, who carries a gun and wears a grotesque mask. "I asked you some questions, old man. Answer me," he continues. "What happened here?" Immer replies. "Marburg, panic, rioting, the National Guard, and then the fucking Chinese! Don't you pay attention to the news, man?" His friend then says, "He still ain't answered you! Make him talk! Torture his old soldier ass!" "Time to sing, old man," says the first thug, as he pulls out a pair of plyers in order to pull out Immer's teeth (Murphy and Zulli 2015, 509–511). Fortunately, for our hero, a flock of flying manta rays appear out of nowhere to gorge themselves on his attackers.

In the world of *The Puma Blues*, arguably the only characters who live by a moral code, apart from Immer himself, are nonhuman. The puma who is at the heart of issue number five, "In the Empire of the Senses," does not kill ungulates for sport, even if she enjoys the sport of it. She does not waste the meat that she kills. Nor does she imprison or torture the deer beforehand. Her moral code is nonhuman but it is strongly felt. It also seems as if the manta rays made a deliberate choice to go after a group of punks but to leave the protagonist alone. Yet by this point Stephen Murphy's eco-pessimism has morphed into eco-despair. What was once highly likely has become inevitable. Not only is humanity is doomed, but we seem hell-bent on taking the rest of the biosphere with us via overdevelopment, toxic chemicals, radioactive waste, and nuclear weapons. Any plants and animals that survive the coming century, the book suggests, will be in no condition to propagate a posthuman utopia. Ultimately, no final hope is given to the reader as the inevitability of collapse is fully certain.

CONCLUSION

There is something masochistic about reading or watching characters who have a genuine appreciation for what's going on around them, but who are unable to do anything about it. Eco-optimistic stories might not always be realistic, but at least they tend to offer concrete suggestions about "what is to be done." While eco-optimist solutions may not be up to the task, they allow for the possibility of human agency. Perhaps surprisingly, post-apocalyptic stories often end up providing rays of hope as well. The destruction that these stories so lovingly depict often gestures toward a brighter tomorrow. The apocalypse can be an act of cleansing, purgation, and rejuvenation, even if—like Moses—the characters themselves won't live to see the new dawn. Eternal-present stories are intrinsically less-than-hopeful, of course, but they don't necessarily foreclose the possibility that at some point a rebellion might break out, often along class lines thereby often retaining a quasi-Marxist edge. The present may extend into the near-future, but that does not necessarily mean that things cannot change for the better at some far off point when a revolution happens.

Conversely, eco-pessimism operates according to a very different political logic than eco-optimism, post-apocalypticism, and eternal-presentism. In eco-pessimist stories, the writer, artist, main characters, and audience are all locked in a downward spiral. Any form of action is pointless and illusory. One name for this kind of storytelling, of course, is horror, and in many ways *The Puma Blues* is a horror comic. While it does not feature stalkers, scream-ers, or conventional monsters, the storyline and imagery generate a sense of uneasiness and paranoia. But it is also a story in which natural landscapes are celebrated, and the main character grows old and dies having spent relatively little time in the company of other people.

Over the course of *The Puma Blues*, Gavia Immer gains insight into the global eco-crisis, as well as a greater sense of self-awareness, but this knowl-edge gives him little or no solace. Nor is he able to influence the course of events. He is powerless, and at most all the reader can say to herself is, "at least someone feels the same as I do." But this emotional connection lacks political purchase. Is such a pessimistic outlook politically counter-productive? Perhaps. Despair, it might be argued, is an indulgence we can ill afford. It might also be worth pointing out that many of the predictions that Stephen Murphy advances in *The Puma Blues* have not—yet—come to pass. The ozone layer has not evaporated, nuclear war has not broken out, and the seas are not devoid of life. But even if Murphy's timetable is off the trend lines, it remains disturbing in its semblance to reality. However, it might not be too late and worth resisting some of the more eco-pessimistic representations within Murphy and Zulli's otherwise compelling work. When activists begin to do just that in their struggles they may find their tactics to prove more successful since lamenting the destruction of the environment alone is never enough.

WORKS CITED

Angus, Ian. 2016. *Facing the Anthropocene: Fossil Capitalism and the Crisis of the Earth System.* New York: Monthly Review Press.

Bissette, Steven. 2015. "Acts of Faith: A Coda." In *The Puma Blues*, by Steven Murphy and Michael Zulli. Mineola, NY: Dover.

Chadwick, Paul. 2006. *Concrete, Vol. 5: Think Like a Mountain.* Milwaukie, OR: Dark Horse.

Chamberlain, Henry. 2015. "Review: *The Puma Blues.*" *Comics Grinder*, November 23. https://comicsgrinder.com/2015/11/23/review-the-puma-blues-the-complete-saga-in-one-volume, accessed on April 28, 2017.

Dueben, Alex. 2016. "Interview: Stephen Murphy Opens Up About Fear and Slivers of Hope in The Puma Blues and Umbria." *Comics Beat*, September 21. http://www.comicsbeat.com/interview-stephen-murphy-opens-up-about-fear-and-slivers-of-hope-in-the-puma-blues-and-umbra/, accessed on December 14, 2016.

Dueben, Alex. 2016. "The Michael Zulli Interview." *The Comics Journal.* July 25. http://www.tcj.com/the-michael-zulli-interview/, accessed on April 20, 2017.

Foster, John Bellamy. 2016. "The Anthropocene Crisis." *Monthly Review* 68(4). https://monthlyreview.org/2016/09/01/the-anthropocene-crisis/, accessed on April 27, 2017.

Groves, Adam. 2015. "*Puma Blues* by Stephen Murphy, Michael Zulli." http://www.fright.com/edge/PumaBlues.htm, accessed on April 27, 2017.

Kermode, Frank. 1980. *The Sense of an Ending: Studies in the Theory of Fiction with a New Epilogue.* Oxford: Oxford University Press.

Klein, David and Stephanie McMillan. 2015. *Capitalism and Climate Change: The Science and Politics of Global Warming.* Seattle, WA: Amazon Digital Services LLC.

Kuper, Peter. 2015. *Ruins.* London: SelfMadeHero.

Malm, Andreas. 2015. "The Anthropocene Myth." *Jacobin*, March 30. https://www.jacobinmag.com/2015/03/anthropocene-capitalism-climate-change/, accessed on April 28, 2017.

McCloud, Scott. 1993. *Understanding Comics: The Invisible Art.* Northampton, MA: Tundra.

———. 2008. *Zot! The Complete Black-and-White Collection: 1987–1991.* New York: HarperCollins.

Miyazaki, Hayao. 2012. *Nausicaa of the Valley of the Wind* (boxed set). New York: Viz.

Moore, Jason W. 2015. *Capitalism in the Web of Life: Ecology and the Accumulation of Capital*. New York: Verso.

Moore, Jason W., ed. 2016. *Anthropocene or Capitalocene? Nature, History, and the Crisis of Capitalism*. Oakland, CA: PM Press.

Morrison, Grant and Frank Quitely. 2014. *We3*. New York: DC/Vertigo.

Murphy, Steven and Michael Zulli. 2015. *The Puma Blues*. Mineola, NY: Dover.

O'Neil, Tim. 2016. "Resurfaced *Puma Blues* Shows Michael Zulli and Stephen Murphy's Audacious Beginnings." *AV Club*, January 26. http://www.avclub.com/article/resurfaced-puma-blues-shows-michael-zulli-and-step-230775, accessed on December 15, 2016.

Rolling Stone. 2014. "Drawn Out: The 50 Best Non-Superhero Graphic Novels." May 5.http://www.rollingstone.com/culture/lists/drawn-out-the-50-best-non-superhero-graphic-novels-20140505, accessed on December 14, 2016.

Royle, Camilla. 2016. "Marxism and the Anthropocene." *International Socialism* 151. http://isj.org.uk/marxism-and-the-anthropocene/, accessed on April 29, 2017.

Sim, Dave. 2015. "Introduction." In Steven Murphy and Michael Zulli. 2015. *The Puma Blues*. Mineola, NY: Dover.

Squarzoni, Philippe. 2014. *Climate Changed: A Personal Journey Through the Science*. New York: Abrams.

Sturgeon, Noel. 2008. *Environmentalism in Popular Culture: Gender, Race, Sexuality and the Politics of the Natural*. Tucson, AZ: University of Arizona Press.

Vaughn, Brian K. and Nico Henrichon. 2008. *Pride of Baghdad*. New York: DC/Vertigo.

Wein, Len and others. 2004. *Star Trek: The Key Collection, Vol 1*. Miamisburg, OH: Checker Book Publishing Group.

Wiacek, Win. 2015. "The Puma Blues: The Complete Saga in One Volume." November 17. http://www.comicsreview.co.uk/nowreadthis/2015/11/17/the-puma-blues-the-complete-saga-in-one-volume/, accessed on April 29, 2017.

Chapter 3

"We Are All Scream!"

Woodgod and the "Animal Superhero"

José Alaniz

You will know what it is like to be an animal only if you are in agony.

(Lamb 2011, 202).

In the early twenty-first century, superheroes—what critic Douglas Wolk called "the public and private shame of American comics"—continued to suffer a crisis of legitimacy inversely proportional to their growing public profile, television ratings and box office clout (2007, 100). As the editors of the landmark scholarly anthology *The Superhero Reader* delicately put it:

> Comics Studies has not quite granted the necessity or even fitness of studying superheroes from aesthetic or humanistic perspectives such as the literary or the art-historical, even though few academics interested in cultural studies would deny the ripeness of the genre for study on semiotic and ideological grounds. Studies of the superhero remain an outlier within the fast-growing literary discourse on comics. As a result, some comics scholars, despite the field's inroads to legitimacy, still continue to decry what they see as the cultural elitism of the academy. The treatment of the superhero is a ready focus for such complaints. In other words, the hoped-for elevation of comics as a research topic has not happened evenly for all genres, or across all disciplines, and the superhero has certainly not been the main beneficiary of that proposition that comics can be art. (Hatfield et al. 2013, xv)

In the years since that anthology's publication, the tide has shifted somewhat, with the recent publication of significant superhero works such as Andrew Hoberek's *Considering Watchmen: Poetics, Property, Politics* (2014), Paul Young's *Frank Miller's Daredevil and the Ends of Heroism* (2016), and Scott Bukatman's *Hellboy's World: Comics and Monsters on the Margins* (2016). More scholars are turning to the superhero genre with the tools of cultural studies, arguing for its primacy as a body genre particularly taken with issues of identity. Especially from the so-called "Silver Age" onward (roughly the late 1950s to the early 1970s), superhero comics displayed increasing attention to race, gender, ability and what Ramzi Fawaz calls "fluxability": a "state of material and psychic *becoming* that endows figures with the capacity to negotiate multiple selves," and to forge alternative communities (2015, 11). As Fawaz writes in *The New Mutants: Superheroes and the Radical Imagination of American Comics* (2015):

> The very fact that superhero comics were conceptually obsessed with phenotypic and physiological difference, expending vast narrative and visual space depicting new species, bodies and identities, meant that the introduction of previously unrepresented differences (whether real-world ones like race or fictional categories like mutation) demanded a substantive recalibration of the social relations between characters, the visual depiction of new distinctions, and a language with which to discuss such differences. (21)

These "new distinctions" even broke the species barrier, most notably in the case of Stan Lee/Steve Ditko's creation Spider-Man (1962) and Lee/Jack Kirby's Black Panther (1966), both for Marvel. Other "animal-heroes," however, have had less stellar receptions such as Frank Robbins/Neal Adams' Man-Bat for DC (1970).

Debuting inauspiciously in a second-tier title during what many critics have come to consider an indifferent decade for superhero comics (the "Bronze Age"), Woodgod never truly rose above his roots. The character first appears in "Birthday!" *Marvel Premiere* Vol. 1 #31 (Mantlo and Giffen 1976). Woodgod is a half-human/half-goat recalls the chimerae of ancient myth, as well as figures from past tales of man tampering with nature such as Mary Shelley's *Frankenstein* (1818) and H.G. Wells' *The Island of Doctor Moreau* (1896). But the swarthy, furry, cloven-hoofed Woodgod most closely resembles the Greek god Pan, though with none of the lustful deity's mirth. All the same, the hero's creation in a lab and subsequent hunting-down by zealous government operatives directly address such sobering topics as animal experimentation, genetic engineering and nonhuman suffering, all just emerging into 1970s mainstream US consciousness.

This chapter examines one of Marvel Comics' most obscure characters through the lens of critical animal studies, tracing Woodgod's story from his debut through his initial and subsequent appearances, in which he escapes human tyranny and (again in a nod to *Moreau)* establishes his own alternative society of animal-people. Woodgod's late 1970s/early 1980s mash-up of animal liberation and superheroics anticipates subsequent, more explicitly politicized series such as Grant Morrison's run on *Animal Man* (1988–1990) for DC. This is true even as it demonstrates the limits of exploring radical politics in a commercial genre popularly associated with children's entertainment. Along the way, my discussion will highlight the curious place of animals in superhero comics and the (in)expressibility of their suffering in a visual-verbal medium. In doing so, my aim is to demonstrate how comic characters can be positioned representationally in order to inspire activism and ecological awareness. Thus, by paying attention to how media matters it can be possible to foster new cultural realities that can pave the way toward total liberation for all.

HUMAN-ANIMAL ONTOLOGY IN WOODGOD

The anthology series *Marvel Premiere,* launched by Marvel Comics in April 1972, earned a reputation over its sixty-one-issue run for middling sales and out-of-left-field characters and storylines. Marvel used the title to reboot characters from series it had cancelled (Doctor Strange) and to experiment with ideas too quirky or risky to introduce anywhere else (Legion of Monsters, 3-D Man). The blog *Bronze Age Babies* called it "the great rotating try-out title" (Karen and Doug 2016).

Issue thirty-one's cover, by legendary artist Jack Kirby promises "the most bizarre superhero of all!" It depicts, under the title "The man-brute called Woodgod," a creature human above the waist, goat-like below, battling men in futuristic environment suits who ride levitating vehicles ("floaters") as they fire their weapons. The cover has some mistakes: Woodgod appears with a light-colored face and torso (the interior pages show him much darker) and he is missing the small horns on his forehead.

The opening page—a four-panel tier giving way to a large splash image—shows a goat-man stumbling, confused, along the empty thoroughfare of a one-street town, his hooves kicking up dust as he approaches. The setting appears rural with mountains in the distance. The dominant portrait, crowned by the title, "Birthday!" depicts the hybrid hero in a tortured pose: his arms outstretched, fists clenched, he howls, "Father!" The artist renders Woodgod as a horned, hairy, dark-skinned Apollo, human torso fused with goat legs—though missing a tail as well as, notably, genitalia. Giffen—at the time an up-and-coming penciller with a stylistic flourish—also does something unusual for a Marvel superhero comics story here: he draws page one's outside panel borders as green woodland foliage. This enacts a visual tension, mirroring the wooded hills that surround the town: civilization ensnared by nature.

Page one's text further complicates the message. The first panel's caption reads: "In the *beginning,* there was no *sound"* (1976). The Biblical associations seem unavoidable, though the figure's resemblance to a satyr belies them, to say the least. The next two text boxes only deepen the mystery:

"There was no *understanding*, for concepts had not yet been *formed*. There was, however, *feeling*.
Pain, for instance. Whimpering, *animal* pain.
And there was Scream ... *Woodgod* was its *name!*" (1976, 1)

Clearly, based on the sophisticated—even obtuse—opening page, Woodgod's first adventure will take readers where no superhero has ventured before.

We soon learn that nearly the entire population of Liberty (eventually revealed to lie in New Mexico) has been wiped out by an accidental release of deadly nerve gas, leaving the place eerily vacant. The scene recalls the premises of such apocalyptic sci-fi yarns as *Where Have All the People Gone* (1974), while Liberty itself uncannily resembles a set for a movie western with the name even suggesting John Ford's film *The Man Who Shot Liberty Valance* (1962). Generic signs for "Barber," "Rooms," and "Grocery" enhance the impression as if civilization itself were somehow a lifeless, paper-thin façade.

In flashback we come to know of Woodgod's origins: created in a secret government laboratory through a "*clone-graft* ... a combination of human and animal *genes*" (1976, 7). The super-powerful creature has no known military purpose—though his "parents," Dr. David Pace and his wife Ellen, work clandestinely for Vertigo Base (later renamed Tranquility Base) on a program to synthesize the nerve gas Purple Mist (1976, 18). The locals get wind of the Pace's experiment and react angrily. The townsman Davis mentions "them *sheep* that jest up an' *died* last when the *gov'ment* people spilled some that *nerve gas* they was workin' on!" (1976, 11). In doing so, it makes an explicit reference to the 1968 "Dugway Sheep Incident" in which over 6,000 sheep were killed near Utah's Dugway Proving Grounds by wayward nerve gas, though the Army has long denied the charge (Robbins 1998). A mob quickly forms and storms the Paces' farm/lab, in the process releasing the Purple Mist and annihilating all life within miles, save for Woodgod and one Liberty resident.

The rest of "Birthday!" shows the semi-intelligent Woodgod's disoriented search for "Father" and his dawning realization of the world's true nature dominated by "Scream," his vague signifier for the unending pain and violence which humans have wrought. In Liberty, he is attacked by Major Del Tremens and his armed "floater" detachment, though with his shell-resistant skin and super-strength he dispatches the soldiers easily. Woodgod walks off at story's end, lost in an insane reality, declaiming, "Man means *nothing! Scream* has taken *Father—scream* will take *Woodgod!* We are *all* Scream!" (1976, 31).

No follow-up to Woodgod's story appeared in *Marvel Premiere*—the issue may have simply violated too many superhero conventions for readers' comfort or interest—though Mantlo did write the character into two issues of *Marvel Team-Up* published a few months later in two subsequent issues (Mantlo and Byrne 1977, A & B). Essentially it was a vehicle for pairing Marvel's most popular hero, Spider-Man, with less well-known figures. The Woodgod storyline produced more than mediocre fare: both the Hulk and Spider-Man stumble on Liberty the day after "Birthday!'s" events and battle the goat-man, then all three battle a vengeful Tremens, who has returned with reinforcements. The flimsy plot basically rehashes the earlier story's events with no new character development, adding only two more famous superheroes. At story's end, Woodgod spares Tremens' life again, and once more wanders off, darkly declaring, "Woodgod will *go!* He will *hide* where *Scream* will never *find* him! But he will come *back,* man, when he is *ready* ... and then *all* will know the *Scream of Woodgod!"* (Mantlo and Byrne 1977b, 31).

Despite such thin narrative gruel, Mantlo's Woodgod stories open an intriguing window into mid-1970s thought on the environment, scientific manipulation of life, and animal pain—all inflected through the sensibilities of a marginal pop culture genre, superhero comics. In doing so, these works set forth a broad-minded if perplexing, utopian if mournful portrait of animal subjectivity and humanity's place vis-à-vis the natural world.

In a fanzine interview, Mantlo detailed the concept behind his creation:

> I was trying to write a character who is born full-grown and has never experienced thought ... Part of his awareness—being half-animal, half-man—is instinctive, intuitive awareness, rather than the rigid, straight-thinking, classical kind of conceptualization a human would have, one that was based on a whole lifetime of experience. ("Woodgod Wanderings" 1976, 23)

As such, the writer crafted Woodgod as a literal man-child, a romanticized savage innocent. Thus, he first appears in the flashback: already almost fully grown, in bandages, lying peacefully in bed as the Paces care for him, wishing him "happy birthday" (1976, 6). Within two days, Woodgod is walking about the Paces' farm-like property, enjoying a sunny day and playing with Muff the dog, saying, "I can ... *walk,* mother! It feels *good!"* (1976, 7). His openness to and acceptance of everything he encounters reflects a radically egalitarian eco-consciousness. As Pace says, "If Muff looks different than us to him, it's not because *dogs* are inferior to *people* ... it's just because that's how things *are!"* (1976, 7).

Sadly, this bucolic "beast boy" setting does not last, as the locals soon attack, shooting the "monster" on sight—introducing two factors that will dominate his existence: *"scream* and *pain* ... a concept joined in an *instant"* (1976, 14). Woodgod wakes to find every living thing he has known consumed by Purple Mist. Running frantically through the forest, he finds only a myriad of lifeless creatures—a literal "silent spring" (1976, 16). Driven to near-insanity by repeated trauma, obsessed with locating "Father," completely lost in a world he does not understand, Woodgod embodies the core fear and suffering of animal being (as well as the modern human's existentialist anxiety). As Mantlo explained:

> [H]is animal consciousness on the verge of panic, having been thrown into something he didn't ask to be in. ... [T]hat part of his consciousness I decided to call "scream." ... By making Woodgod crazy I want to set him totally apart from the whole universe. From his vantage point of separateness he can examine it. ... By being so totally *other,* I put Woodgod outside, and use him as a way to examine both himself and the sphere. (1976, 23)

Disarray, bewilderment, wild shifts in mood and consciousness come to predominate in the half-animal subject's psyche. Giffen's art visualizes these swings in three-panel sequences that show Woodgod's eyes growing red and opaque. In the first such sequence, an attack by the sole survivor in Liberty sets off the goat-man's anger. In the descending panels his face becomes darker and pupils disappear, replaced by solid red as he utters, "You are *not* my father! You are merely *man* ... like *other* men! Your *ways* are the ways of *pain"* (3)! He then knocks the attacker through a shop window.

Another strategy, the split portrait, signals Woodgod's fundamental hybridity and divided self. These range from a panel in which the three-day-old creature stares at himself in a mirror, asking, "Father, is that *me?"* to the more commonly utilized bifurcated visage of the full-grown specimen, often in moments of rage (1976, 11). In these "half-head shots," Woodgod's face is split exactly down the middle by panel borders. For example, during the battle with Tremens and his men, the wrathful red-eyed satyr challenges an approaching floater (*"More?* You want *more,* man?") in not one but two portraits, both cut off by the extra-thick panel borders which enclose the central action (1976, 26). Woodgod's head seems to partly float in the negative space of the margin, effectuating a graphic match with Mantlo's "totally *other"* identity.

Both approaches for representing the hero's "wild" conflicting natures appear in the scene in which he engages and kills a crazed dog on the streets of Liberty. As Woodgod strangles the mutt, Giffen shows his frenzied emotional state through a triple-portrait, heads once again floating in borderless white space as the eyes go red, each face looking more "beastly" than the one adjacent. The captions announce: *"[S]cream* goes mindlessly *berserk* as *animal* takes over ... hands reaching up to *grip* ... to *twist* ... scream screaming *out* again as animal *breaks* animal" (1976, 10). A sickening sound effect ("Snap") tells us the victor of the strange contest.

Interrupted by a flashback, the scene concludes with the image of Woodgod crouched over the dead canine, the background formed by a split portrait of his face, sundered down the middle by the panel gutter. The text box declares: "The dog was *dead* now ... his spine bent back *behind* him. *Part* of Woodgod *cried. Part* of him did *not*" (1976, 16). And indeed, the left half-portrait (with a blue background) shows a tear racing down Woodgod's cheek, while the other half-portrait (greenish background, with "power lines" emanating from his head) shows him dry-eyed.

These strategies for representing a quasi-animal consciousness, predicated on a false dichotomy (humans can feel sympathy, animals do not or cannot), reflect Mantlo's simplistic dualism. As he told an interviewer: "The innocent Wood God is looking for his father while the savage Wood God is tearing something apart because that something is attacking him" ("Woodgod Wanderings" 1976, 23). Yet the comics' depiction of a non-human being's utter terror, split consciousness and feral lashing-out at an overwhelming reality does offer tantalizing views of something deeper: animal suffering, reified in Mantlo's concept of "Scream." In exploring this notion further, we will detour to a discussion of the human and nonhuman experience of pain.

"THEIR ENTIRE UNIVERSE IS THE PAIN"

Scholarly treatments of pain in literature have tended to focus on the issue of its representability: does such a subjective state have a linguistic correlate? For Elaine Scarry, whose landmark *The Body in Pain: The Making and Unmaking of the World* reframed the debate for a generation, the answer is no (1985). Pain belongs to the realm of the inexpressible, disarticulation, the non-verbal. As she put it, pain leads to an "immediate reversion to a state anterior to language" (1985, 4). Sarah Mintz succinctly summarizes the argument: "For Scarry radical pain is a radically private experience whose sensations, wholly unavailable to language, eradicate the individual's capacity to think, feel, even perceive anything other than the pain itself; pain is a totalizing force that damages imaginative potential and constricts and pacifies the sufferer" (2013, 4).

All the same, pain and suffering do appear as subjects throughout the history of literature. Enkidu the wild man, from the epic *Gilgamesh,* wastes away in bed after being fatally cursed by the gods: "For twelve long days/he was deathly sick, he lay in his bed/in agony, unable to rest,/and every day he grew worse" (Mitchell 2004, 149). The tragic ending to Ernest Hemingway's *A Farewell to Arms*, uses the repeated phrase "Give it to me" and its variations (referring to an analgesic respirator mask) to figure an excruciating birth gone awry (1929). Superhero comics, too, know trauma. In "The Coming of the Hulk," Bruce Banner screams for hours upon hours after exposure to a Gamma bomb blast (Lee and Kirby 1962).

In short, the literary preoccupation with "suffering narratives" have complicated Scarry's "inexpressibility" and "pain as annihilation of speech" thesis. Scarry's approach, Mintz contends, makes the problem of representation less about some essentially elusive quality in *pain* than an anxiety about the ambiguity of *language.* Like pain scales that require patients to categorize feeling in terms of single words ("throbbing," "stinging," "burning"), Scarry's formulation sidelines the intricacies and imprecision of narrative in favor of a language that, in naming objects, would verify reality and guarantee knowledge—but then finds language insufficient because it cannot reliably identify what pain feels like (2013, 5).

As demonstrated by the field of narrative medicine, verbalizing pain and illness, assigning it a role and meaning, holds real value for patients and their caregivers. Furthermore, writing on the "inexpressible" as it relates to comics, Hillary Chute convincingly argues: "[T]he force and value of graphic narrative's intervention, on the whole, attaches to how it pushes on conceptions of the unrepresentable that have become commonplace in the wake of deconstruction, especially in contemporary discourse about trauma" (2010, 2).

Still, the fraught linkage between language and pain has troubling consequences, especially for discussions of the nonhuman. As ethicist Bernard Rollin reminds, "[T]he International Association for the Study of Pain (IASP) definition of 'pain' until very recently required language as a necessary precondition for the ability to feel pain (shades of Descartes)," insisting that both animals and neonatal human infants felt no discomfort, and thus required no anesthesia during surgery (2011, 432).

Setting aside the "speechlessnes" of animals (a controversial subject which has absorbed Jacques Derrida, among others), scholars like Rollin have sought to reorient the debate to one of sentient *mattering.* With reference to Aristotle's notion of *telos,* Rollin notes:

> If we raised pigs, for example, under totally natural conditions, satisfying all
> aspects of pig nature, from nest-building to rooting, we could say we understand
> "happiness" relative to that animal. When we fail to meet the needs flowing

from the *telos,* we harm the animal. While we do not have a word for the mattering implicit in failing to allow a pig to forage, or build its nest, as we keep them in modern confinement agriculture, we can plainly see that each of these failures to meet what the animal is by nature is going to create a harm we are guilty of committing. The word "pain" simply does not capture the myriad ways different treatments affect animals. (2011, 427)

What Rollin calls "negative mattering" reaches its zenith in physical abuse, because of the totalizing nature of nonhuman suffering: "[a]n animal *is* its pain, for it is incapable of anticipating or even hoping for cessation of that pain ... their entire universe is the pain, they can have no *hope!*" (2011, 431). We find the most utter hopelessness in this regard in the institution of science, with its purview "to narrow the possible meanings of the word *life* ... and reduce it to a set of predictable biological procedures" (Pick 2011, 144). This best allows it to carry out its task: "the ceaseless production of a clear differentiation of species" (Pick 2011, 141).

Here Sunaura Taylor's work on the similarities in the outlook toward animals and disabled people bears mentioning; she emphasizes the frequent overlaps in language: "The medical profession's gaze on disability is calculated, measuring, labeling, and dissecting. The disabled person becomes a body to be cropped, numbered, labeled—not unlike a butcher's diagram" (2011, 194). Indeed, we can read Woodgod as a disabled human hero as much as an "animal" hero.

Nowhere do we see this "scientific" worldview more forcefully expressed than in animal experimentation. In her discussion of Frederick Wiseman's 1974 documentary *Primate,* Anat Pick calls it "the traumatic text par excellence" for how it lays bare the unspeakable (2011, 146). To her, this means not only the "speechlessness" of animals but modernity itself and its latent instrumentality toward them, along with the ways in which it "primarily transforms living bodies into mastered and dispensable stuff and into sets of abstract scientific calculations" (2011, 146).

The Paces' own experiments to create a "clone-graft" likewise appear unconditionally informed by "institutional" thought—even though Mantlo and Giffen portray the scientist couple as benevolent, parental figures (1976). In fact, Woodgod's origins echo those of Superman with his parents, Jor-El and Lara, in the genre's ur-text. Nonetheless, Pace works "in absentia" from Tranquility Base on a project to synthesize a lethal nerve gas. The accident that unleashes the Purple Mist, causing mass death, only shows that the deceased Pace "*succeeded* at his job a bit *too well*" (1976, 18). Even when seeking to create life rather than end it, the tragic outcome points to the ineluctable logic of the institution to degrade and destroy.

"WE ARE ALL SCREAM"

Woodgod, product of a hellish experiment on human and animal genes, is born a tortured soul, a "beast boy" doomed to forever bear the onslaught of a merciless reality he cannot comprehend. His attempt to grasp this impossible predicament gives rise to Scream, his expression for the confusion and anguish of creation, the disorienting horror show brought forth by humanity.

Literally, in the case of "Birthday!'s" first scene: wandering the near-lifeless town, as noted, Woodgod encounters the sole human survivor of the Purple Mist—who promptly attacks him as a "damned *monster!*" A rock flung by the stranger strikes Woodgod in the temple, provoking the first three-panel transformation of his eyes to red. The caption reads: *"Rock* gives rise to *scream* … scream to *pain* … and *pain* gives way to *understanding."* This understanding leads the goat-man to fight back against his oppressor, presumably killing him.

What Woodgod "understands," he feels—at a deep, visceral level. "Birthday!" presents his knowledge as pure, perceptual, emotional animality. Mantlo says as much when he characterizes Scream as "an awareness of some part of his being reacting to his external surroundings" ("Woodgod Wanderings" 1976, 23). At some foundational level, the story tells us, nature itself is "reacting" through Woodgod.

Certainly in "Birthday!" and in the character's other early appearances, the authors take great pains to buttress a dichotomy between man/science and nature/animal, extending Pick's "ceaseless production of a clear differentiation of species" (2011). The former, in classic Romantic fashion, represent evil, corruption, the fall. The denizens of Tranquility Base (still called Vertigo in the initial story) live and work in an ultra-sleek, mechanized, unnatural space, and dress in futuristic turtlenecks. Moreover, the "scientific" gaze has colonizing ambitions vis-à-vis nature: page eighteen shows Tremens and his agents remotely observing Woodgod via satellite. The goat-man's image appears framed by machine circuits which form the panel borders—in chilling contrast to the "foliage-borders" of his first appearance on page one. Giffen also inserts these "mechano-panel borders" on page twenty-two, depicting Tremens and his team as they prepare to confront their foe.

Woodgod's appearance, recalling "wild" freedom-loving satyrs and Sasquatches, advances his side of the dichotomy: an unspoiled nature resistant to man. His simplistic, quasi-dissociated speech further cements this association. Unlike Tremens, who speaks in clipped, no-nonsense militaristic cadences, Woodgod's halting, repetitive sentences recall those of the Incredible Hulk ("Hulk smash," "Hulk the strongest one there is," etc.), another "creature hero" born of misguided science, who also frequently tangled with the military (Hatfield 2012, 116). And certainly his adversaries see in him a sub-human aberration, as clear from the epithets hurled at him throughout his first three appearances. In "Birthday!" humans call him "critter" (1976, 3) "damned monster" (1976, 3), "freak" (1976, 14) "that thing" (1976, 18), "freaking thing" (1976, 27), "monster" (1976, 30). In "Nightmare in New Mexico" *(Marvel Team-Up* # 53) "B.E.M." (bug-eyed monster) (1977, 26) and in "Spider in the Middle" *(MTU* #54) 30 "You stinking animal!" (1977, 30), to cite only a few instances.

Expressing the instrumental-minded outlook of animals which Rollin terms "negative mattering," Tremens attempts to rocket Woodgod, Spider-Man and the Hulk into space "for *experimental purposes,* of course!" even calling them "experimental *test animals*" (Mantlo and Byrne 1977a, 15; 23). Such an abjected status as absolute other provokes an extraordinary response: the totalizing, world-destroying horror of Scream. Both the process and the name suggest yet another late 1960s/early 1970s cultural staple as provenance for Woodgod: psychotherapist Artur Janov's Primal Therapy, in which the patient expels their personal neurosis through intense, loud emotional expression. Janov propounded his theories in his touchstone book, *The Primal Scream—Primal Therapy: The Cure for Neurosis* (1970). As practiced at his Primal Institute in Los Angeles throughout the decade and beyond, his deep-therapy approach sought to bypass the intellect so as to contact some authentic traumatized self buried by decades of neglect and repression—and then release the pent-up "primal pains" through extreme vocalization (337).

Primal Therapy, what Brian Williams and Paul Edgar call "an amalgam of the ideologies of the 1960s youth movement translated into therapeutic terms," exploded into the mainstream when celebrities such as ex-Beatle John Lennon and artist Yoko Ono went through Janov's program (2008, 1). In particular I want to stress the therapy's "primal discourses," with their "aggressive rejection of reason and rationalism," which privileged "feeling" over intellectualizing and the "talking cure" of traditional psychoanalysis (Williams and Edgar 2008, 10). The Primal Scream was a sort of anti-language, a non-speech that gave voice to unalloyed pain: "The basic unit of Janov's therapy, 'primals,' can be a violent phenomenon, often frightening to those seeing them for the first time, as they involve the full expression of the emotion that was repressed at the time of the trauma" (Williams and Edgar 2008, 19).

Though Primal Therapy would fade as a cultural reference point after the 1970s, it was blossoming into full flower immediately prior to "Birthday!'s" publication; Woodgod's Scream—betokening the animal consciousness thrown into shrieking panic, its terror before man's cruelty overflowing its banks—derives in part from Janov's contentions on the psychic wounds inflicted by modern life.

These wounds become literal in the climax to "Birthday!" that assembles many of the aforementioned verbal-visual strategies to convey Mantlo and Giffen's dualistic vision of human/nonhuman life. As Woodgod battles the floaters, he uproots a telephone poll to swat one of the machines out of the air. "I did not *ask* for this, man!" he yells. "*You* gave Scream to *Woodgod! You!*" Split into another odd "double-portrait" in the page's bottom tier, he kills "Doc," declaring, "Man is *born* of *Scream* … man *dies* of *Scream!* Go to *Scream,* man!" (1976, 27).

Tremens, his entire detachment wiped out, desperately fires his cannons as Woodgod barrels toward him, explosions erupting all over his body. The captions read: "The scream of *mortar fire* … kicking the floater *back* with each *burst* … ripping the purple *dust* … tearing *blood/muscle/bone* in a symphony of *scream. Animal. Animal. Animal. Scream!*" (1976, 30). In the middle, page-width panel, a red-eyed Woodgod reaches toward the reader with both hands, power lines bursting behind, giving full vent to his range through trans-speech: "Eeeeeeaarrhhahh!" This appears in large bold letters with no word balloon, like a sound effect, marking the vocalization's unmooring from anything human—the "Scream" of "primal pains" (1976, 30).

In the final panel, which takes up more than half the page, Woodgod (the "total animal") pounces on Tremens (in his helmeted environment suit the "total machine"), dislodging him from the floater. Giffen does at least two things here that suggests we should read this image as the triumph of the goat-man's nonhuman nature—his having gone "total animal." Firstly, Woodgod's pose duplicates almost exactly that of the rabid dog which had attacked him earlier (1976, 10). Secondly, Giffen depicts the action in Dutch angle, the ground seeming to rear up from the right corner—indicating the animal/nature's rejection of the floater's "logical" human-made equipoise.

Nevertheless, in the end, humanity's order seems restored, as signaled by a twelve-panel grid. It is perhaps the most "logical," utilitarian, "equi-poised" type of page composition in comics, in which each panel gives equal weight to every turn of the narrative. Though at first we find Woodgod on the verge of achieving his full revenge, declaiming, "*Scream,* man! *Taste Scream! Drink Scream! Scream!*" as he prepares to slay Tremens, by the final frame a dejected Woodgod, his back to us, walks off into a pale blue void, muttering, "We are *all* Scream!" The "beast boy" abandons the battlefield, leaving a bewildered and vengeance-bent Tremens in the dust (1976, 31). Besides reproducing the exact image from the end of Spider-Man's origin (with its well-known quote about "great power" and "great responsibility"), Woodgod's tiny portrait in the final panel conveys an even more existential message than its famous predecessor: no one and no thing, neither through reason nor madness, can ever escape the Scream in us all.

CONCLUSION: DOES THE BEAST BOY SPEAK?

> When I first created Woody (back in *Marvel Premiere* #31) I wanted
> to portray him as a child-innocent, rapidly maturing due to bio-
> genetics, but with an animalistic, pathological side that takes over in
> moments of anger/tension/rage, etc. I wanted to personalize that side
> of my creation, so I called it … scream.
>
> Bill Mantlo and John Byrne, "Nightmare in New Mexico!"
> in *Marvel Team-Up* (1977, 18)

In the middle of Woodgod's final showdown with Tremens and his men, a subtle inversion takes place. The besieged goat-man threatens, "I will *kill* you, man! *I will kill you!* No more *scream,* man! No more *pain!*" (1976, 26). Note that he speaks of "man" in abstract terms; Woodgod resolves to avenge himself on the killer of his father, "man" (i.e., the species), much as humans might use the word "animal" as an umbrella term for all nonhuman beings (a piece of discursive sleight-of-hand warned against most notably by Derrida).

Lori Gruen writes that such muddled generalization pervades the discourses even of those who seek to better the lot of nonhuman life:

> [M]uch of the animal rights literature focuses on aggregations and abstractions
> in … important and sometimes problematic ways. Particular individuals and
> their relationships are lumped together as mass terms, for example farmed ani-
> mals, companion animals, research chimpanzees, and suffering, pain, and death
> are generalized over. (2014, 129)

Woodgod, an obscure minor figure in the Marvel Comics Universe, reverses those terms, casting humanity writ large as the pest, the interloper, the problem. This animal-inflected story shows the potential of comics' image-text strategies, as well as the very real limits posed by the superhero genre, for representing nonhuman alterity "justly." Indeed, can an animal-positive vision ultimately be squared with superheroes at all?

Setting aside the quasi-fascist roots of the genre, and its traditional celebration of white, male bodies and violent domination that are taken up elsewhere in this book, superheroes comprise a profoundly anthropocentric practice. "Ani-drag" characters such as Mighty Mouse, Captain Carrot and Rocket Raccoon can be said to only reinforce, rather than challenge, the argument although others in this collection argue elsewhere.

And "Birthday!," we should throw up our hands and admit, does not function as a superhero story at all. Woodgod bears none of the key traits that Peter Coogan's taxonomy identifies for indisputably "qualifying" as a superhero: powers, identity, mission, costume. Likewise, one can see Coogan's discussion of the Hulk and how he similarly does not really "fit" the super-hero mold, yet whose prominence in the Marvel Comics Universe compels inclusion (2006, 41). Like other "creature-heroes," the goat-man defies more superhero conventions than he upholds, betraying his Gothic/sci-fi origins. Most "natural/animal" heroes such as Swamp Thing, Tigra, Man-Bat, Man-Thing, and the more recent Silverclaw tend to operate in this way: as destabilizing forces at the fringes of their respective superhero worlds.

Woodgod would remain an ancillary figure isolated from the rest of the Marvel milieu even after his return from hiatus, in a storyline spread over *The Incredible Hulk* Vol. 1 (Mantlo and Buscema 1980). He has undergone some radical changes: having lost the fixation on "finding Father," he has gained super-intelligence, becoming patriarch to a new race, the Changelings. Woodgod in essence takes up the mantle of the scientist, producing his own animal-human hybrid life forms through mastering and exceeding the Paces' techniques; whatever else he represents, Woodgod seems obsessed with creation, perpetuation. Needless to say, his speech now more resembles Reed Richards' than the Hulk's.

Not unlike that other Marvel life manipulator, the High Evolutionary, the goat-man now enjoys a separatist existence with his creations, safely ensconced in a remote Colorado valley. Despite his attempts at establishing an egalitarian utopia, hierarchies form (lizard-people and lion-people seemingly placed below bird-people and centaurs) and mutiny erupts. The "Valley of the Changelings" deteriorates from a Fawazian queer alternative community to a Gothic plot strongly recalling H.G. Wells' *The Island of Dr. Moreau.*

Woodgod's trajectory from inarticulate chattel to learned intellectual and statesman tracks that of Frederick Douglass, but it also bolsters the ineluctably human-centered biases of his creators, betraying the central paradox of the "animal superhero." The term is an oxymoron. For all that, "Birthday!" deserves its status as a precursor to comics that pursue the representation of "real" animal ontology more imaginatively, such as Stephen Murphy/Michael Zulli's *The Puma Blues* (1986/2015), Grant Morrison and Frank Quitely's *We*[3] (2005), and Nick Abadzis' *Laika* (2007).

Woodgod—a symbol of nature produced as much through science as nature—represents the utopian gonzo freedom of the satyr and wild man, the funky folkloric unboundedness of Bigfoot, refracted through the deep-therapy 1970s, and tempered with the nation's incipient pangs of conscience over the suffering of nonhuman life. He is a flawed, superhero embodiment of animal life's unspeakable pain, its Scream, long unheard by humanity, brought to life through the fantasy of the it-narrative, "the autobiography of something not human, formerly inanimate but now inspired with enough passion, reason and speech to launch upon its own story" (Lamb 2011, xxxviii). In fact, "the most bizarre super-hero of all" comes with a warning it behooves us to heed: "We are *all* Scream!" (Mantlo and Giffen 1976, 31).

More than anything, this realization allows readers to have an interconnected understanding of ecology instead of prioritizing the humanism of the individualized ego. With such a reoriented understanding it can be possible to foster new waves of activism for total liberation beyond the pages of Marvel's comic books alone.

WORKS CITED

Benson, Thomas W. 1985. "The Rhetorical Structure of Frederick Wiseman's *Primate.*" *Quarterly Journal of Speech.* 71(2): 204–17.

Boggs, Colleen Glenney. 2013. *Animalia Americana: Animal Representations and Biopolitical Subjectivity.* New York: Columbia University Press.

Buhs, Joshua. 2011. "Tracking Bigfoot Through 1970s North American Children's Culture: How Mass Media, Consumerism, and the Culture of Preadolescence Shaped Wildman Lore." *Western Folklore* 70(2): 195–218.

Chute, Hillary L. 2010. *Graphic Women: Life Narrative and Contemporary Comics.* New York: Columbia University Press.

Coogan, Peter. 2006. *Superhero: The Secret Origin of a Genre.* Austin, TX: Monkey Brain Books.

Fawaz, Ramzi. 2016. *The New Mutants: Superheroes and the Radical Imagination of American Comics.* New York: New York University Press.

Gruen, Lori. 2014. "Facing Death and Practicing Grief." *Ecofeminism: Feminist Intersections with Other Animals and the Earth,* edited by Carol J. Adams and Lori Gruen, 127–141. New York: Bloomsbury.

Hatfield, Charles. 2012. *Hand of Fire: The Comics Art of Jack Kirby.* Jackson: University of Mississippi Press.

Hatfield, Charles, Heer, Jeet, and Worcester, Kent. 2013. *The Superhero Reader.* Jackson: University of Mississippi.

Howe, Sean. 2012. *Marvel Comics: The Untold Story.* New York: Harper Press.

Husband, Timothy, Gilmore-House, Gloria, and Cloisters. 1980. *The Wild Man: Medieval Myth and Symbolism.* New York: Metropolitan Museum of Art, 1980.

Janov, Artur. 1977. "Towards a New Consciousness." *Journal of Psychosomatic Research* 21(4): 333–9.

Karen and Doug. 2016. "Who's the Best … Marvel Premiere Premiere?" *Bronze Age Babies,* July 9. http://bronzeagebabies.blogspot.com/2016/07/whos-best-marvel-premiere-premiere.html

Lamb, Jonathan. 2011. *The Things Things Say.* Princeton: Princeton University Press.

Maggs, Barbara Widenor. 1976. "Reljković, Satyrs, and the Enlightenment in Eighteenth-Century Croatia." *The Slavic and East European Journal.* 20(4): 437–450.

Mantlo, Bill and Sal Buscema. 1980a. "The Changelings!" *The Incredible Hulk.* 1(253), October, 1980: 1–31.

————. 1980b. "The Changelings! – Part II." *The Incredible Hulk.* 1(254), November: 1–31.

Mantlo, Bill and John Byrne. 1977a. "Nightmare in New Mexico!" *Marvel Team-Up.* 1(53), January: 1–31.

————. 1977b. "Spider in the Middle!" *Marvel Team-Up.* 1(54), February: 1–31.

Mantlo, Bill and Keith Giffen. 1976. "Birthday!" *Marvel Premiere.* 1(31), August: 1–31.

Mintz, Susannah B. 2013. *Hurt and Pain : Literature and the Suffering Body.* London: Bloomsbury Academic.

Mitchell, Stephen. 2004. *Gilgamesh : A New English Version.* New York: Free Press.

Pick, Anat. 2011. *Creaturely Poetics: Animality and Vulnerability in Literature and Film.* New York: Columbia University Press.

Robbins, Carla Anne. 1988. "Army's Huge Supply of Nerve Gas Poses Unnerving Questions—"'What About the Sheep?' Asks Member of Civilian Panel; Incineration Stirs Up Fear." *Wall Street Journal,* June 1: A1.

Rollin, Bernard. 2011. "Animal Pain: What It Is and Why It Matters." *The Journal of Ethics.* 15(4): 425–37.

Scarry, Elaine. 1985. *The Body in Pain: The Making and Unmaking of the World.* New York: Oxford University Press.

Taylor, Sunaura. 2011. "Beasts of Burden: Disability Studies and Animal Rights." *Qui Parle: Critical Humanities and Social Sciences* 19(2): 191–222.

Tolstoy, Leo, and Katz, Michael R. 1991. *Tolstoy's Short Fiction: Revised Translations, Backgrounds and Sources, Criticism.* New York: Norton.

Williams, Paul and Brian Edgar. 2008. "Up Against the Wall: Primal Therapy and 'the Sixties'." *European Journal of American Studies.* 3(2): 1–22.

Wolfe, Cary. 2008. *Animal Rites: American Culture, the Discourse of Species, and Posthumanist Theory.* Chicago: University of Chicago Press.

Wolk, Douglas. 2007. *Reading Comics: How Graphic Novels Work and What They Mean.* Cambridge, MA: Da Capo.

"Wanderings." 1976. *Foom Magazine* Woodgod. 1(13), March: 23.

Chapter 4

Making Superheroes of Children

The (Mis)Use of Nonhumans in Inspiring Childhood Development

J. L. Schatz

INTRODUCTION

Popular culture in general, and children's media in particular, are saturated by themes of superheroes saving the environment from destruction, and animal protagonists rescuing their loved ones from disaster. Children are continually taught that mistreating animals is something only a villain would do. This can be seen in the exposure of vivisection labs in MGM's *The Secret of NIMH* (1982), the awareness about the fur industry in Disney's *101 Dalmatians* (1961), and the knowledge about the pet industry in Pixar's *Finding Nemo* (2003). Sadly, many of these same children continue to eat meat, buy shoes made from leather, consume resources in disastrous ways, and run out to buy fish only to kill them by flushing them down the toilet to emulate the film (Flynn and Hoffman 2003). This disconnect between what children see on the screen and what they do in reality is vexing. For one, given the media's influence over children's perception of gender, beauty, and race it is odd that the media would not have the same power to influence children's perception about species. Secondly, it speaks to the inability for children to change patterns of behavior that are often controlled by both parents and governing institutions. Finally, it demonstrates that, even in spite of multiple positive representations that encourage children to fight against animal and environmental injustice, other hegemonic norms and media messages hold more power in solidifying speciesist behavior at large. Nevertheless, this chapter will argue that it remains possible to use media representations in order to critically teach students and children how to alter their practices and become the heroes they watch on the screen, and read on the page.

A foundational assumption to this chapter, and for this book at large, is that media matters, and that human decisions to consume it are no more neutral than the consumption of the dead bodies produced by factory farms. To an obvious extent, the media's ability to influence people's attitudes and how individuals shape their sense of self is profound. If it weren't, advertising companies would not spend billions each year to win over young consumers (Lagorio 2007). To a lesser known extent, comics in relation to gender have "revealed that, for male readers, ... regular reading of these series is not part of a process of inculcation of roles but one of learning of a historically new and complex masculine identity" (Maigret and Libbrecht 1999, 10). In fact, as early as 1944, *The Journal of Educational Sociology* put out a special issue on "The Comics as an Educational Medium" with articles dedicated to their impact on childhood development. Unfortunately, there has been very little work to date that has investigated the question of superheroes and comics in relation to the formation of human identity as a species. This omission is particularly disastrous because

> cultural norms perpetuate values that define good and evil, normal and abnormal, human and "animal" in ways that condone oppression and shape speciesist attitudes and behaviors. Studying these normative forms of popular culture tells us about the humans who consume and produce them. Additionally, consuming and producing is an activity that influences one's choices and simultaneously (re)creates culture, both of which are paramount in unraveling the constructions that give rise to non/human oppression. (George and Schatz 2016, xiv)

To this end, whether it is the light-hearted action of the *Puppy Buddies* series (2006–2013), featuring live-action dogs that speak and have super powers, or *A Dog's Purpose* (2017), which questionably abused a dog to produce a feel-good film, children are constantly inundated by the heroism of animals and the call to save them (Alexander 2017). This inundation, rather than merely being a hindrance to education, can help parents and educators use what is being internalized to foster critical conversations about food, clothing, and other forms of consumption.

The second foundational assumption to this chapter is that the transformative possibility of using comics and superheroes exists regardless of the creator's intent. This is not to say the creator's intent is irrelevant. Rather, it is to say that how it gets internalized and interpreted can have an impact regardless of any premeditated desire for that impact to have occurred. In one sense, which would resonate with those in literary disciplines, this chapter firmly disagrees with Roland Barthes' belief that a writerly understanding of texts is more important (1973). Instead, this chapter believes that the readerly model of interpretation can better produce critical praxis and novel modes of education. In another sense, Judith Butler in relation to language argues that even if we concede ... that the injurious connotation is inevitably retained ... it does not follow that such words can have no other connotation. Indeed, their repetition is necessary ... in order to enter them as objects of another discourse. ... The possibility of decontextualizing and recontextualizing such terms through radical acts of public misappropriation constitutes the basis of an ironic hopefulness that the conventional relation between word and wound might become tenuous and even broken over time. (1997, 100–101)

To put it differently, even when the intent of the filmmaker or writer isn't to raise awareness about the treatment of nonhuman animals, their use of both literal and metaphorical animals creates the critical repetition necessary to challenge human supremacy. In fact, given how often nonhumans are rendered absent in language and representation, it is all the more frequent that animal metaphors and fictions go unattended (Adams 1990, 40–64). Therefore, by making these absences in intent present in interpretation it becomes possible to redeploy tired stereotypes and violent training techniques through fostering an awareness of what so often remains unnoticed.

The final foundational assumption to this chapter is that speciesism as it currently exists is morally untenable, threatens the planet with its wanton disregard for nonhuman life, and requires both immediate action and education to change the situation. Unfortunately, "secrecy serves to conceal the details of the horror from all but those who must participate in it to keep the cogs of the machinery running smoothly ... [and] to protect the very profitable institutionalized cruelty to animals as it exists today" (Spiegel 1996, 80). This is why Ag-Gag laws are increasingly being implemented across the United States and why the Motion Picture Association of America's seal of approval, which comes from the American Humane Association, only covers the treatment of animals when the camera is rolling (Schatz 2013). In both cases, consumers lose the will and information necessary to challenge these practices when they are denied the knowledge of what goes into raising animals for food and entertainment. Fortunately,

I find it hard to imagine how somebody could know something about gross animal abuse and exploitation ... and not see it as part of a larger circle of violence [where they] ... majority of publicly traded corporations and industries will do anything to make a profit. They will torture animals while construing and presenting it as human entertainment. They will chop off the tops of majestic mountains. They will use child labor, then claim that a portion of their proceeds go to children's causes. They will literally kill people, or at least create conditions to all but ensure people's deaths, when facing the consequences of doing so is cheaper than other alternatives. (Gorski 2014, 5)

These corporate practices don't occur in isolation. Rather, they occur in large part because consumers remain complicit in this violence when they don't critically interrogate their consumption habits regardless of their intent to inflict violence and ecological damage. In short, so long as moviegoers continue to flock to the theaters to see films that require animal abuse to create, or reproduce speciesist themes in content, the media will subsequently produce more in the name of profit. Fortunately, by using the pop culture mediums that already influence children it is possible to begin these conversations and debates that can change the global leaders of tomorrow. And, in doing so, it is possible to alter the fictions put forward that will ultimately influence subsequent generations.

With these assumptions in mind, it is also important to clarify how this chapter deploys the term superhero since it goes beyond merely wearing a cape or having the ability to fly. To this end, it has often been impossible to define what precisely makes one a superhero despite several anthologies devoted to the concept. This is in large part because of the difficultly in defining what constitutes being a hero in the first place. In DC's trailer for their 2017 movie *Justice League*, when asked what his superpowers were, Batman replies with all seriousness, "I'm rich." While Batman is the focus of other chapters in this book, it will suffice to point out that, despite using this moment as comic relief in an otherwise action-packed preview, Batman's seriousness is what makes it funny because the question of what makes one a superhero is very much up for debate. As my son describes it, there are the "possible superheroes" who buy or fight their way into power and the "impossible superheroes," who have more extraordinary powers. This chapter will not make a distinction between these two types of superheroes when using the term. Rather, it will include all characters—both fictional and nonfictional—who perform heroic feats outside of what is possible for most viewers and readers to realistically achieve, even if it is technically possible. In the eyes of many children consuming media these are all superheroes and potential role models to be emulated regardless of any singular power.

However, the upcoming sections of this chapter will still make some divisions between types of superhero narratives. This is done so as to lay out a means to utilize the concept of "heroes" in order to talk about Critical Animal Studies in a way that resonates with children and young adults based upon the particular genre. Obviously, depending on the particular piece of popular culture there are different methods of communication that make sense to use over others. Inasmuch, this chapter will tackle three types of animal hero representations and ways to engage them in a critical form of praxis. The first includes the human-as-savior genre, which predictably features human heroes saving animals in films like *Legally Blonde 2* (2003) where Elle Woods works within the legal system to ban animal cosmetics testing. In this category the idea of what makes one a "hero" goes beyond having more traditional superpowers. The second includes talking animal and animated films, such as *Homeward Bound* (1993) or *The Lion King* (1994), as well as ones where nonhuman animals are literally superheroes, as in the case of the *Super Buddy* films (2006–2013). The third includes human-animal mutants, which features comics like *Teenage Mutant Ninja Turtles*, and a host of others where animals are anthropomorphized to have the desire and feelings of humans. In each instance, it is imperative to realize that, beyond any specific superhero, there is a reality that has material consequences for the nonhuman animals represented and forced to act upon the screen. When talking with students or children about media representation it is crucial not to forget this point for some poststructuralist retreat into discursive semantics alone.

Of course, given the nature of this chapter, this is not to say interrogating discursive or ontological formulations of the world are irrelevant. Quite the contrary, one of this chapter's foundational assumptions is precisely that discursive disseminations of popular culture shape how identity categories are ontologically formed through speciesist tendencies. Nevertheless, it is to say that if our discursive or ontological interrogations cannot produce a will to challenge the hegemonic structures they are interrogating then they cease to have value since they forfeit any potential for radical praxis. As such,

> "the animetaphor is ... never absorbed, sublimated, or introjected into the world but rather incorporated as a limit[.] ... The animetaphoric figure is consumed literally rather than figuratively" ... [by] always pointing to a space (even if it is always already in language) outside of language, exposing the limits of language. ... Animals in language rest at the edges of the mouth, my mouth; I taste the failure of language to describe animals, and savour the presence of real animals flanking my sentences, my words. My language cannot digest the tissue and meat of nonhuman animals—a meal that cannot be digested. (Hayward 2008, 259–260)

This existence of the real nonhuman beyond the absent referents created in language and media therefore demands a necessity for academic discourse to move its goal beyond mere education alone, and rather toward transformation instead. No doubt, this is the very premise of this chapter's third foundational assumption on the need for change. To this end, "total liberation pedagogy does not seek to just destabilize human power in the abstract, but roots this in the need to support cultural and political practices that actively seek to overthrow speciesist relations across society" (Kahn and Humes 2009, 182). Using superheroes, comics, and popular culture to move beyond the animetaphors and to the more literal "meat of the matter" can help forward a total liberation pedagogy, but only so long as these dialogs are understood as never being neutral. Rather, they must always be about more than just the individual hero, film, or comic in question.

HUMANS-AS-SAVIORS: THERE'S A SUPERHERO IN US ALL

There are no shortages of films that portray humans as saviors of nonhuman animals. It happens in *Free Willy* (1993), *Legally Blonde 2* (2003), *Project X* (1987), *Gorillas in the Mist* (1988), among many other films that portray humans as the central figures in advancing nonhuman liberation. In one sense, these films offer an easy starting point for conversation since they outline how the mistreatment of animals is wrong, and feature a plot that leads a human hero to stop these horrific practices. At the same time, many of these films place the potential for agency far beyond what most people can do. In this regard, these movies can often serve to anesthetize the belief that change is within anyone's individual power. In short, there is also the risk that many of these films, while outwardly challenging individual segments of animal oppression, ignore the infrastructural reality that traps modern civil society within speciesism. In fact, all too often the resolution of these narratives includes the freeing of a single animal or the enactment of a series of piecemeal laws, such as with *Legally Blonde 2* (2003) that abolished cosmetic testing. Nevertheless, "the history of ... legislated 'reforms' of inherently abusive situations are largely ineffective. In the short term, they do little to reduce suffering. In the long term, they increase suffering by re-legitimizing exploitation, thereby sustaining the situation that causes all the suffering" (Dunayer 2004, 65). Such stories also limit the ability for large-scale change because they make change seem easy to accomplish, thereby making people assume protections are already in place because they are so obviously needed. Therefore, dialog about the human-as-savior superhero must not merely cast the protagonists as the only form of heroism that students and children can emulate. Instead, those heroes ought to be contextualized within the world the children and students live within, as well as how actual engagement with altering consumption practices can be made.

Regrettably, in many of these human-as-savior motifs there is a belief that at the end of the saga the battle has been won. This creates the belief that it only takes one act to solve injustice. Further still, oftentimes the environment or species is saved not because of any intrinsic value but because they provide utility for human survival and enjoyment. For instance, "the chief problem with 'Gorillas in the Mist' is that it banalizes its heroine; it turns her into one of us. And by all accounts Fossey was anything but ordinary" since not everyone has the ability to pick up and go study mountain gorillas in Rwanda (Hinson 1988). In *Free Willy* (1993) the heroism of freeing an orca from captivity is not something many kids can risk taking on, even though there would be no need for orca captivity in the first place if children weren't encouraging their parents to buy tickets to Sea World.

> It's as if everyone can get on board with respecting rivers and mountains but still want to eat, experiment on, wear, and be entertained by animals. Left ecological concerns stem not from any kind of deep respect for the natural world, but rather from a position of "enlightened anthropocentrism" … that understands how important a sustainable environment is for human existence. … Moreover, it is far easier to "respect nature" through recycling, planting trees, or driving hybrid cars than it is to respect animals by becoming a vegan who stops eating and wearing animal bodies and products. (Best 2006)

And so, while not everyone might be able to work in a military nuclear testing facility studying radiation on chimpanzees like Helen Hunt and Matthew Broderick in *Project X* (1987), everyone can abstain from purchasing products that are needlessly tested on animals. Even more radical films such as *Bold Native* (2010), which endorses tactics by the Animal Liberation Front, falsely place the emphasis on singular acts of heroism rather than the sustained effort of people refusing to consume factory-farmed flesh. This is not to say we do not need these other heroes as well. Certainly, activists who risk their freedom to release animals in vivisector labs and on factory farms deserve credit. However, teaching about these heroes still requires teaching both the limits of individual action and the steps that people can do to immediately decrease their complacency in speciesist institutions of violence.

In order to fill what's missing from the films above it is useful to teach students and children the concept of a "macroaggression" to help them "understand … mindless participation in or compliance with big, systemic forms of oppression rather than interpersonal forms of bias or discrimination. It shares with 'micro-aggression' the quality of not necessarily being purposeful" (Gorski 2014, 6). Just as the intent of the filmmaker or writer is secondary to how it is interpreted, and internalized by its audience, one's intent to participate in violence is secondary to one's actual participation in that violence since its internalization is literally the digested lives of nonhuman animals.

> In other words, despite all my recycling, walking, and other environmentally conscious practices, I could have decreased my carbon footprint much more drastically had I simply eaten less food produced on factory farms. … My intent, when I did consume factory-farmed products, was not malicious, but my impact was malicious. By enjoying the convenience of factory-farmed meat, I deprived the most marginalized people, not to mention other marginalized living beings, of their vital needs in order to satisfy my trivial need for cheap ice cream or omelets or bacon cheeseburgers. (Gorski 2014, 10)

By demonstrating these connections to students and children, it becomes possible for them to realize how their consumption reinforces the current villainy that these heroes are fighting against. Therefore, by first refusing to participate in these macroaggressions students and children are not only empowered to make change in their own lives but then often become the everyday heroes who encourage others as well. Fortunately, "above all else, animal agriculture fears exposure. The industry can exist in its present form only as long as the public is kept in the dark about animal treatment. ... Many people, especially the young, who learn about factory farming will ... do everything possible to drive this industry out of existence" (Marcus 2005, 123–124). Critical conversations over film and popular media helps to create that exposure because it ensures the everyday violence served onto people's plates is seen as the dead bodies they are, instead of the mere meat of the dish.

TALKING AND ANIMATED ANIMAL HEROES: EVERY NONHUMAN IS A SUPERHERO

Talking animal heroes are abounding as well. Whether it be from classics like *Flipper* (1964–1967) and *Lassie* (1954–1974), or the more recent *Super Buddy* (2006–2013) phenomenon, there is no shortage of popular cultural representations of animals acting to save their human companions. While not all these heroes actively speak, they are all anthropomorphized to have human emotions and motivations. Beyond the live-action dubbing of animal heroes there are a host of animated films that feature nonhuman creatures talking like humans while fighting for the planet. Whether this be *FernGully* (1992), which tackles both deforestation and vivisection, or *The Fox and the Hound* (1981), which questions the practice of hunting, nonhuman animals are often represented as the heroes children identify with. To this end, "animation ... can provide a rich archive for an alternative politics of embodiment, reproduction and non-reproduction. ... The porous boundary between ... the animal and the nonhuman are simply recruited for the continuing reinforcement of the human, the heteronormative and the familial" (Halberstram 2008, 266). Such animated works serve as entry points into talking about the embodiments thrust upon the nonhuman world and the human viewer's expectations for it. Ask what it means to be "human" and what makes for a "species." And, while there are a handful of scientific answers to how species has been defined differently over time, what makes for the category of "human" in the world of animation like *Zootopia* (2016), *Epic* (2013), *Finding Nemo* (2003), and countless others is very much up for debate. "In other words, while it is true that reproduction and kinship relations become more and more obviously artificial, the concept of the 'human' tends to absorb the critique that inevitably follows from the natural and it does so because we reinvest so vigorously and so frequently in the scaffolding that props up our flailing humanity" (Halberstram 2008, 266). Consequently, the solutions offered in many of these films are not only often-extraordinary feats but also piecemeal solutions that expose the very failures of such humanism. This was the case with *Finding Dory* (2016) where, even as the fish aim to escape the aquarium, aqua-captivity is redeemed through its contributions to oceanic science.

Another example of inadequate solutions in media is *The Circle of Life* (1995), a 20-minute short featuring Timon and Pumbaa from *The Lion King* that as of 2016 was still being shown at Disney World's Epicott Center. In the film's conclusion on how to solve the world's environmental problems, the short suggests investment in alternative energy and other technological solutions. This leaves children with the belief that the only way to tackle big ecological issues is to rely on science, technology, and economic development instead of anything immediate or more revolutionary. At no point is there any mention of the fact that, just outside the gates of *The Circle of Life* (1995), Disney patrons are offered the bodies of dead animals to be consumed. And, while Disney World does raise many of their own animals and grows over thirty tons of fruits and vegetables to sell on their resorts, the scale of their operation, which includes serving 1.2 million pounds of turkey annually, still requires the use of industrial farming methods beyond Disney's innovations (Levy 2015).

> To make the point about the interrelationships here in a simple but crucial way, consider that no society can achieve ecological sustainability if its dominant mode of food production is factory farming. The industrialized system of confining and fattening animals for human food consumption, pioneered in the US after World War II and exported globally, is a main cause of water pollution (due to fertilizers, chemicals, and massive amounts of animal waste) and a key contributor to rainforest destruction, desertification, global warming, in addition to being a highly inefficient use of water, land, and crops. (Best 2006)

In these moments, it's worth reminding children and students that whatever heroic feat any protagonist might achieve in helping save the environment that, if one really cared about the environment, they can begin by saving it through decreasing their meat consumption. In fact, there is no better way someone in their daily life can save animals, or the environment, than by stopping to pay people to kill and destroy them. At the same time, these efforts to cut out meat consumption do not have to come at the expense of other efforts to combat species injustice or environmental destruction. However, when the only conversation that is foregrounded is the larger engineering and structural solutions, such as alternative energy, children and students miss the opportunity to understand how they are actively participating in the structures they seek to resist.

When these nonhuman heroes are not animated there is a need to engage with a pressing conversation around the exploitation and abuse found within live animal usage for entertainment. For a start, "animal cruelty has been a fact of life on productions since the inception of Hollywood. ... Nearly 100 horses died during the shooting of 1959's Ben-Hur alone" (Baum 2013). "The American Humane Association's (AHA) 'No Animals Were Harmed' seal of approval is extremely misleading to producers and audiences alike. AHA doesn't monitor the living conditions of animals off set, during pre-production training, or when they're taken from their mothers" (PETA 2017). Even when animal actors are taken care of, their captivity, consent, and what becomes of them afterwards are all too often unknown by the general public. In most situations, animal actors are abused and tortured in the process of training them to perform and are slaughtered if they can't do their tricks well enough (Baum 2013). Ric O'Barry, who "pioneered the underwater training of dolphins for the American film and television show *Flipper*," after the fact regrets his participation despite the love and care he expressed for Suzy, the dolphin who played Flipper (*The Independent* 2009). "The turning point for O'Barry came in 1970 ... [when] Suzy retired and remained in the Miami Seaquarium where she was looked after by O'Barry. He had started to notice her unhappiness ... and when she died in his arms, he was convinced she'd committed suicide" (*The Independent* 2009). After that moment, O'Barry went on to engage in direct action against the annual dolphin hunt in Taiji, Japan, where the majority of the world's dolphins for entertainment and oceanic science come from. While the feature-length documentary *The Cove* (2009), which documents O'Barry's actions, definitely falls within the human-as-savior genre, his voice and actions against the exploitation of animals for entertainment should not be understated. Ensuring children and students know that the animal actors they see on the screen live very different lives when the camera isn't rolling is essential in fostering the praxis necessary to see beyond the uplifting anthropomorphized narratives at play.

In the end, whether the characters are animated or played by live animal actors, the environmental themes within them mustn't be forgotten for the more limited message of justice they so often promote. When even *Finding Dory* (2016) failed to increase awareness around how aquariums more often than not imprison animals in horrific ways, despite featuring a plot focused on a fish trying to escape the aquarium, it is up to parents and educators to ensure that the larger message of total liberation is understood by children and students alike. This is especially true at the point when "'Finding Dory' could not have been created without the real life creatures which inhabit Monterey Bay Aquarium" and was used as an advertisement by aquariums across the United States as advertising to drive up attendance (Hilario 2016). Continually reminding kids about the real-world consequences of their consumption, as well as media production, is vital in helping use the words of both animated and talking animal heroes in a way that can truly foster change beyond a few hours of family bonding on a rainy day.

HUMAN-ANIMAL MUTANTS: THE HYBRIDITY OF IDENTITY

In many human-animal mutant stories, such as in *Teenage Mutant Ninja Turtles*, the powers attained come from some scientific experiment gone awry or through an accident. In some cases, it causes turtles to become more human and in other cases, such as with Spider-Man, it causes humans to become more animal-like. In both situations, the line between human and nonhuman blurs in order to create a new category of hero who fights for humanity, despite often being excluded from it. Certainly, the repeated theme of protecting a human civilization bent on either exterminating or commodifying the nonhuman world is worth questioning. To this end, "the superhero mythos depicts a fanciful world of perfect heroes and colorful villains but also depicts a world reflecting the dominant values of American society. ... We are being told that we must preserve the status quo ... [and that] threats to the status quo must be extinguished. ... The dominant hegemony is safe in the hands of the comic book superhero" (Vollum and Adkinson 2003, 105). For example, while protecting Earth from Shredder and Krang only supports the diary, pepperoni, and sardine industries that the ninja turtles love, one should question if such hybrid heroes are only saving the world for the already-speciesist establishment that relishes things like pizza and turtle soup. As such,

> Genomics and biotechnology generally are fetishized by scientists and policy makers as the means by which to reinvent capitalism as a new more efficient and environmentally benign project often under the banner of the knowledge based bio-economy[.] ... With such examples capitalist biopolitics suspends a moral human/animal binary in order to promote capitalization ... and is arguably informed by the historical lineage of discursively placing various classed and racialized human others as "closer to animal." In this manner capitalism strategically employs contradictory accounts of human/animal difference that are enabling for various development and accumulation projects. (Twine 2012, 13)

This fetishization of technology as the answer in reality extends itself into the fictions of heroism because without its accidents the world would be lacking the mutants necessary to save it. However, if the technological logic of capitalist accumulation isn't halted, the world these mutated heroes act so desperately to save will be lost to speciesist attitudes that will inevitably doom it to extinction regardless. This is crucial since "one of the sites for this ongoing negotiation and management by intellectuals of the shared ideology is the media of which popular cultural texts such as superhero comics are a part" (McGuire 2014, 13).

Put simply, "the environmental crisis can be directly linked to anthropocentric views of the world. The perception that value is located in, and emanates from, humanity has resulted in understanding human life as an ultimate value, superior to all other beings" (Sivil 2001, 110). Merely extending the amount of time the planet has to survive without addressing the root of the problems misses the point, which is precisely why these heroes must continually fight ever-greater villains and worsening circumstances. Hence, even if these heroes uphold a conservationist or preservationist approach to the world, instead of the expansionist approach of capitalism, the endpoint is the same. No doubt, "all three approaches are informed by anthropocentric assumptions. This results in a one-sided understanding of the human-nature relationship. Nature is understood to have a singular role of serving humanity, while humanity is understood to have no obligations toward nature" (Sivil 2001, 112). Preserving the world to admire for human inspiration, or conserving it for sustainable human use, still necessarily places the nonhuman world under the mastery of human desire. Even when heroes guard against the worst of those desires and ambitions—the ones that explicitly threaten the planet—they often don't guard against the more everyday banal desires of humanity. Ultimately, "this ensures that human duties retain a purely human focus, thereby avoiding the possibility that humans may have duties that extend to nonhumans. This can lead to viewing the nonhuman world, devoid of direct moral consideration, as a mere resource with a purely instrumental value of servitude" (Sivil 2001, 112). Ensuring we fight these larger transformational struggles is essential for dislodging the very speciesism these human-animal hybrids strive to challenge.

Of course, not all human-animal superheroes come from scientific accidents. There are many who get their powers from mysterious artifacts, as is the case of DC's Vixen, other wordly capabilities, such as the Wonder Twins or Beast Boy, or through some spiritual intervention, as in the case of Animal Man. Once again, all these characters beg the question of where their human self ends and their nonhuman self begins since they all play with the hybridity of identity. With both Animal Man and Vixen it is the human who increasingly becomes animal in order to achieve their powers. In these instances, one can remain attentive to the way this hybridity blurs the species line rather than reinforces it because becoming animal-like is not perceived as negative. Here, "this use of technology to distinguish between nature and culture obscures the very real and energetic invention and use of technology by nonhuman living organisms ... as well as the extent to which so-called human technologies actually mimic technology already invented by other species" (Hird 2008, 241–242). From this perspective, interactive communication between humans and animals allows these hybrid heroes to go beyond either species alone. This can be understood as similar to a

> reworking [of] Butler's performing bodies to include nonhuman material agencies involved in the process of the active and not just discursive materialization ... beyond its assumed anthropomorphic limitations. Thus matter is not delimited to the linguistic or discursive acts or to the humancentred vision of the organic body. ... By assigning no priority to a given materiality or discursivity ... intra-actions are constraining activities that do not determine the future, but rather remain uncertain because of the intra-activities of phenomena—which entail human, nonhuman, cyborgian forms of agency: an enactment or doing. (Parisi 2008, 286–287)

In turn, it is not so much the power of these heroes to become nonhuman that gives them their strength but rather the cyborgian agency they claim in their becoming. These enactments of performativity are possible beyond the idea of shapeshifting literal form because altering the conception of how "the human" is constructed makes it possible to forego the pre-significations that affix a lower status unto nonhuman beings to begin with.

CONCLUSION

Of course, there are countless other formulations of superheroes and means by which to talk about them. Therefore, the above should be taken more as a suggestive springboard rather than a totalizing way to approach superheroes and Critical Animal Studies. The one tenant, however, that must remain consistent through all approaches though is the non-neutrality of media as an event and our choices of how we consume it. At the same time, the reality beyond the screen should not over-determine or distract from the analysis of characters and themes within these stories. Rather, talking with children through fiction gives a basis in which they can approach complex questions of morality and consumption at large. No doubt,

> fiction does mold us. The more deeply we are cast under a story's spell, the more potent its influence. In fact, fiction seems to be more effective at changing beliefs than nonfiction, which is designed to persuade through argument and evidence. Studies show that when we read nonfiction, we read with our shields up. ... But when we are absorbed in a story, we drop our intellectual guard. ... Fiction enhances our ability to understand other people; it promotes a deep morality that cuts across religious and political creeds. ... Fiction ... increases ... empathy and reinforces an ethic of decency that is deeper than politics. (Gottschall 2012)

While children and students might not be aware of how all the industrialized practices they participate in drive ecological destruction, they can readily grapple with the moral questions put before heroes who fight any number of villains to stop injustice. By using fiction as their springboard for understanding and activism, students and children can reimagine the ways they desire to interact with the world. Thus, in these conversations the point is not to dwell on the logocentric details of why factory farming is destructive and vivisection is often unnecessary. Instead, it is to posit the fictional universe as the locus of conversation while making one aware of the off-screen implications of the violence sustaining that universe.

Ultimately, it is worth remembering this chapter's three foundational assumptions in approaching how one teaches Critical Animal Studies and heroism because they can serve as a foundation to other disciplines of teaching media studies as well. The first, most obviously, is that media matters because it deeply informs and implicates the people who consume it. More specifically, "the current popularity of superhero movies seems to demonstrate the hold the genre has on the public, and these movies take up current real-world issues" (Rosenberg and Coogan 2013, xviii). The second premise is that the power of interpretation lies with the reader, and not with the creator of any given text. This premise is crucial since it helps to teach children and students that the way they understand the world matters and that things can change, instead of reinforcing the belief that "this is just the way things are." When students feel empowered to interpret the media they can then go on to use those skills to deconstruct and challenge the way specific policies and educational disciplines are constructed because everything is open for interpretation. And, finally, that we can no longer passively wait for the problems of social injustice and environmental crisis to solve themselves on their own. If we don't act there soon won't be a habitable world to interpret in the first place. In short, the planet is in need of superheroes but those heroes now must become the individuals who normally sit back and passively consume. Finding teaching mechanisms to break that passivity has to be a top priority for educators in order for the critical praxis necessary to challenge the current hegemonic makeup of civil society.

To put it simply, superheroes serve as an ideal starting point for getting children and students engaged with learning and taking action. In fact, "comics have emerged as a strong literacy tool both in the official school curriculum and in the after school movement ... [and] are particularly motivating for reluctant readers[.] ... As vehicles for discussion, comics offer a gateway to ... move [students] from passive consumers of texts to active producers of knowledge" (Seelow 2010, 57). The willingness of students to engage with the fantastical feats of humans-as-saviors, the comedy and action of talking animal and animated films, and the hybridity of mutation demonstrates the ability for children to engage in complex conversations. There is no need to preserve some sort of innocence in children by hiding the reality that inspired these fictions, and which inspire reality in turn. In fact, the sooner these conversations can be had the better so that, when children do have the ability to increasingly control their participation in the world, they have thought about what the consequences of those actions are. To begin these conversations with the fictions of superheroes, as well as the real-world heroes that inspired them, enables a more novel mode of reflection that is more adaptable to a variety of situations since the emphasis is not set on any one particular real-world detail. Instead this method of education encourages the critical thinking skills necessary to adapt to the ever-changing environment of hegemonic violence. "Presently, humanity faces an unprecedented ecological threat of global proportions, a problem of our own creation. We need to act differently, which requires thinking differently first" (Checkett 2001). To think differently requires going beyond the realm of what is possible or arguable for today because we are fighting a much larger battle over the fate of the planet and the very existence of tomorrow.

WORKS CITED

Adams, Carol. 1990. *The Sexual Politics of Meat: A Feminist-Vegetarian Critical Theory*. New York: Continuum International.

Alexander, Bryan. 2017. "PETA calls for boycott of 'A Dog's Purpose' after disturbing video surfaces." *USA Today*, January 18. https://www.usatoday.com/story/life/movies/2017/01/18/peta-calls-boycott-dogs-purpose-after-disturbing-video-surfaces/96736184/

Barthes, Roland. 1973. *The Pleasure of the Text*. New York: Hill and Wang.

Baum, Gary. 2013. "No Animals Were Harmed." *Hollywood Reporter*, November 25. http://www.hollywoodreporter.com/feature/

Best, Steven. 2006. "Rethinking Revolution: Animal Liberation, Human Liberation, and the Future of the Left." *The International Journal of Inclusive Democracy* 2(3). http://www.inclusivedemocracy.org/journal/vol2/vol2_no3_Best_rethinking_revolution.htm

Butler, Judith. 1997. *Excitable Speech: A Politics of the Performative*. New York: Routledge.

Checkett, John-David. 2001. *The Green Goddess Returns: Batman's Poison Ivy as a symbol of emerging ecofeminist consciousness*. Boca Raton: Florida Atlantic University.

Dunayer, Joan. 2004. *Speciesism*. Derwood, MD: Ryce publishing.

Flynn, Kathleen and Allison Hoffman. 2003. "Fish Flushers Learn Life Does Not Imitate 'Nemo.'" *LA Times*, June 26. http://articles.latimes.com/2003/jun/26/local/me-nemo26

George, Amber and J. L. Schatz. 2016. *Screening the Nonhuman: Representations of Animal Others in the Media.* New York: Lexington Books.

Gottschall, Jonathan. 2012. "Why fiction is good for you." *Dallas News*, May 25. http://www.dallasnews.com/opinion/sunday-commentary/20120525-jonathan-gottschall-why-fiction-is-good-for-you.ece

Gorski, Paul. 2014. "Consumerism as Racial and Economic Injustice: The Macro-aggressions that Make Me, and Maybe You, a Hypocrite." *Understanding and Dismantling Privilege* 4(1): 1–21. http://www.wpcjournal.com/article/view/13097

Halberstam, Jack. 2008. "Animating Revolt/Revolting Animation: Penguin Love, Doll Sex and the Spectacle of the Queer Nonhuman." In *Queering the Non/Human*, edited by Myra Hird and Noreen Giffney, 265–281. Burlington, VT: Ashgate Publishing Company.

Hayward, Eva. 2008. "Lessons From a Starfish," In *Queering the Non/Human*, edited by Myra Hird and Noreen Giffney, 249–263. Burlington, VT: Ashgate Publishing Company.

Hilario, Arturo. 2016. "Monterey Bay Aquarium's Influence on Finding Dory." *El Observador*, May 19. http://el-observador.com/2016/05/19/monterey-bay-aquariums-influence-on-finding-dory/

Hinson, Hal. 1988. "Gorillas in the Mist." *Washington Post*, September 23. http://www.washingtonpost.com/wp-srv/style/longterm/movies/videos/gorillasinthemistpg13hinson_a0c8cc.htm

Hird, Myra. 2008. "Animal Trans." In *Queering the Non/Human*, edited by Myra Hird and Noreen Giffney, 227–247. Burlington, VT: Ashgate Publishing Company.

The Independent. 2009. "Dying to make us happy: The bloody truth behind the dolphinarium." October 10. http://www.independent.co.uk/environment/nature/dying-to-make-us-happy-the-bloody-truth-behind-the-dolphinarium-1799837.html

The Journal of Educational Sociology. 1944. "The Comics as an Educational Medium" 18(4). December. http://www.jstor.org/stable/i313687

Kahn, Richard and Brandy Humes. 2009. "Marching Out From Ultima Thule: Critical Counterstories of Emancipatory Educators Working at the Intersection of Human Rights, Animal Rights, and Planetary Sustainability." *Canadian Journal of Environmental Education* 14: 197–195. http://files.eric.ed.gov/fulltext/EJ842748.pdf

Lagorio, Christine. 2007. "Resources: Marketing To Kids" *CBS News*, May 14. http://www.cbsnews.com/news/resources-marketing-to-kids/

Levy, Justin. 2015. "10 things you may not know about food at Walt Disney World." *WESH News*, July 13. http://www.wesh.com/article/10-things-you-may-not-know-about-food-at-walt-disney-world/4443472

Maigret, Éric and Libbrecht Liz. 1999. "Strange Grew Up With Me: Sentimentality and masculinity in readers of superhero comics." *Réseaux. The French journal of communication* 7(1): 5–27. http://www.persee.fr/docAsPDF/reso_0969-9864_1999_num_7_1_3347.pdf

Marcus, Erik. 2005. *Meat Market: Animals, Ethics, and Money.* Boston, MA: Brio Press.

McGuire, John. 2014. *With us or Against us? Hegemony and Ideology within American Superhero Comic Books 2001–2008.* http://researchdirect.westernsydney.edu.au/islandora/object/uws%3A34600/datastream/PDF/view

Parisi, Luciana. 2008. "The Nanoengineering of Desire." In *Queering the Non/Human*, edited by Myra Hird and Noreen Giffney, 283–309. Burlington, VT: Ashgate Publishing Company.

PETA. 2017. "Animal Actors." April 20. d/l: http://www.peta.org/issues/animals-in-entertainment/animal-actors/

Rosenberg, Robin and Peter Coogan. 2013. *What is a Superhero?* Oxford, UK: Oxford University Press.

Schatz, J. L. 2013. "Speciesist Fiction and the Ethics of the Hobbit." *Critical-Theory.com*, April 16. http://www.critical-theory.com/speciesist-fiction-and-the-ethics-of-the-hobbit/

Seelow, David. 2010. "Voices from the Field the Graphic Novel as Advanced Literacy Tool." *Journal of Media Literacy Education* 2(1): 57–64. http://digitalcommons.uri.edu/cgi/viewcontent.cgi?article=1027&context=jmle

Sivil, Richard. 2001. "Why we need a New Ethic for the Environment." In *Protest and Engagement: Philosophy after Apartheid at an Historically Black South African University*, edited by Patrick Giddy, 103–116. Washington, DC: The Council for Research in Values and Philosophy.

Spiegel, Majorie. 1996. *The Dreaded Comparison: Human and Animal Slavery*. New York: Mirror Books.

Twine, Richard. 2012. "Revealing the 'Animal-Industrial Complex'–A Concept & Method for Critical Animal Studies?" *Journal for Critical Animal Studies* 10(1): 12–39. http://www.criticalanimalstudies.org/wp-content/uploads/2012/10/JCAS+Volume+10+Issue+1+2012+FINAL.pdf#page=13//jl

Vollum, Scott and Cary D. Adkinson. 2003. "The Portrayal of Crime and Justice in the Comic Book Superhero Mythos." *Journal of Criminal Justice and Popular Culture* 10(2): 96–108. http://www.albany.edu/scj/jcjpc/vol10is2/vollum.html

Part II

Chapter 5

Dilemmas of Animal Rights in the *Animal Man* Comic Book Series

Márcio dos Santos Rodrigues and
Matheus da Cruz e Zica

INTRODUCTION

This chapter explores the connections between activism in defense of animal rights and American comic books. This is crucial in understanding how culture informs the tenants of animal liberation activism. In order to achieve this objective, we critically engage with many of the comics found in the twenty-six issues of the *Animal Man* comic book series, written by the scottish author Grant Morrison, and illustrated by Chas Truog and Doug Hazlewood between 1988 and 1990. The purpose of this discussion is to understand to what extent Morrison's work can be understood as a political act because it is subscribed in a terrain of dispute and negotiation that reproduces, on a cultural level, dilemmas regarding animal rights. In the comic *Animal Man*, Morrison argues for animal liberation while presenting a story that revolved around Buddy Baker, "an out-of-work, married-with-children, third-rate super-hero who becomes involved with animals rights and finds his true vocation in life"(Morrison 1991, 5–6). This narrative was also distinct from those seen in superhero stories up to that moment and was different from stories about characters with animal powers. It is this connection between humans and animals, that Morrison complicates, that becomes one of the main themes explored throughout the series.

In this chapter we use particular analysis conventions (both structural and narrative ones) in which we can gleam some sort of access to the context as an evidential paradigm in which "small details" are understood as more "revealing details" (Ginzburg 1989, 96–125). Here we consider *Animal Man* not only for its ideas—but also for what is implicit, as its own reason for being and existing. Comics are also considered a place of dispute, but also negotiation, which reproduces the fundamental conflicts of society at cultural levels, not being seen as an instrument of domination. This is what Douglas Kellner considers products of media culture (2001). Here, we present the same concern proposed by Kellner, to understand how cultural texts diffused by the media—such as comics—in political struggles (consciously or not) can both (re)assert conservative positions and introduce more liberal paradigms (2001). Such concept would bring up certain interpretations that tend to regard media genres not only as merely "ideological," "alienating," and "childish" but also as solely "repositories" of social representations and not as a type of practice that could modify social aspects.

Noticing this other way of speculating about the social world, which is a comic book story, is not a simple task, because they express ways of registering experiences that we are not familiar with (Groensteen 2006). Morrison constantly mentions that what goes on inside the pages of his comics is not even more or less real than what we call reality. As Peter Burke mentions in his book, *Eyewitnessing*, images "provide access not to the social world directly, but to a contemporary vision of that world" (2004, 236). The same occurs in *Animal Man* because Morrison actively contributes to the way our perception is shaped, through the visions or representations they construct. Thus, we are given the task of entering the pages of *Animal Man* and evaluating what is witnessed, without neglecting the way it is done—even if, at first, that reality seems to be "unrealistic" or merely a daydream. Both of them, whether fictional or otherwise would have their own rules, which could expand beyond any mere dichotomy between the two just as with the human and animal.

Thus, when looking into the "reality" of comic books, in the capacity of historians, we should not simply analyze it looking for possible reflexes of the "real world." It is necessary to understand how that reality works. In other words, it is important to try to understand its "internal logic," why it works that way, and how it participates in the social world. Even though it is a fairly introductory study—in the sense of starting, rather than concluding—the goal here is to contribute to the field of Critical Animal Studies (CAS), calling the attention to a source that is scarcely studied. It is also intended to contribute to the study of representations and how the implicate praxis beyond the page as well. It is also intended to contribute to the study of how representations within comics can implicate praxis beyond the page.

Although ecological movements were formed in the 1970s and early 1980s, and earlier forms of human-animal and environmental studies arose in the wake of the discussion raised by such movements, there are still few scholars of the field that investigate, particularly, materials, such as the comic books. There are also few works regarding the relationship between comics and ecological themes. They are not very interested in connecting the analysis of textual and imagistic content of comic books to the context in which they were produced, most of them only consider comics a support and means of information. Comic books are able to interfere in society insofar as they evoke controversies and engender opinions (Duncan and Smith 2009, 246–268). Superheroes in general, and Animal Man in particular, can help rise up against pre-established meanings as it struggles to make come to light ways that are relegated to secondary plans in the social world. Being neither neutral nor impartial, comics and graphic novels help raise questions that, in one way or another, matter and belong to their time. Thus, when analyzed, as a source, not just as a form of communication, we cannot ignore comics as a medium, even if they are fictional. Much more than applying theories, a possible analysis of *Animal Man* as a source would be an effort to find some representative aspects of the social world to which they refer to. No doubt, this is what forms the basis for an effective form of critical praxis. Before all else, it is necessary to consider that these series are practices that make use of socially constructed representations.

OBJECTIFYING "THE MAN WITH ANIMAL POWERS"

On the first page of the first issue of *Animal Man*, "The Human Zoo," we see a sequence in which an enigmatic character walks toward San Diego (1988a, 1). By the end of the page the narrator asks, the powerful question: "Why did we ever come down? Why did we come down out of the trees?" (Morrison 1988a, 1). Before providing any further discussion on the page that follows, we are introduced to the protagonist of the series, Bernhard "Buddy" Baker— Animal Man—trying to save his neighbor's cat, who is stuck in a tree. The fact that Morrison introduced Buddy on top of a tree is quite significant. It might be due to the fact that "Animal Man" would come to embody the connection between humans and nature, with particular regard to the links built over time between humans and animals.

Interestingly, this connection—which, apparently, passed unnoticed and ended up being claimed by the environmental movement as a whole during the 1980s—is reinforced by a "small detail" / "a revealing detail" (Ginzburg 1989, 96–125). This is the sentence the neighbor said, suggesting that Buddy should be careful, because falling from the tree would represent a huge fall as "it's a long way down!" In this part, quite metaphorically, Morrison conveyed an ecological speech or message. "Falling from the tree" is a metaphor that leads us to think about the reasons why humans established a false dichotomy between themselves and animals when they came down from the tree and started to walk upright. Morrison discusses the ontological and epistemological basis that would justify the differentiation between, on the one hand, what humans proudly call a way of life in culture and, on the other, the animals, remembered by a supposed anomie. Morrison shows with the passage that the separation between humans and nature represented a fundamental sin that separated humans from the rest of the natural world. The dichotomy between humans and animals is thus presented as an obstacle that prevents humans from rising and overcoming their moral fall. The author seeks in this passage to make readers reflect on the question of the mysterious figure and on why Buddy so quickly appears in the tree. The narrative sequence thus reveals a pretension to change the understanding of a traditionally accepted human/nature dichotomy, constructing for her a representation that makes it immoral. This is the key that will allow the representation on the fall from the trees as unacceptable and tragic.

The "man with animal powers" was created by Dave Wood and Carmine Infantino, in September 1965, for the *Strange Adventures* magazine, #180. In the original version, when Buddy witnessed the fall of an alien spacecraft, he was exposed to radiation and from then on he acquired animal powers. In Morrison's version, Buddy dies because of the radiation and is revived by aliens. In Morrison's version the aliens rebuilt Buddy's body in order to resuscitate him, so that he could absorb not only the animals' skills but also their sentience. When *Animal Man* was created in the early 1960s, it did not achieve great success as several characters with powers similar to those of animals had already existed from Ant-Man to Spider-Man, among numerous others. Thus, the idea of one of them to have animal powers was not something that seemed to arouse greater attention. This lack of popularity is what made the original version have only five issues. Soon after, Animal Man would become a "second-tier" character, being almost forgotten, until it gained notoriety in Morrison's hands. A large part of the reason for the success of the *Animal Man* series in the 1980s is due to the fact that Morrison addressed controversial and important discussions at that time. The writer presented something that his readers were semi-familiar with and grappled with ideas surrounding human identity and the treatment of animals that intrigued them. As a result, Morrison's *Animal Man* achieved a huge popularity at that historical moment and was successful with both critics and the public. One of the unique aspects of the world is the powerful and clear political intention that the writer builds by centering activism in defense of animals to the story. Walter Benjamin shows us that the art of storytelling is the art of telling experiences (1969). For Benjamin, "the storyteller takes what he tells from experience—his own or that reported by others. And he in turn makes it the experience of those who are listening to his tale," which in our case is those who are reading (1969, 87).

In fact, Morrison joined the Animal Liberation Front Supporters Group (ALF SG), which was an organization founded in 1982 that used principles of "direct action" and allegedly promoted the "illegal activities involving the rescue/release of animals from places of abuse and suffering" (Liddick 2006, 41). As such, *Animal Man* can be considered a work of autobiographical fiction—along the lines described by Colonna—since Morrison uses a fictional character whose existence is realized through the language of comics to speculate about social problems of his interest (2004). In other words, Morrison turns to Buddy as an alter ego and makes him a means to insert himself on dilemmas of animal rights by discussing whether it is possible or not to stop consuming meat or other animal products. In issue #17, there is a sequence in which Animal Man sees his son, Cliff, eating a burger (1989c, 9). Morrison uses exactly this passage to point out to the reader his position on meat consumption. Here Morrison unites theory with practice. Animals, as in the case of chickens, pigs and cows are systematically slaughtered through an industrial logic. In doing so, the author highlights the relationship between livestock slaughter and more serious environmental impacts such as deforestation and the increase of carbon dioxide levels in the atmosphere. It is not without purpose that issue #17 is entitled "Consequences." Further, in issue #26, "Deus Ex Machina," the last issue Morrison wrote, the writer apologized to readers for making the series a sermon (1990, 13). Morrison, like Buddy, decided to become a vegetarian. In the introduction that was originally published in *Animal Man* Book 1 Morrison mentions: "shortly after beginning to work on ANIMAL MAN, I joined the Animal Liberation Front Supporters Group and I ate my last ever steak. Since then I've survived exclusively on water, grass, peanuts and the kindness of strangers" (Morrison 1991, 7). In the last issue he wrote, he criticizes himself as a participant in speciesist practices, and discusses the reasons why he went on to change his eating habits.

CONTROVERSIES AND DILEMMAS IN SCENE

In an interview with Lisa Brown published in the journal *Antennae*: *The Journal of Nature in Visual Culture*, Morrison does not mention the arguments of philosopher-activists who influence the debate about animals rights and animal studies, such as Peter Singer and Tom Regan (2009, 82–87). Morrison does claim to have watched, as a boy, the 1981 documentary *The Animals Film*, directed by Victor Schonfeld. He states that this film was decisive in his writing for *Animal Man* as well as *We3*, which is the focus of another chapter in this book. Although there is no direct evidence of the influence of these thinkers, Morrison made use of representations that are spread by the social imaginary to build something that is understandable to most of his readers. Those representations may not necessarily be derived from his interpretation of the works of authors such as Singer and Regan, but they are part of the same discursive web and aim to produce the same effects. Despite availing himself of those authors' reading and not of what is conveyed as common sense, Morrison would end up proposing a new interpretation for animal rights. Cornelius Castoriadis pointed out that "every symbolism is built on the ruins of earlier symbolic edifices and uses their materials, even if it is only to fill the foundations of new temples" (1997, 121). Following this line of reasoning, we would be led to more than simply identify the network of references which Morrison uses to build his plots, but also to notice how he modifies it. Operating through slips and cuts, the writer inscribes the matter they deal with in their work (activism) in a system of references to other discursive repertoires (the anarchist ideal, for example). Here, it is not possible to assume an idea of convergence, but of the evolution of new and multiple meanings that are linked to others and, therefore, would ultimately reframe the social imaginary around the issue of animals.

For instance, Morrison at no point even uses the term "speciesism" though he represents this concept through several "speciesist" characters in *Animal Man*: the hunters that appear in the first three issues, the fox hunters in issue #10, and the inhabitants of an island having a dolphin hunt in issue #15. In this issue, "The Devil and the Deep Blue Sea," a dolphin tells about the annual killing party in a fishing village (1989b, 8). Morrison, by way of this passage, highlights the cruel conditions that animals are subjected to, and shows the speciesism is a sadistic expression. Morrison reflects on aspects of human perversity and violence to question whether we should be faithful to traditions and laws or to their own principles. The atrocities presented in issue #15 aims to make the reader identify with the animals. Morrison discusses whether animals may have equal or potentially even more consciousness than humans. However, in considering them as sentient beings, the author states that at minimum the welfare needs and the vital interests of animals must be respected. What Morrison puts in evidence is whether "rights" can be extended to animals. When someone says that they have no rights they are saying that they do not count and are not worthy of moral consideration. Such an individual is then considered inferior, useless, and ultimately expendable. Sadly, this is exactly what happens with animals on a regular basis.

THE ETHICAL LIMITS OF DIRECT ACTION

The series continually engages in tension around "reformists/welfarist" and "abolitionists" stances. This is particularly the case in the issues that relate to lab animal liberation. In issue #17, Buddy is participating with activists in a sabotage to free monkeys with their eyes stitched shut, and after freeing the confined monkeys, one of the activists decided to pour gasoline in the laboratory and set it on fire (Morrison 1989c, 7). Even though Animal Man questions this act at first, he later decides, "to wash his hands of it" (Morrison 1989c, 7). The primary ethical question raised in this issue is: when, if ever, is violence needed to bring about justice. The writer had asked such a question in the second issue. In the letters section, Morrison informs us that *Animal Man* permitted him not "only to deal with the animal abuses that I find personally disturbing and indefensible but also to question the morality of the more extreme activists, some of whom are talking about killing scientists and poisoning foodstuffs" (1988b, 25).

By making such a stance clear from the beginning of the series, the author ends up providing *Animal Man* room to articulate, on a cultural level, dilemmas around the question of the animal. And when they do appear, such controversies also inform us about society, particularly for the concepts of "right" and "wrong" that are also elaborated by society. The first issues written by Morrison already presented this tension, putting the Animal Man against a "villain," the B'wana Beast, whose only motivation is to fight the cruelty against the animals. A gorilla is captured by scientists. In response to the arrest, the "villain" decides to take revenge on the kidnappers. For the antagonist the abolition of any kind of exploitation against animals would be the only view acceptable. It is a question of extirpating sufferings that are imposed on animals, even if to resort to violence. This entry of the antagonists is an expression of the tensions of the animal liberation movement around the principle of equal consideration of the animals, be it of the sufferings or the interests. The tensions translate over the disagreement concerning the basic notions of what is morally right. By participating in a relationship mediated by violence, humanity is corrupted. Denunciation is only possible if animal abuse is pointed out as divergent to what makes us human. The assumption of the equality of animals authorizes their insertion in a universe of rights, in which they would be beneficiaries of rules that prevent their exploitation, as also pointed out by Amy J. Fitzgerald and David Pellow in a chapter published in *Defining Critical Animal Studies* (2014, 28–48). Here an intersectional perspective is delineated, enlarging and making more complex the production of inequalities. Similarly Morrison questions the power relations between species and their impacts on everyday experiences between human and animals. The practical result of this multifaceted operation would be the attempt to denature animal exploitation and to destroy the notion that animals would be distinct beings. The effect of denaturalization would be the possibility of denunciation and mobilization in favor of animal rights. For this, Morrison shows, is how the worldview of Buddy moves from a liberal and utilitarian perspective to a radical position.

SCIENTIFIC EXPERIMENTATION

Animal Man was also a means used by Morrison to comment on how animals are used for experimental purposes of any kind. In several moments during the series, animals are seen suffering and in pain at laboratories as the one shown on the cover for *Animal Man* #17, drawn by Brian Bolland, in which Animal Man holds a baby monkey with sewn eyes (Morrison 1989c). With this cover, Morrison is explicitly referring to the study conducted by the University of California Riverside with monkeys (Guither 1998, 223). On April 20, 1985, Animal Liberation Front activists invaded laboratories, and there they found an infant monkey that was alone in a cage with its eyes stitched closed (Potter 2011). On the cover, Animal Man's features imply that he is in more pain while the infant monkey still tries to look peaceful, even though their eyes are sewn shut. That cover lends itself to an explicit critique of such systematic use of animals in scientific research.

At the beginning of the series, Buddy represented the Singer's views. Singer in 2006 argued that in some situations animal experimentation can be ethical as in the use of primates as laboratory animals in research to minimize the effects of Parkinson's disease. Singer says in this occasion: "I do not think you should reproach yourself for doing it, provided ... that there was no other way of discovering this knowledge. I could see this as justifiable research" (Smith 2012, 31). In the first issues there was no singular ethical position assumed by Animal Man in regards to the use of animals for scientific purpose, as the character adopted Singer's positions. In issue #1 Buddy is called to help in the investigation of a crime in which monkeys appear forming a unique creature. Buddy at that time did not care a lot about using animals for drug tests. He did not wonder if there were ways to conduct experiments without animals, moreover the tests had the goal to cure HIV. The tension perceived in this passage is that of utilitarianism. The cure for AIDS would produce a greater good for those involved, even if it were necessary to inflict suffering on animals. This is what we see in Singer's propositions. Regan criticized Singer's utilitarian bias, which focuses on the interests and means and not the needs of nonhumans. After the incident involving monkeys for laboratory tests and the confrontation with the B'wana Beast, Animal Man breaks with the utilitarian logic, inasmuch as the ability to put oneself in the animal's place makes the hero's focus on the needs of animals. Into the molds of Critical Animal Studies, the hero starts to establish a real approximation at the intimate level with animals and his stance before the world is completely altered. Buddy not only extracts from animals the powers, but also becomes able to feel what they feel. This was the most significant change introduced by Morrison, something that the original version of the 1960s was not capable.

Likewise, this ability makes Animal Man rethink his relationship with the world, with others and himself. The first change that Animal Man adopts is to combat the speciesist practices in his daily life. A drastic change in diet is the first strategy of action; something that Morrison explores on the daily level of people's lives. In this way, he starts to defend, like Regan, "the total abolition of the use of animals in science; the total dissolution of commercial animal agriculture; the total elimination of commercial and sport hunting and trapping" (Guither 1998, 20). Ideas and perceptions on the environment appear from the first issue written by Morrison. In issue #4, named "When We All Lived in the Forest," Animal Man meets the B'wana Beast (Morrison 1988d). B'wana Beast journeys to America to rescue his pal Djuba, a gorilla, who has been captured by scientists from S.T.A.R. Labs in San Diego and infected with a variety of anthrax. Djbuba is considered by the scientists as "missing link" between humans and their apelike ancestors and his capture awakens the fury of "The White God of Kilimanjaro." B'wana Beast fails to save Djuba and he ends up being infected by the virus. On the verge of death in Animal Man's arms, he states the following:

> P-Paradise ... we were given paradise ... and we turned it into an ... abattoir ... Everywhere we go ... we leave things bleeding and screaming ... we're murdering the world ... we have to be stopped ... mankind has to be stopped ... Buh-Before there nothing left ... we thing we own the world But ... but ... Ohh! Oh God, we've ... Fallen so far ... and there's still ... still ... there's still ... no ... Bottom. (Morrison 1988d, 17)

The suffering expressed in B'wana Beast's speech, added to the use of biblical metaphors (like that of a lost paradise), allows not only to touch the piety of readers, but mobilizes a supposed religiosity by the analogy between the ordeal or the martyrdom or even the redemption that would die for the liberation of animals. Morrison presents the postulation that the damage that men do to animals is unjustifiable. Thus, the sense of animal liberation proposed in the B'wana Beast's speech would be to correct the world so that it became consistent with the imperatives of morality and harmony with animals.

Although characters like those only have "concrete existence" on comic books pages, they correspond to a deliberate attitude to represent the authors' opinion on a state of affairs they do not agree with. A sentence such as the one above appeals to the reader's sensitivity, trying to emphasize the importance of changing their attitude toward animals. For the scholars of critical animal studies, it would be meaningful for many reasons. First, it counts on a political intention—the sentence seeks to persuade the reader by confronting the dominant worldview and claiming it is not valid. It can be seen as a complaint, as a warning for some situations, expressing the view that comic books can serve as a means to change the world. Second, it helps promote the existence of an untouched nature (reference to Paradise) tainted by the hands of people who insist on transforming it into a "slaughterhouse." Third, it expresses a sense of guilt when putting some thoughts into why people do that. Buddy also has the ability to interact with nature through the connection he establishes with the morphogenetic field of Earth, an energy field that articulates all the biophysical spheres that bind humans to animals. Morrison, by conferring this ability on Animal Man, reinforces the representation of nature with a network established by organisms that depend on each other. The hero goes so far as to tell his son in the passage from issue #17: "Humans can think Things through. You've got to understand that nothing exists in a Vacuum, Cliff. Everything is connected. Certain Events have certain Consequences" (Morrison 1989c, 10). All forms of life would be interdependent in the conception of the Animal Man. Morrison highlights that when we experience a greater integration with our animality, our perception would open up, allowing us to access dimensions never before explored. A new sensibility opens the character's mind to what passes through an animal's consciousness, what an animal can suffer and compels him to reconsider his priorities as a superhero.

CONSUMING ANIMALS

Other comic books dealing with animal rights include *Badger*, created by Mike Baron in 1983. One of *Badger*'s covers, issue #25 ("The Duck Lady"), represents hunters as sadistic individuals who hunt for the pleasure of killing (Baron 1987). The duck-hunting season pictured on the cover in question utilizes a savage taste. Baron is mentioned in issue #5 by Morrison in a scene where Buddy demands that his family all become vegetarian as well (Morrison 1988e, 6–8). In this scene, while confronting his family, Buddy wears a shirt with a badge similar to Badger's (Morrison 1988e, 9).

Morrison by dressing Buddy in a shirt that has a symbol, which resembles the one Mike Barron's character wears, draws a parallel with the "environmentalist" vision presented in an unpretentious way in *Badger*; and the fact that Buddy seems—as Badger—senseless in the eyes of his family. When Buddy discarded all food of animal origin from the pantry and imposed eating habits on his family without consulting them, he acts like an activist who has just been converted to the cause instead of one who is versed in the nuance of animal rights. This results in him trying to convince everyone around him through a zealous and moralistic appeal to justice. From the first frame to the last one in the sequence that juxtaposes Buddy trying to "convert" his family with an announcement of a religious preacher on television asking for money from the ones who believe in it. Right after that, we see Buddy trying to convert and "demonizing" all those who eat meat.

The boycott on meat consumption in *Animal Man* does not simply appear as linked to a matter of diet or eating habits, but it is also configured as an option aimed at political and moral demobilization of the meat and fur industry. The boycott on clothes that have fur as raw material is also presented, particularly when Buddy chooses to wear a synthetic leather jacket as part of his uniform. When in issue #5 he asks if his wife has "any kind of idea of the terrible conditions these animals live in before they get dragged down to the slaughterhouse and turned into somebody's groceries," he reflects on animal bonding being associated with hierarchies established in terms of power (Morrison 1998e, 8). The animals would find themselves in a lower hierarchical position of great vulnerability and impotence. The criticism here rests on the human freedom and the different ways that they harm the rights of others.

CONCLUSION

In the 1970s, different social actors—civil rights activists, feminists, ecologists, pacifists, anarchists, etc.—directed their attention to animal rights. Opposed to the dominant consensus that objectifies animals, defining them as mere properties and resources, these different actors elaborated a variety of reasons to prevent humans from legitimating animal exploitation, confinement, removal of their environment, slaughter, and consumption. One of them suggests that animals have rights due to the fact that they live on Earth, sharing this condition with humans. Therefore, they should have the same rights. In line with this process, UNESCO proclaimed, in January 1978, the Universal Declaration of Animal Rights, highlighting that "all animals are born with an equal claim on life and the same rights to existence," among other things (article 1).

Behavior and sensibility changes toward animals, as the ones listed above, have existed for a long time, as stated by Keith Thomas in his excellent book *Man and the Natural World* (1983). More recently, it has also been studied by Anthony J. Nocella II and others in *Anarchism and Animal Liberation* (2015). The fight nowadays known as anti-speciesism, presents a strong connection with libertarian actions. It is clear that, in some currents of the animal rights movement, anarchist ideas are present and active (Best 2009, 189–199). The complaint against forms of social coercion, characteristic of anarchism, is transposed to that of the animal question. In the anarchist current of the animal rights, freedom ends up being extended to animals and should not be shared only with the humans. However, if there is a movement in defense of animals, it is by virtue of its collective character and, largely, by its inclusion in the ecological movement. While there is extensive literature about animal rights, few works present a strict concern for historically situating this phenomenon. Fortunately, newer contemporary works seek to build different perspectives about the animal-human relationship. Like Morrison, scholars of Critical Animal Studies examine the dilemmas that shaped our understanding of animals.

However, we should consider the emergence of the movement in question as linked to the involvement of other subjects, much more than signaling an origin derived from a single pole and, therefore, liable to be refuted. It is worth considering the movement based on a single pattern as we would be facing the most diverse reasons, several times irreconcilable. First of all, it is agreed and evaluated that the movement in question cannot be interpreted in a monolithic way. As there is not just a movement for animal rights it would then be more acceptable if we used movements—in the plural. Therefore, every claim drawn upon by each social actor must be interpreted as linked to certain situations rather than a consolidated theoretical framework. Operating through comic book fiction, *Animal Man* is part in this ongoing process. The struggle for animal rights makes *Animal Man* a megaphone for the construction of environmental ideas, and in the plot we have hard attacks on the way humans impact other living beings. Accompanying Buddy Baker enables the reader to confront speciesist conceptions. Animal Man becomes aware of multiple forms of discrimination against animals and from then combat the cyclically perpetuated oppression by systems of speciesism, hopefully enabling readers to do the same.

The criticism outlined in its pages, when assuming a pamphleteer tone, points to alternatives that can be built in the relationship humans have with nonhuman animals. By looking to this fictional universe is become possible to forge a path forward within the nonfiction of reality. It also allows for imaginative reconfigurations of what animal rights activism can look like when shedding the speciesism of many mainstream approaches. However, even more important, *Animal Man* helps to serve as inspiration to new waves of readers to realize how animal liberation is a key component to any struggle for justice.

WORKS CITED

Baron, Mike. 1987. "The Duck Lady." *Badger* #25. July. Chicago: First Comics.

Benjamin, Walter. 1969. "The Storyteller: Reflections on the Work of Nikolai Leskov." In *Illuminations: Essays and Reflections*, edited by Hannah Arendt, 83–110. New York: Schocken Books.

Best, Steve. 2009. "Rethinking revolution—Total liberation, allience politics, and prolegomena to resistance moviments in the twenty-first century." In *Contemporary*

Anarchist Studies: An Introductory Anthology of Anarchy in the Academy, edited by Randall Amster et al, 189–199. New York: Routledge.

Best, Steve and Anthony Nocella II. 2004. *Terrorists or Freedom Fighters?: Reflections on the Liberation of Animals.* New York: Lantern Books.

Brown, Lisa. 2009. "Grant Morrison: We3." *Antennae 9*: 82–87.

Burke, Peter. 2001. *Eyewitnessing: The Uses of Images as Historical Evidence.* New York: Cornell University Press.

Castoriadis, Cornelius. 1997. *The Imaginary Institution of Society.* [Translation of *L'institution imaginaire de la société,* Paris: Seuil. 1975]. Cambridge, MA: MIT Press.

Colonna, Vincent. 2004. *Autofictions & autres mythomanies littéraires.* Auch: Tristram.

Duncan, Randy and Matthew J. Smith. 2009. *The Power of Comics:* History, Form and Culture New York, Continuum.

Fitzgerald, Amy J. and David Pellow. 2014. "Ecological defense for animal liberation: A holistic understanding of the world." In *Defining Critical Animal Studies,* edited by Anthony Nocella II et al., 28–48. New York: Peter Lang Publishing.

Flükiger, Jean-Marc. 2009. "The Radical Animal Liberation Movement: Some Reflections on Its Future." *Journal for the Study of Radicalism* 2(2): 111–132.

Freeman, Carrie Packwood and Jason Leigh. 2013. "Consuming Nature: Mass Media and The Cultural Politics of Animals and Environments." In *Ignoring Nature No More: The Case for Compassionate Conservation,* edited by Marc Bekoff and Sarah M. Bexell, 257–270. Chicago: University of Chicago Press.

Ginzburg, Carlo. 1989. *Clues, Myths, and the Historical Method.* Baltimore: Johns Hopkins University Press.

Groensteen, Thierry. 2006. *Un objet culturel non identifié* ["An unidentified cultural object"]. Angoulême: Éd. de l'An 2.

Guither, Harold D. 1997. *Animal Rights: History and Scope of a Radical Social Movement.* Cardondale: Southern Illinois University Press.

Kelnner, Douglas. 2011. *A cultura da mídia—estudos culturais: identidade e política entre o moderno e o pós-moderno.* [Media Culture—cultural studies: identity and politics between modernism and post-modernism]. Bauru, São Paulo: EDUSC.

Liddick, Donald R. 2006. *Eco-terrorism: Radical Environmental and Animal Liberation Movements.* Westport, CT: Praeger Publishers.

McCance, Dawne. 2013. *Critical Animal Studies*: An Introduction. Albany: SUNY Press.

Morrison, Grant. 1988a. *Animal Man #1:* "The Human Zoo." September. New York: DC Comics.

———. 1988b. *Animal Man #2:* "Life in the Concrete Jungle." October. New York: DC Comics.

———. 1988c. *Animal Man # 3:* "The Nature of the Beast." November. New York: DC Comics.

———. 1988d. *Animal Man #4:* "When We All Lived in the Forest." December. New York: DC Comics.

———. 1988e. *Animal Man #5:* "The Coyote Gospel." December. New York: DC Comics.

———. 1989a. *Animal Man #10:* "Fox on the run." April. New York: DC Comics.

————. 1989b. *Animal Man #15*: "The Devil and the Deep Blue Sea." September. New York: DC Comics.

————. 1989c. *Animal Man #17*: "Consequences." November. New York: DC Comics.

————. 1990. *Animal Man #26*: "Deus Ex Machina." August. New York: DC Comics.

————. 1991. Animal Man Book 1 Trade Paper Back. July. New York: DC Comics.

Potter, Will. 2011. *Green Is the New Red: An Insider's Account of a Social Movement Under Siege*. San Francisco: City Lights Books.

Regan, Tom. 1985. "The Case for Animal Rights." In *Defense of Animals*, edited by Peter Singer, 13–26. New York: Basil Blackwell.

Singer, Peter. 2010 . *Libertação animal* [*Animal Liberation*]. São Paulo: Editora WMF Martins Fontes.

Sunstein, Cass and Martha Nussbaum. 2005. *Animal Rights: Current Debates and New Directions*. New York: Oxford University Press.

Smith, Wesley J. 2012. *Rat is a Pig is a Dog is a Boy*. New York: Encounter Books.

Thomas, Keith. 1983. *Man and the Natural World: Changing Attitudes in England 1500–1800*. Oxford: Oxford University Press.

White, Richard. 2015. "Animal geographies, anarchist praxis and Critical Animal Studies." In *Critical Animal Geographies: Politics, Intersections, and Hierarchies in a Multispecies World. Routledge Human-Animal Studies Series*, edited by Kathryn Gillespie and Collard Rosemary-Claire, 19–35. London, Routledge.

Chapter 6

We3 and the Violence of Sentimentality

Allison Dushane

We3, a comic miniseries written by Grant Morrison and illustrated by Frank Quitely, focuses on a trio of household pets transformed into military weapons. The cover of the 2005 compilation of the three issues, serialized by Vertigo in 2004, depicts them in the classic attitude of superheroes. Three animals—a dog, a cat, and a rabbit—pose together, heads held high, gazing into the distance with noble and stoic expressions. Each of their bodies is encased in a power suit and each of their heads is adorned with a crown of glowing wires, suggesting the technologically enhanced mantle of a self-made hero like Ironman or Batman. However, these unconventional superheroes haven't chosen to modify their bodies and minds in the pursuit of justice or revenge. Rather, their experimental transformation into cyborgs is the outcome of an agenda that harnesses animal lives toward human ends. *We3* chronicles their adventures as they escape from a government research facility and search for their true "home." In the foreword to *Defining Critical Animal Studies*, David Nibert argues that the Military Industrial Complex (MIC) and the Animal Industrial Complex (AIC) function as "mutually reinforcing systems of domination—continuing the inextricable link between the oppression of other animals and human violence" (2014, x). The form and the narrative of *We3* illuminate the multiple forms of violence perpetuated by this link; as it denounces the experimentation on and use of animals by the military, *We3* also protests against widespread instrumental exploitation of animals in human culture.

We3 performs another layer of critical work by exposing the anthropocentrism that often drives cultural representations of animals in media as well as their interpretations in academic scholarship. Anthropocentrism is "an ideology of human supremacy that advocates privileging humans ... to maintain the centrality and priority of human existence through marginalizing and subordinating nonhuman perspectives, interests and beings" (Weitzenfeld and Joy 2014, 3). Critical Animal Studies presents an alternative to traditional animal studies, which tends to reinforce anthropocentrism by reducing animals to "reified signs, symbols, images, words on a page, or protagonists in a historical drama" (Best et al. 2007). In *What is Posthumanism?*, Cary Wolfe points out that an increased attention to the animal as a topic of study runs the risk of simply perpetuating anthropocentric, or human-centered, perspectives: "Just because we direct our attention to the study of nonhuman animals, and even if we do so with the aim of exposing how they have been misunderstood and exploited, that does not mean that we are not continuing to be humanist—and therefore, by definition, anthropocentric" (2010, 99). The media theorist Jean Baudrillard, in "The Animals: Territory and Metamorphoses," a brief chapter in his landmark *Simulacra and Simulation*, claims that such anthropocentric representations of animals are actually a form of violence (1995). As he puts it, "our sentimentality toward animals is a sure sign of the disdain in which we hold them" (1995, 134). That is, the impulse to humanize nonhuman animals, instead of contributing to their liberation, actually serves to mask and diminish the violence that has historically been inflicted on them in the service of human ends. *We3* makes a significant contribution to the work of critical animal studies by rendering the metaphorical violence of sentimentality visible in order to draw attention to the literal forms of violence perpetuated by the pervasive appropriation of animals by popular culture in the service of human interests.

How does *We3*, then, by representing animals as superheroes, not simply repeat this anthropocentric violence? Through a more sustained engagement with Baudrillard and Wolfe's posthumanist approaches to animal studies, I argue that the minimalist dialogue and exaggerated representations of violence that characterize the aesthetic of *We3* can also be read as a self-reflexive critique of the violence that is sustained and perpetuated by sentimentalized representations of animals. That is, instead of merely repeating the tropes of sentimentality that serve as markers for the history of violence, or disdain, of animal life, *We3* works through formal elements unique to the medium of comics in order to draw attention to the metaphorical violence of making animals speak. I begin by surveying the role that anthropomorphic animals have traditionally played in comics and establishing how *We3* represents its animal protagonists with a self-conscious awareness of this tradition. I then turn to a more extensive engagement with Baudrillard's essay and a reading of *We3*'s representation of talking animals in order to explore the link between anthropomorphism and violence. Focusing on a reading of the innovative panel structures and surreal depictions of violence that characterize the aesthetic of *We3*, I argue that the comic places its audience in the position of the objectifying gaze of sentimentality in order to draw attention to and critique anthropocentric perspectives. To conclude, I consider how the ending sequences of *We3* can be productively read alongside posthumanist ethical systems that question the validity of an ethic founded on the anthropocentric discourse of "rights."

Instead of simply representing the violence inflicted on animals by human beings in order to evoke sympathy, *We3* critiques the historical tendency of its own medium to erase the agency of animals by anthropomorphizing them. In *The Power of Comics*, Randy Duncan and Matthew J. Smith outline the history of "funny animal comics," beginning with the earliest, which, "like the fables that preceded them, always focused on some moral lesson" (2008). As animal comics developed, they served as "equipment for the imagination, allowing readers to break free of an otherwise confining life," providing a "quality of wish fulfillment" similar to superheroes. They have continued to serve, often satirically, as figures to illuminate the "idiosyncrasies of human society" and "explore the human condition" (2008, 208). In *Animal Stories: Narrating Across Species Lines*, Susan McHugh observes this phenomenon on a wider scale, arguing that animals in cultural narratives in diverse forms of media—including film, novels, visual art and video games—tend to "emerg[e] as significant figures ... only in terms of metaphor" (2011, 488). Reviews of *We3* comment on how Morrison and Quitely counter this tendency while still eliciting sympathy for the animals, citing the effective tension between the series' realistic and understated rendering of the animal characters and its unapologetic and exaggerated portrayals of violence. For example, in the *Comics Authority Review*, Keith Dooley writes that *We3* is "a book that will bring tears to readers' eyes." Not only are the depictions of violence "visceral, realistic and extremely graphic," they serve to elicit a sympathetic response toward the animal protagonists: "The effects of the violence and their escape from captivity on the animals is harrowing, with Quitely's depiction of each animal's face showing depths of despair and desperation" (2014). However, as Kenneth Volk points out, "the genius of Morrison's story is that he mostly resists the impulse to anthropomorphize his nonhuman characters" (2005). He draws attention to how the aesthetic features of *We3* work not only to generate sympathy, but to draw the reader's attention to "the way animals perceive the world." In particular, the innovative panel structures make for an "unnerving contrast" between the "story's political conflict" and the "lost pets' simple biological drives." Instead of serving as mere proxies for human fears and desires, the animals in *We3* are depicted as agents with distinct and idiosyncratic instincts and affects.

The visual aspect of comics makes it an ideal medium through which to reveal and unsettle the dominance of anthropocentric perspectives. The original issues of *We3* feature covers that depict the animal protagonists through the eyes of their human owners in the form of posters declaring them

"Missing" or "Lost." The cover of issue one depicts a "medium size dog—brown Labrador mixed," with head cocked, tongue lolling out, and eyes looking up with a blank expression. The poster offers a reward for information leading to the return of "Bandit." Likewise, issues two and three offer rewards for a sleeping cat named "Tinker" and a rabbit named "Pirate." In the first series of panels, the perspective shifts from human to animal, as the trio of cyborgs tracks and assassinates their target, supervised by a tactical team in a van labeled "Pet Supplies" (2005, 1.1–1.10). Their mission culminates in a two-page splash panel, which depicts a hail of bullets as they make contact with a human body that explodes into chunks of flesh riddled with bloody holes (2005, 1.6–1.7). This opening sequence stands in stark contrast to the "friendly & approachable" Bandit on the cover. In short, the graphic violence of the assassination is disturbing, in part, because it is carried out by a house pet, previously humanized by the missing posters: innocent, helpless, and adorable. As the team returns to their research facility, the military officers in charge are giving a senator a tour. While they all observe a group of "rat biorgs" busily working to assemble a jet engine, one of the scientists remarks that "replacing an expensive and outmoded workforce with efficient animal slaves is only one very small application of our research and development program" (2005, 1.14). Suddenly, one of the rats accidentally kills another with a drill, prompting them to remark "say hello to man's new best friends" (2005, 1.15). This brief exchange illuminates the deeply ambivalent cultural status of animals; they are regarded simultaneously as disposable components of a capitalist system and revered as human companions.

In *Simulacra and Simulation*, Baudrillard considers the systemic origins of the ambivalent roles that animals play in human culture (1995). He argues that, whereas in pre-capitalist cultures the killing of animals was surrounded by more intimate rituals of symbolic exchange, contemporary sites of animal "sacrifice" such as laboratories and factory farms, operating behind closed doors and on an incomprehensible scale, erase the possibility for a recognition of their agency or their suffering (1995, 134–137). Sentimentality toward animals emerges as a widespread cultural cover up for the invisibility of this suffering. In Baudrillard's account of the signification of animals, one of the defining features of animals is their refusal of incorporation into human systems that organize power through language: "They, the animals, do not speak. In a universe of increasing speech, of the constraint to confess and to speak, only they remain mute, and for this reason they seem to retreat far from us, behind the horizon of truth" (1995, 137). He reads the silence of animals as an affront to the hegemony of human reason: "In a world bend on doing nothing but making one speak, in a world assembled under the hegemony of signs and discourse, their silence weighs more and more heavily on our organization of meaning" (1995, 137). The roles that animals play in human culture are all instrumental:

> Certainly, one makes them speak, and with all means, some more innocent than others. They spoke the moral discourse of man in fables. They supported structural discourse in the theory of totemism. Every day they deliver their "objective"—anatomical, physiological, genetic—message in laboratories. They served in turns as metaphors for virtue and vice, as an energetic and ecological model, as a mechanical and formal model in bionics[.] ... In all this—metaphor, guinea pig, model, allegory (without forgetting their alimentary "use value")—animals maintain a compulsory discourse. Nowhere do they really speak because they only furnish the responses one asks for. (Baudrillard 1995, 137–138)

We3 draws attention to the ways in which the agency of animals is always filtered through the anthropomorphic lens of language. As Baudrillard puts it, "our sentimentality toward animals is a sure sign of the disdain in which we hold them. It is proportional to this disdain. It is in proportion to being relegated to irresponsibility, to the inhuman, that the animal becomes worthy of the human ritual of affection and protection" (1995, 134). Following this logic, sentimentalized representations of animals like the one on the missing poster can be interpreted as signs of the same attitude toward animals that allows for the enslavement and violence toward animals taking place in the research facility.

The technology that enables the animals to speak serves as an ironic commentary on the compulsory discourse of animals in popular culture. Bandit, Tinker and Pirate, to whom the human researchers refer by the project name WE3, are each equipped with technology that translates their attempts at communication into human speech. Instead of complete sentences and witty rejoinders, the animals speak in stilted words and phrases that reveal a limited understanding of the human speech that surrounds them. In lieu of names, they refer to themselves and each other with the numbers they have been assigned at the facility. The animals' unconventional spelling and awkward to nonsensical grammar is rendered in distinct all-caps font and through a greater number of speech bubbles than the human characters. In this essay, quotations from the text employ parentheses to indicate the speech bubbles when the animals are speaking in order to highlight this difference. When the tour arrives at a room marked "Animal Weapon 3," the senator is introduced to Bandit, or 1, and his companions, 2 and 3. The senator is at first intrigued to meet 1, but is horrified and frightened when his greeting, "Hello, boy. And how are you today?" is met with an (almost) human: "(I.M. GUD.) (R.U. GUD 2?) ('MR. WAH-SHING-TON.')" (2005, 1.16–1.17). As the humans discuss the decommissioning of the project as if the animals cannot hear them, Tinker the cat is preoccupied with their smell "(MMMMEN ST!NK!) (BOSSSS! ST!NK!)" and her hunger "(HUNGRY)." Meanwhile, Bandit expresses confusion "('DEE-COMM-ISH.') (?WORD?)" and Pirate voices the simplest of desires "(NO.) (GRASS.) (EAT.) (NOW.) (EAT.)" (2005, 1.18). These features not only to highlight the fact that these particular animals have been modified from their natural state, but also to comment on the artifice of talking animals as a pervasive cultural trope. The presence of animals with the ability to actually speak is perceived as a threat to human dominance. The military officer justifies his decision to decommission the animals, partially on the basis of their capacity for language: "You may see that as a triumph for techno-biological know-how but I'm looking at three **pissed** little animals[.] ... [W]hat kind of lunatic would teach a killing machine to talk?" (2005, 1.19). The silence of animals presents one kind of threat to human assumptions of meaning and truth; however, there is nothing more threatening than a military weapon, once relegated to the "compulsory discourse" of metaphor and experiment, suddenly furnishing his own response. In addition, his invocation of the long history of conceiving the animal as "machine" underscores a human-animal binary that is often established using the criterion of language.

Resisting the compulsory discourse demanded of them in the research facility, the animals carry out their escape in silence. This sequence, which unfolds over three two-page spreads comprised of discrete shots of security camera footage, emphasizes a distinctly nonhuman mode of viewing. Each page is divided into a 3x5 grid that intersperses the narrative recorded by the security footage from different parts of the facility with individual close-ups of each animal's face, focusing on the eyes. The lower right hand corner of the fourth page features a close up of the bared fangs of an animal; this image collapses the previous focus on each character into a single blurred expression of instinctual animal rage. On the culminating pages, the animals move through the facility, leaving a trail of bodies in their wake (2005, 1.20–1.25). The concluding sequence of issue one, which follows WE3 after they escape from the facility, continues to portray the animals acting according to their own instincts. The rabbit, confused, defers to his companions. The dog, sniffing the air, repeatedly insists that they go "(HOME)." The cat stalks and kills a bird mid conversation, insisting "(2 STAY. EAT HERE)" (2005, 1.31). The final page provides a vertical panorama of a forest that dwarfs the small animals at the bottom as helicopters loom overhead. The cat watches his companions move forward, with a single speech bubble: "(WE3 NO HOME NOW)" (2005, 1.32). The placement of the speech bubble makes the speaker as well as the meaning of the statement ambiguous. It could possibly be Tinker arguing that WE3 is already home, or Bandit insisting that they are not home yet. The ambiguity suggests another reading: collectively, the animals know that no "home" exists for them in their technologically humanized state.

The layouts and aesthetic composition of individual panels work in concert with the stylized dialogue to decenter anthropomorphic perspectives. *We3* experiments with the phenomenon of "closure," defined by comics scholar Scott McCloud in *Understanding Comics* as "the phenomenon of observing the parts but perceiving the whole" (1994, 63). The cognitive experience of reading comics is heavily influenced by the design and placement of panels, which can range from the linear and the straightforward to the abstract or deliberately disordered. In particular, the transitions between panels influence the audience's experience of the narrative, as they continually construct meaning across the "gutters," or spaces between the panels, where "human imagination takes two separate images and transforms them into a single idea" (1994, 66). The innovative panel structures that display the violence that dominates issue two, as the military attempts to hunt down and destroy WE3, illuminate the difference between animal and human modes of perception. Within the research facility, the scientists try to communicate the danger that the animals pose to their human pursuers. In addition to their technological enhancements, "the dog alone is equipped with ground-to-air missiles," they have a fundamentally different mode of operating in the world: "even their senses are different from ours. They're much faster than any human. They experience time and motion differently" (2005, 2.4). One particularly arresting two-page layout superimposes images of WE3 colliding with military tanks and personal with mini-panel squares that focus in on specific details. A bullet approaching a soldier's face, a detached human foot, and other bits of bodies and machinery all disorganize a linear reading of the action as the snapshots disorient human temporal and spatial perspectives (2005, 2.6–2.7). Another two-page layout features Tinker the cat in the upper left hand corner, poised above a series of rectangular panels that record the successive moments of his assault on a group of soldiers. Tinker enters and moves through and between the panels, appearing in the gutters while the soldiers remain with their confines, further suggesting that the animals perceive the world on different terms as they break the traditional "rules" of closure (2005, 2.10–2.11). By frustrating the expectations of closure, these sequences question the dominance of the human imagination.

The sequences in this issue seem to revel in gore; human and animal flesh and blood are liberally splashed throughout the pages. However, their distinct design suggests that this gore is engineered not simply for thrills, but in order to invoke a form of disgust that serves to challenge sentimental, anthropocentric perspectives toward animals. Anthropocentrism takes multiple forms, which all rely on some kind of separation into categories based on specific qualities. Human-animal dualisms, for example, position "humans over and above all other animals, radically separated into two homogeneous, opposing kinds." Human animal–continuums place "humans and animal others along a scale," hierarchically ranking humans and animals alike based on their perceived value. Both forms privilege a certain set of characteristics, in particular the capacity for "self-realization and self-determination" (Weitzenfeld and Joy 2004, 6). Jonathan Gaboury convincingly argues for *We3* as an "example of aesthetic violence that destabilizes gratuitousness by meticulously hybridizing its violent agents, its hapless victims, and its page layouts" (2011, 1). In his reading of these sequences, the complex fragmentation involved in *We3*'s vivid portrayals of violence dissolves the individuality of their subjects. Tinker, for example, has "ceased to be a subject of narration," as her activity on these pages represents "lightness and viciousness in the abstract." The meticulously rendered scenes of violence in *We3* are disturbing in part because they frustrate a clear sense of cause and effect: "there are no actors, no subjects, because cat, dog, and rabbit are always in-between and on-the-run, blending and corrupting their instinct with technology" (2011, 30). The hybridization between and the dissolution of human and animal subjects that Gaboury observes in these sequences is one way that *We3* critiques anthropocentric perspectives. The depictions of violence in *We3* collapse distinctions between animal and human actions and intentionality; violence itself emerges as a phenomenon that itself erases self-realization and self-determination. In these violent episodes, the line between good and evil becomes as blurry as the lines between human and animal, as the sentimental portrait of a peacefully sleeping Tinker that graces the cover of the issue in the form of a missing poster is replaced with a killing machine.

The form and the narrative of *We3* work together to draw attention to the violence that links the human treatment of animals to the violence perpetuated by ethical systems founded upon the discourse of human rights. Dismantling such systems, which support human-animal dualisms and continuums alike, is one of the key aims of Critical Animal Studies. In his introduction to the essay collection *Philosophy and Animal Life*, Cary Wolfe argues that "problem with both sides" of the animal rights debate in traditional philosophy "is that they are locked into a model of justice in which a being does or does not have rights on the basis of its possession (or lack) of morally significant characteristics that can be empirically derived" (2008, 13). He offers one alternative through a reading of the philosopher Cora Diamond's work, which reframes the ethical relationship between humans and animals around the "fundamental question of *justice*" in place of "rights" (2008, 10). In Diamond's "Injustice and Animals," she asks the question: Why do we respond emotionally, and morally, to the treatment of animals, particularly as tools of research? She argues that the realization of the "horror at the conceptualizing of animals as putting nothing in the way of their use as mere stuff" is linked to our "horror at human relentlessness and pitiliness in the exercise of power" (2001, 136). Our "capacity to respond to injustice as injustice" is not fully rational, but based on "a recognition of our *own* vulnerability" (2001, 121). *We3* invites the audience to respond emotionally to the vulnerability we share with animals, to not only pity the animals situation as research subjects, but to witness the injustice of a system that exercises power over human and animal subjects alike.

The role that the animals play in *We3* is a reminder of the disposable nature of all life from the perspective of the linked military industrial and animal industrial complexes. As Baudrillard puts it: "Everything that has happened to them has happened to us. Our destiny has never been separated from theirs, and this is a sort of bitter revenge on Human Reason, which has become used to upholding the absolute privilege of the human over the bestial" (1995, 133). His argument about the sentimentalization of animals traces this process through to its logical end, in the tendency for culture to simultaneously humanize and denigrate animals in the process of privileging "Human Reason," or an empirical determination of rights, over the "bestial" that unites human and animal life. The violence of sentimentality is the violence of a culture that assigns value to humans and animals alike on the basis of attributes that have use value in capitalist systems. Yet, no life—human or animal—is assured safety from such violence, although the deaths of some are recognized and mourned more than others.

Issues two and three of *We3* stage multiple deaths, nonhuman and human alike, that elicit a spectrum of responses. After WE3 defeats the initial assault of the soldiers, the military unleashes another weapon: the rats from the research facility, armed with their jet construction tools. They attack, and die, as an undifferentiated swarm, going unrecognized as individuals like Bandit, Tinker and Pirate despite their shared experience as experimental subjects (2005, 16–19). As the action takes place on an elevated train track, an approaching train swerves and collapses into a pile of wreckage from below, from which Bandit tries to rescue a dead man, saying to himself "(GUD DOG.) (HELP MAN.)" This man is the first of the casualties that had nothing to do with the initial conflict. The next are a man, his son and his dog, armed with a shotgun, that have the misfortune of encountering WE3 on a dark stretch of road; when the man shoots and wounds Pirate, Bandit and Tinker enact instinctive revenge, dismembering animal and human alike. This time, Bandit repeatedly chastises himself, repeating "(BAD DOG.)" (2005, 2.29). In desperation, the military unleashes Animal Weapon 4, an imposing bull mastiff that stalks WE3 in silence; Animal Weapon 4 ultimately kills Pirate, unleashing the wrath of Tinker and Bandit, as Bandit continues to chant "(BAD DOG.)" (2005, 3.14–3.15). The death of Pirate is arguably the climax of the series, the death that elicits the most sympathetic response from the reader in part because Pirate, Bandit and Tinker are characterized through their speech and the narrative as victims and superheroes. Pirate's death elicits more sympathy from human readers than that of the undifferentiated rats or Animal Weapon 4, who silently occupies the role of a villain, because the operation of sentimentality has placed these animals on an anthropocentric hierarchy.

Yet, through the pervasive and disturbing scenes of violence that cross boundaries between human and animal, military and civilian, *We3* invites the audience to critique this response. That is, by sentimentalizing its animal protagonists through a technology that literally makes them speak, a technology developed in the service of a system that privileges profit and power over life, *We3* exposes the hierarchical valuation and devaluation of life signaled by sentimentalized portrayals of animals. In *The Animal that Therefore I Am*, Jacques Derrida muses on the possible source of an ethics that moves away from an excessive reliance on "pathos" (2008). Rather than focusing on recounting images of the "industrial, mechanical, chemical, hormonal, and genetic violence to which man has been submitting animal life for the past two centuries," he asks us to reconsider the nature of the pathos on which animal rights discourse depends: "If these images are 'pathetic,' if they evoke sympathy, it is also because they 'pathetically' open the immense question of pathos and the pathological, that is of experience of this compassion" (Derrida 2008, 26). He begins with a reading of Jeremy Bentham's landmark 1823 *Introduction to the Principles of Morals and Legislation*. Derrida argues that Bentham's text changed "the very form of the question regarding the animal" (2008, 27). Through a reading of Bentham, Derrida argues that, "the question is not to know whether the animal can think, reason, or speak, etc.," but instead, the "*first* and *decisive* question would rather be to know whether animals *can suffer*" (2008, 27). The point of changing the animal question is not to engender more pity toward animals, but turn the question of suffering around to confront the illusory foundation of human reason as a faculty that holds power over nature:

> "Can they suffer?" amounts to asking "Can they not be able?" And what of this inability [*impouvoir*]? What is this nonpower at the heart of power? What is its quality or modality? How should one take it into account? What right should be accorded it? To what extent does it concern us? Being able to suffer is no longer a power; it is a possibility without power, a possibility of the impossible. Mortality resides there, as the most radical means of thinking the finitude that we share with animals, the mortality that belongs to the very finitude of life, to the experience of compassion, to the possibility of sharing the possibility of this nonpower, the possibility of this impossibility, the anguish of this vulnerability, and the vulnerability of this anguish. (Derrida 2008, 28)

Sentimentality, or pathos, depends on a power differential between the sympathizer and the recipient of sympathy. Anthropomorphism is grounded in this essential power differential, which is created by privileging qualities such as abstract reason and the capacity for language. By moving away from the discourse of "rights" and toward acknowledgment of the shared "nonpower" that characterizes "the finitude of life," a form of compassion that doesn't depend upon anthropocentric hierarchies may be generated between human and nonhuman animals.

We3 further dismantles the violence of sentimentality by enacting scenes of the shared vulnerability between humans and animals. In the opening sequence of issue three, before they fight Animal Weapon 4, WE3 hide out in an abandoned building. A homeless man finds them, and is met with hostile responses, particularly from Bandit: "(RRRRRR)(MAN GO!)" The man responds: "I ain't your master boy. You aint mine. He is horrified by both the cruelty indicated by their technological mantles and their speech: "Goddamn, look what they did to you!. What kinda sicko penned you all up in there. Talking animals. I need liquor. And tools" (2005, 3.2–3.3). As he exits through an alleyway, he refuses to give up the animals to the military and police representatives that are searching for them. They offer him a bribe with a dose of condescension: "—sorta money you could **use**. Guy like you" (2005, 3.5). His refusal is an act of protest that acknowledges his place in an oppressive power structure, a place that he shares with the animals. "Yeah. Yeah. I sure could," he responds, followed on the next page with a quick turn "But ... Nah ... I seen nothin' you fascist pig assholes" (2005, 3.5–3.6). When he returns, after the climactic scenes of violence, Bandit and Tinker have managed to shed the artificial "coats" that supply their armor and weaponry as Bandit utters the combined statement and question: "(IS COAT NOT WE.)" (2005, 3.25). The man returns, first glimpsed in the form of ominous boots seen approaching as Tinker stalks and kills prey to bring to his companion, unfettered by the artificial external shell, but still equipped with the head electrodes that allow the remaining members of WE3 to speak to one another.

The most powerful way in which *We3* moves from the repetition of mere pathos to the demonstration of compassion is through its ending. The last remnant of their technological enhancement to be removed, the element that forced them to speak, is a sign that the animals have truly escaped. In the final pages, the man sits with Bandit and Tinker, now naked and silent; he has presumably used tools to remove the head electrodes, the last remaining evidence of their former slavery. Instead of pathos, *We3* ends with an image of shared vulnerability. The homeless man, a human being viewed with either pathos or disdain by a capitalist system of power, recognizes the finitude that he shares with the animals that suffer alongside him in a culture organized by a hierarchy of instrumental reason. This image not only completes the journey of the animals, but also underscores the journey that *We3* encourages its audience to take: to fundamentally shift their perspective toward nonhuman animals from sentimentality to compassion.

WORKS CITED

Baudrillard, Jean. 1995. *Simulacra and Simulation*. Ann Arbor: University of Michigan Press.

Best, Steve and Anthony Nocella II, Richard Kahn, Carol Gigliotti, and Lisa Kemmerer. 2007. "Introducing Critical Animal Studies." http://www.critical-animalstudies.org/wp-content/uploads/2009/09/Introducing-Critical-Animal-Studies-2007.pdf

Derrida, Jacques. 2008. *The Animal That Therefore I Am*. New York: Fordham University Press.

Diamond, Cora. 2001. "Injustice and Animals. *Slow Cures and Bad Philosophers: Essays on Wittgenstein, Medicine and Bioethics*. Durham: Duke University Press.

Dooley, Keith. 2014. "Review: 'WE3.'" *Comics Authority*. February 19. https://comicsauthority.com/2014/02/19/review-we3/

Duncan, Randy and Matthew J. Smith. 2009. *The Power of Comics: History, Form & Culture*. New York: Continuum.

Gaboury, Jonathan. 2011. "The Violence Museum: Aesthetic Wounds from *Popeye* to *We3*." *ImageTexT: Interdisciplinary Comics Studies*. 6(1).

McCloud, Scott. 1994. *Understanding Comics: The Invisible Art*. New York: Harper Perennial.

McHugh, Susan. 2011. *Animal Stories: Narrating Across Species Lines*. Minneapolis: University of Minnesota Press.

Morrison, Grant, and Quitely, Frank. 2005. *We3*. New York: Vertigo.

Nibert, David. 2014. "Foreword." In *Defining Critical Animal Studies: An Intersectional Social Justice Approach for Liberation*, edited byAnthony J. Nocella II, John Sorenson, Kim Socha, and Atsuko Matsuoka, xiii–xi. New York: Peter Lang.

Wolfe, Cary. 2008. "Introduction: Exposures." In *Philosophy and Animal Life*, edited by Stanley Cavell, Cora Diamond, John McDowell, Ian Hacking, and Cary Wolfe, pp. 1–41. New York: Columbia University Press.

———. 2010. *What is Posthumanism?* Minneapolis: The University of Minnesota Press.

Wolk, Douglas. 2005. "The uses of cuteness: kitties, ducks, babies and a ninja." *The Washington Post*. October 9. http://www.washingtonpost.com/wp-dyn/content/article/2005/10/06/AR2005100601550.html

Weitzenfeld, and Joy. 2014. "An Overview of Anthropocentrism, Humanism, and Speciesism in Critical Animal Theory." In *Defining Critical Animal Studies: An Intersectional Social Justice Approach for Liberation*, edited by Anthony J. Nocella II, John Sorenson, Kim Socha, and Atsuko Matsuoka, 3–27. New York: Peter Lang.

Chapter 7

White God

Rethinking Human and Nonhuman Subjectivities through Underdog-Superhero Narratives and Ahuman Theory

Chantelle Gray van Heerden

THE ANIMAL AS CATALYST

Patricia MacCormack, in *The Animal Catalyst*, writes that the "persistently met-amorphic contortions of all grammatical varieties of the word 'animal' fascinate contemporary thought in a unique way" (2014, 1). But despite this fascination and even rigorous critique of our relationship to and with nonhuman animals, dominant mainstream ideologies and practices continue to produce and repro-duce hierarchical relations with inherent and normalized violence. Certain medi-ums such as film, however, have the capacity to disrupt our thinking through an immediacy of the event so that the primacy of human subjectivity becomes questioned more or less intuitively. Such a distribution could have the power to change the ways in which people interact with the nonhuman world in prac-tice. This is particularly successful through superhero and underdog-superhero narratives. Examples include *Benji the Hunted* (1987), *Free Willy* (1993), *The Whale Rider* (2002) and so on. In these animals take on a more prominent role, although the animal subjectivities often remain narrated from a human point of view. Movies such as *Dawn of the Planet of the Apes* (2014) and *War for the Planet of the Apes* (2017) engage more thoughtfully with nonhuman actors as agents with relational sentience, portraying them as heroes, underdog-heroes, villains and a combination of these. That the ape agents are anthropomorphized is problematic, of course, and raises important questions about our ability and willingness to think animals, animal agency and animal relationality in terms other than human. This is also an important reason why animal subjectivity should remain a key area of investigation, but the films do allow for a view of animals—or at least apes—as *more than*. The 2015 Hungarian film, *White God*, moves beyond a strictly anthropomorphized representation of animals (at least as much as this is possible), and narrates the story of a mixed-breed dog, called Hagen, in such a way that the human and animal subjectivities are ontologically equiponderated. The movie's rejection of the primacy of human subjectivity can thus be viewed as a movement toward ahuman theory, a silencing of the human that effectuates an "opening to the expressive potential of the other" (MacCormack 2014, 3). Having a larger scale adoption of this viewpoint would better allow activism to produce an ethic of total liberation.

While I will concentrate on the underdog-superhero configurations in *White God*, the central argument of this paper is grounded in Gilles Deleuze and Félix Guattari's notion of "becoming-animal" (1987). Moving away from the centrality of semantic representations, becoming-animal denotes a reciprocal relationality—that is, the becoming-human of the animal and the becoming-animal of the human. Brian Massumi, for example, argues that such "reciprocal imbrication of difference" signals a "mutual inclusion" on the animal continuum (2014, 4). But even though this concept allows us to think through the nature of our relationship to and with nonhuman animals, I argue for a deeper understanding through which to reconceptualize negotiated and non-negotiated processes of human and nonhuman subjectivities. To do so, I consider the possibilities offered by ahuman theory to account for "humanity's accursed excess of power" (MacCormack 2014, 1). Because, in this way, we might begin to prefigure our conceptions and subjectivities around nature and ecology in such a way that they are grounded in ontological equality and function within a relational epistemology. This is beautifully illustrated through the underdog-superhero canine uprising in *White God*, specifically when Hagen is abandoned by his guardian and has to learn to fend for himself. In time, he attracts some 250 cross-breeds who start an underdog revolt in Budapest. What I hope, like Massumi, is to show how *White God* might help us envision an altogether different politics, "one that is not a human politics of the animal, but an integrally animal politics, freed from the traditional paradigms of the nasty state of nature and the accompanying presuppositions about instinct permeating so many facets of human thought" (2014, 2). Such a maneuver can help foster a collective form of praxis that may, in turn, produce intersectional awareness so that one's own justice does not come at the expense of a more encompassing liberation for all.

BECOMING-INTENSE, BECOMING-ANIMAL, BECOMING-IMPERCEPTIBLE

Memories of a Moviegoer

The acclaimed motion picture, *White God* (*Fehér isten*, 2014, Kornél Mundruczó), is a fine example of a movie with a nonhuman hero: a dog. A pack of dogs. My memory of it is still fresh.

The opening scene shows the streets of Budapest, mostly empty (abandoned, we will later learn), except for a young girl on a bicycle, crossing the Széchenyi Chain Bridge. On the other side we see her turning a corner. The sparseness is interrupted as a pack of dogs come running at the girl. The scene is cut and the title sequence is shown. When we next see 13-year old Lili, she is playing with Hagen in a park. They are about to be moved to Lili's estranged father's apartment because her mother, a college professor, is on her way to Sydney to pursue her career. We first meet Lili's father, Daniel, on the job where he—a slaughterhouse inspector—is supervising the evisceration of a cow. We watch the skinning, follow the movement of the meat saw as the brisket is cut down the middle. The carcass is hoisted and the viscera falls out. Daniel monitors the process right up to the end and declares that the meat is "Suitable for consumption." This is our first insight into the main leitmotif of the film: the assumed and unquestioned dominion of humans over animals.

Outside, Lili is waiting with Hagen and her mother. The parent-switch is made, but Daniel is not happy about the dog. We see them enter his apartment. A nosy neighbor tells him that "Mutts have to be reported." The apartment is small. *Dreadful Oedipal atmosphere.* Father and pre-pubescent daughter will have to share the double bed. Then there is the individuated animal, the family pet; "sentimental, Oedipal animals," Deleuze and Guattari tell us, "each with its own petty history, 'my' cat, 'my' dog" (1987, 240). These animals, these pets "invite us to regress, draw us into a narcissistic contemplation, and they are the only kind of animal psychoanalysis understands, the better to discover a daddy, a mommy, a little brother behind them" (Deleuze and Guattari 1987, 240). The nosy neighbor, as the viewer by this times suspects, reports the dog and Daniel is heavily fined for harboring the mongrel. He orders Lili to get rid of Hagen but Lili cannot stand the thought of impounding her companion. Instead, she takes him to her music class and tries to hide him in the closet. When Hagen inevitably disrupts the class, the teacher admonishes her and instructs her to take him out. In defiance, she too leaves the class. This is the final straw for Daniel and when he finds them after searching for hours, he abandons Hagen on the side of the road. Hagen sets off in pursuit, but the car is too fast and he loses them.

Here the narrative diverges so that the single thread becomes two: Hagen's and Lili's. On the one hand, we have Hagen, the underdog (abandoned dog), wandering the streets. On the other hand, we have Lili (abandoned daughter) in a downward spiral, trying desperately to deal with her loss. We follow Hagen as he meets up with a pack of street dogs in search of food. The pound's dog-catchers arrive, but Hagen is lucky enough to escape because an old man hides him under a blanket. The old man is not a friend, however. "We are both hungry dogs," he tells Hagen and sells him to a Turkish restaurant owner for a plate of food. The restaurateur, in turn, sells him to a dog-fighter.

To everyone's surprise, Hagen the "lapdog"—now called Maxi—wins the fight. A skirmish ensues between the humans and Hagen takes the opportunity to escape, though his freedom is short-lived as the dog-catchers trap him soon after and drop him off at the pound.

The story is interrupted several times so that we can follow Lili, now desperately trying to find Hagen. First there is the acting out, then the reunions: father-daughter, teacher-student, Lili-Hagen. But before we get to the grand finale, Lili is chosen to play the lead part in a performance of Wagner's *Tannhäuser*. There are a number of Wagnerian themes in the film. For example, Hagen is a character from *Der Ring des Nibelungen* (*The Ring of the Nibelung*), the last of Wagner's four-series opera entitled *Götterdämmerung* (*Twilight of the Gods*). Wagner's *Tannhäuser* also elicits primary themes found in the film: the tension between sacred and sacrilegious love, and the redeeming, emancipatory potentiality of love. It is fitting, then, that we see Hagen break free from the pound during Lili's performance of *Tannhäuser* while the music slowly builds. It is violent, bloody. Here Hagen becomes the second kind of animal Deleuze and Guattari describe: "animals with characteristics or attributes; genus, classification, or State animals; animals as they are treated in the great divine myths, in such a way as to extract from them series or structures, archetypes or models" (1987, 240–241). Hagen as Cerberus, guardian of the dog underworld/underdog world. Emboldened, the other dogs follow suit. *They multiply.* The viewer is given no explanation as to how it is they know, why it is they join, perhaps to convey a language that humans are not privy to, a sense that we cannot easily slot into our own paradigms and agendas. We are simply made to watch as one dog, then another, then several more join this moving mass. Soon around 250 dogs are united in an uprising which changes the domestic cityscape into a cataclysm of canine insurrection.

We hear a television presenter say that the pack "acted not like animals, but a well-organized army." We hear surprise in his voice. When the cur revolution reaches the concert in which Lili is performing and she realizes that Hagen is one of the pack, she sets off on her bicycle to find him. Finally, the third kind of animal emerges; the "more demonic animals, pack or affect animals that form a multiplicity, a becoming, a population, a tale" (Deleuze and Guattari 1987, 241). No longer do we see an undifferentiated mass following a single leader, but a pack with all its implied immanent and emergent modes of organization and interwoven processes of differentiation. In what seems to be a cinematic feat, we watch the dogs move from hunting mode to one of cease-fire as they lay down in unison to Lili's trumpet-playing (reminiscent of the Pied Piper of Hamelin). Lili experiences a pause in her destiny, in her becoming-dog. Finally, Lili and Daniel too lie down flat on their stomachs—an unmistaken gesture of human genuflection.

It is like a tale; it is never disturbing. It is all there: there is a becoming-animal not content to proceed by resemblance and for which resemblance, on the contrary, would represent an obstacle or stoppage; the proliferation of [dogs], the pack, brings a becoming-molecular that undermines the great molar powers of family, career, and conjugality; there is a sinister choice since there is a "favourite" in the pack with which a kind of contract or alliance, a hideous pact, is made; there is the institution of an assemblage, a war machine or criminal machine, which can reach the point of self-destruction; there is a circulation of impersonal affects, an alternate current that disrupts signifying projects as well as subjective feelings, and constitutes a nonhuman sexuality; and there is an irresistible deterritorialization that forestalls attempts at professional, conjugal, or Oedipal reterritorialization. (Deleuze and Guattari 1987, 233)

Memories of Becoming-Animal

In *What Animals Teach Us about Politics*, Massumi reminds us that the "law of competition has had to bow before a healthy dose of cooperation, whose crucial contributions to evolution are now widely acknowledged, with symbiosis accepted as the very origin of multicellular life" (2014, 1). Incidentally, Peter Kropotkin wrote about this as early as 1902 in his book, *Mutual Aid: A Factor of Evolution*, but even though the concept and practice of mutual aid continue to be essential to contemporary anarchist politics and praxis, this is not necessarily reflective of popular consensus. More recently, Elizabeth Grosz explores the limitations of neo-Darwinian conceptions of adaptive conformity in *Chaos, Territory, Art* (2008). Further, *In Becoming Undone*, Grosz looks at animal sexuality to call into question the idea that chance mutation is the sole source for variation, arguing convincingly for its creative underpinnings by drawing on animal courtship practices (2011). Massumi, however, argues that while sexual selection "expresses an inventive animal exuberance attaching to qualities of life with no direct use value or survival value," it does not account for "'lower' animals that persist in multiplying asexually" (2014, 2; 3). For this reason, he focuses on animal play in an extended thought experiment on animal politics, drawing on the work of Gregory Bateson (1972), Jane Bennett (2010), Deleuze and Guattari (1987), Lynn Margulis (1999), Martin A. Nowak and Roger Highfield (2011), and so on. While I cannot here recount the entire argument, I want to focus on his twelfth proposition in which he states that "animal politics is a *politics of becoming*, even—especially—of the human" (Massumi 2014, 50). He qualifies this proposition by stating in the first supplement that while "the becoming-animal of the human is entered upon by necessity," and the "recourse to animality is a strategy of survival," the requisite nature thereof "does not contradict its creativity" (Massumi 2014, 55). What we have here, then, are at least two important points: (1) the conditions pertaining to the becoming-animal of the human and, in particular, the kinds of conditions needed for producing a politics that "reestablishes ties with our animality" the creative underpinnings of both the becoming-animal of the human and the becoming-human of the animal (Massumi 2014, 38); and (2) This, importantly, is not about *resemblance*, as Deleuze and Guattari tell us, but about *movement* which qualitatively changes the great molar (standardized, normative) structures, flows and processes of the world. In other words, the becoming-animal of the human is not about zoomorphism any more than the becoming-human of the animal is about anthropomorphism. Rather, it is about finding a way to conceive of a subjectivity where the human does not precede the nonhuman in its being; that is, through becoming.

So what are the conditions for producing a politics that restores ties with our animality through becoming-animal? Deleuze and Guattari write:

> A becoming-animal always involves a pack, a band, a population, a peopling, in short, a multiplicity. ... What we are saying is that every animal is fundamentally a band, a pack. That it has pack modes, rather than characteristics. ... We do not become animal without a fascination for the pack, for multiplicity. (1987, 239–240)

Multiplicity—and in particular pack multiplicities—is, then, the first condition for the becoming-animal of the human. Here multiplicity should not be understood in terms of quantity. As Deleuze and Guattari tell us, it is neither about the one nor the multiple, neither the fragmented nor the divided and, in this sense, does not reference the prior unity of either a subject, an object or a higher totality. Instead, a multiplicity is constitutive and comprises "determinations, magnitudes, and dimensions that cannot increase in number without the multiplicity changing in nature" (Deleuze and Guattari 1987, 8; 24). Grounded in the thought of Elias Canetti, Deleuze and Guattari identify two modes of multiplicity which apply here: mass or crowd multiplicities and pack multiplicities. The greatest difference between these modes can be said to lie in the fact that pack multiplicities are "constituted by a line of flight or of deterritorialization that is a component part of it," whereas mass multiplicities characteristically territorialize so that even lines of flight (or qualitative bifurcations) become structured around molar forms of organization (Deleuze and Guattari 1987, 33). However, these modes are not to be conceived of as binary opposites, but as a continuum within a single assemblage.

In *White God*, the pack multiplicity plays an important role in Lili's becoming-animal. Importantly, she does not *resemble* a dog in any way. She does not act like a dog or live like a dog. She does not bark or walk on all fours. There is no imitation of the dog. Instead, there is a becoming part of the pack that initiates the becoming-animal of the human, allowing for a mode of subjectivity beyond the human individual, to intensive connection. Hagen has already forged the pack multiplicity, is *himself* a pack multiplicity, even without the presence of the other dogs (a pack multiplicity is not about numbers; it is a substantive). Lili, however, is still part of the crowd, the mass multiplicity, at the time when the canine insurrection erupts, although she has already moved to the edge of the mass multiplicity. We see her moving further away from edge of the mass to the edge of the pack when, after the interruption of the concert, she leaves the music hall in an attempt to find Hagen. The alliance is initiated here as Lili deterritorializes the mass multiplicity by leaving the crowd to go in search of Hagen. The coalition is sealed when, face to face with the dog-mob, she lies down in the street, now one of the pack, now effectuating her becoming-animal, now further deterritorializing even the pack multiplicity.

I want to take a step back again to think for a moment about crowds and packs and the conditions for creating a politics which, through the becoming-animal of the human, establishes a zone of indiscernibility between human and nonhuman animals—between Lili and Hagen. "Urban crowds," writes Andrea Mubi Brighenti "emerged as social actors ... in the wake of the French Revolution" (2010, 292). As a result, most "observers regarded crowds as excessive and dangerous," to be viewed as little more than mobs who are "potentially very close to an overthrowing force" (Brighenti 2010, 292). So even though crowds were increasingly investigated by criminologists, general physicians and specialists, such as neurologists, sociologists, psychologists, and so on, it was always in an attempt to control them. Canetti became vexed by these limited approaches and sought new ways to describe the behavior of crowds in terms of their desire investments—an element also referred to by Deleuze and Guattari. In a description of a workers' demonstration in Vienna on July 15, 1927 in which Canetti participated, he recalls the unity and heterogeneity of the crowd which, for him, is "achieved in neither the parts nor the whole" but, instead, "lies in the *movement* of the whole and its parts" that Canetti conceives of as a wave (Brighenti 2010, 292). He writes, "During the following years and then again and again later on, I tried to grasp the wave, but I have never succeeded. I could not succeed, for nothing is more mysterious and incomprehensible than a crowd" (Canetti 1999, 488). Here we distinguish the second and third conditions of the becoming-animal of the human; the second being that it is driven by a desire investment, and the third being that it involves movement (or speed, as I shall show)—movement being that which institutes the war machine, producing the circulation of impersonal affects so as to disrupt signifying projects and subjective feelings, creating something entirely new.

Memories of a Molecule

In the introductory chapter of *A Thousand Plateaus*, Deleuze and Guattari state that there are only machinic assemblages of desire and collective assemblages of enunciation (1987, 22). Machinic assemblages denote flows, bodies and processes, as well as their structurations and affects, while collective assemblages of enunciation refer to discursive and symbolic orders and practices. Later on, in the chapter entitled "Micropolitics and Segmentarity," they write:

> Why does desire desire its own repression, how can it desire its own repression? The masses certainly do not passively submit to power; nor do they "want" to be repressed, in a kind of masochistic hysteria; nor are they tricked by an ideological lure. Desire is never separable from complex assemblages that necessarily tie into molecular levels, from microformations already shaping postures, attitudes, perceptions, expectations, semiotic systems, etc. (1987, 215)

What we see here, first of all, is that desire, for Deleuze and Guattari, is not an undifferentiated mass of energy (1987, 215). Desire is also not understood in terms of an internal lack as in Lacan, nor as regulated by an external law as in Plato, nor as repressed as in Freud. Instead, they conceive of desire as machinic; that is, as a constituent component of that part of the infrastructure located concurrently at the intersection between the "contents and expression on each stratum," and which is capable of autopoiesis and generating feedback (Deleuze and Guattari 1987, 73). At the same time, this machinic dimension is in complex relations with another kind of assemblage—collective assemblages of enunciation—with which it is co-imbricated and even co-constitutive. As a result of these complex generative-feedback systems, it becomes possible that desire can desire its own repression. But while it is easy to conceive of desire desiring its own repression in terms of the molar, Deleuze and Guattari argue that this may in fact be the result of a molecular line of flight.

The molar, as may have become clear by now, indicates the major components of our lives and typically contributes to what we perceive of as our identity, for example our profession, nationality, sex and gender, class, race and so on. The molecular, on the other hand, is more imperceptible, "traveling at speeds beyond the ordinary thresholds of perception" and denotes lines of deterritorialization that may bring about changes in the lattice of molar organization. These are variations that cause fissures in our thought and action and may be due to large movements, such as Occupy, in which people practiced radically different ways of being; or it may be something seemingly innocuous, such as having a conversation with a friend that challenges a normative conception, catalysing an altogether different kind of subject position. Every society, every individual, every process and every relation is "supplied by both segmentarities simultaneously" (Deleuze and Guattari 1987, 213). The difference is that molar currents have a propensity for territorialization and reterritorialization, and are thus arranged so as *not* to "disturb or disperse, but on the contrary to ensure and control the identity of each agency, including personal identity" (Deleuze and Guattari 1987, 195). The concurrent molecular flows, on the other hand, are more transitory, fluid and supple and tend toward deterritorialization so that they become amenable to variation, modification and even lines of flight. These three kinds of lines (molar, molecular and lines of flight) are important in terms of desire investments and becoming-animal because becoming-molecular, Deleuze and Guattari contend, is the "next step" in becoming-animal and lies the farthest from the system of stratification and codedness or molar terrorialization (Deleuze and Guattari 1987, 248). This difference in actualized desire, as it pertains to becoming-animal, can be seen in three films: *Black Swan* by Darren Aronofsky (2010), *The Falls* by Peter Greenaway (1980), and *White God*.

Deleuze and Guattari warn of two dangers in becoming-animal, as Simone Bignall argues: "on the one hand, the process may be stifled by the capturing of new forces and their reterritorialization by existing forms; the second occurs when the process is so disruptive of one's existing set of affective relations that one spirals into a line of abolition" (2013, 133). In other words, the first signals a desire for the molar and the second signals a molecular desire, but one which is so deterritorialized that the line of flight becomes a line of abolition or line of death. Peter Greenaway's film, *The Falls*, is a good example of a line of flight that becomes reterritorialized around molar identities. The film, which is scripted in documentary style (while simultaneously disrupting the genre), captures the after-effects of what is known as the Violent Unknown Event (VUE). This event is never fully depicted or described, though it is said that nineteen million victims were affected in a number of ways, all of which relate in some manner to birds. The ninety-two interviewed "victims" all have surnames beginning with the letters FALL and are said to have the following symptoms, representative also of the other affected sufferers: quadrimorphism (four sexes, rather than two), immortality (deaths now occur due to fatal accidents or diseases), bird-like physiological mutations, related pathological conditions (especially what is known as "patagium fellitis" or "skin-wing aggrievement"), and a sudden erasure of people's mother tongues so that all sufferers now speak one of the ninety-two new languages produced by the VUE.

The becoming-bird of the victims is stunted, however, when the line of flight is reterritorialized as "an identification with a bird" (Blake 2010). For example, the victims continuously, but unsuccessfully (except for Melorder Fallaburr who can apparently fly), attempt to "achieve physical flight" rather than producing "an equivalent to flight or cultivat[ing] a sublimated form of flight such as singing like a bird" (Blake 2010). We see this identification in other ways too. For example, interviewee number fifteen, whose name is Starling Fallanx, was a "singer, firework-enthusiast, wanderer, collector [and] authority on the nightingale" before the VUE. Thereafter, we are told, "she can no longer taste salt, open her eyes under water, wear velvet next to her skin or smell hawthorn blossom," although "she is still able to teach her daughters to whistle the thirty-two songs of the nightingale and astonish them by locking her Achilles tendons to grip apples with the soles of her feet." A jazz singer before the VUE, the event presents Starling with an opportunity to further deterritorialize her singing through her becoming-bird but, instead of taking flight in this way, she desires a more molar actualization, teaching her daughters how to whistle like a nightingale, a skill she had even before the VUE. We see here a clear example of how desire can desire its own repression.

Darren Aronofsky's film, *Black Swan*, is an example of the second danger related to becoming-animal, namely a desire for abolition. The plot revolves around the New York Ballet's controversial production of the well-known Tchaikovsky ballet, *Swan Lake*. The main character, Nina (Natalie Portman), also chosen for the lead role in the ballet, is required to perform the parts of both the White Swan (Odette) and the Black Swan (Odile). This doppelgän-ger theme of the ballet recurs throughout the film, tracing "Nina's desperate efforts to meet the demands of this doubled characterization" (Bignall 2013, 122). When we meet Nina, she is in her early twenties, yet still living with her overbearing mother (Barbara Hershey). Fully Oedipalized, she is presented as timid, weak even, though courteous and respectful. A good, obedient, hard-working daughter. A perfect Odette. The ballet director, Tomas (Vincent Cas-sell), demands ever-more from Nina's performance. When he criticizes her characterization of Odile while praising Lily (Mila Kunis), her understudy's performance, Nina visibly begins to fall apart. Desperately clinging to her prima-ballerina status and fueled by a jealous fascination, Nina commences a relationship with Lily. In a defiant act, Nina goes clubbing with Lily. Now we see Nina taking drugs, hallucinating the Black Swan, dancing sensually, eventually having sex with Lily.

> In the act of sex, Nina and Lily share a mutual becoming-swan. Lily's tattooed wings become feathered, while Nina's eyes turn swan-red and her skin becomes goose-fleshed. Their bodies merge and become indistinct in the encounter that transforms them. It is only when Nina wakes alone in her room, which is barri-caded from the inside, we realize that Nina has hallucinated this night of sexual liberation and self-transformation. (Bignall 2013, 124)

This initial becoming-swan is then further deterritorialized and taken to its logical extreme in the final scenes of the movie. On the day of the ballet's opening performance, we see Nina plucking a single black feather from her back, while her feet are shown to be webbed, her eyes red. Later, on stage, we see her skin transform and become swan-textured, a full plumage eventually bursting forth. But this flight into the Black Swan comes at a high price. An earlier scene in the dressing room shows Nina killing her nemesis, Lily, but the final act reveals that she has, in fact, fatally wounded herself, that she was merely hallucinating the presence of Lily. The creative becoming process has turned deadly. "I was perfect," Nina says, taking her final breath. Such undifferentiated deterritorialization takes place, Deleuze and Guattari tell us, when desire—when a line of flight—turns into a line of abolition or death because a "minimum of strata, a minimum of forms and functions, a minimal subject from which to extract materials, affects, and assemblages" has not been retained (1987, 270). As Bignall argues, "rather than extending the existing territory of her identification with the White Swan to also become the Black Swan, Nina wholly abandons her little-girl self and replaces this identity with an erotic alter-ego" (2013, 129).

In *White God*, we witness a more successful process of becoming-animal. The primary motif of the film, as I mentioned earlier, is the presumed and undisputed dominion of humans over animals. The theme is concretized through, for example, a new law in Hungary that allows only purebreds and designates the molar "class stratification" of dogs, as well as the species stratification of human and nonhuman animals (Dowd 2015). Lili's "ownership" of, and later alliance with, a mongrel thus indicates a molecular oscillation. Daniel's profession demonstrates the brutality and normalized violence of this human/nonhuman stratification, later manifested through the vicious dog fights. This, in turn, is molecularized through the eventual canine insurrection which allows for a line of flight and a questioning of the primacy of human subjectivity. The title of the film, which is not elucidated in any way in the movie itself, may "be a tip of the hat to Samuel Fuller, whose 1982 race-relations allegory *White Dog* takes a similarly conflicted view of the relationship between man and his supposed best friend" (Lodge 2014). In this film, based on Romain Gary's 1970 novel with the same title, the viewer watches the struggle between a black dog trainer, Keys (Paul Winfield), and a "white dog"—a dog trained to attack black people, but also literally a white Alsatian in the movie. The hierarchical race relations in *White Dog* are echoed in the hierarchical animal-human relations in *White God*, although the undertone in the former is perhaps even more menacing than that portrayed by the canine uprising in the latter, with the implication at the end of the film being that the white dog has been re-programmed to become a "black dog"—a dog who attacks white people. This may, furthermore, be seen as commentary on desire and how desire is collectively shaped, produced, reproduced, and challenged. In *White God*, it is especially in and through the reciprocal becoming

of Hagen and Lili that we see the tension of the desire investment. In Hagen
we have, on the one hand, his desire to be "owned"—or at least cared for—by
Lili and, on the other, his later desire to be free, to be part of the pack, to be
Lili's equal. The former desire is a *portrayed* desire, of course, and one which
has become so accepted as to be unseen. And it is, I would argue, specifically
this "desire" by pets to be owned or cared for by humans that underpins the
entire narrative of *White God* in its questioning of the primacy of the human.
Donna Haraway argues that subjects "do not preexist their constitutive intra-
action at every folded layer of time and space" (2008, 32). This, she contends,
justifies "the primacy of 'being with'" between human and nonhuman animals (Sands 2014, 56). Such "becoming-with" has also been termed "mutual
interspecies ownership" (Maher 2014, 30).

However, this seems to me a fundamental misunderstanding of the immanent reciprocity of becomings, as well as a denial of the (skewed) power relations between humans and animals as they currently exist. *White God* deeply
questions that such a "mutual ownership" could ever be the desire of the animal. At any rate, how do we know? Our musings can only ever "remain within
a dialectic logic of alterity that is essentially bordering on a narcissistic mirror where the animal's absolute otherness compels the human toward either
assimilation or self-reflection, rather than grace" (MacCormack 2014, 8). It is
a reflection of our own desire investments, rather than that of animals. Such an
imposing of human forces leads to a domestication of energies (or, as in *White
Dog*, the barbaric honing of energies), so that the relation is necessarily that of
a human relation to and with the dog, despite claims of mutuality. Becoming-
animal has "nothing to do with a sentimental or domestic relation," but neither
does it have anything to do with State animals" (Deleuze and Guattari 1987,
244). It is not enough to move from the Oedipalized relation to the symbolic
relation—Hagen as Lili's beloved pet to Hagen as Cerberus, guardian of the
dog underworld/underdog world. There has to be an "undoing of us, whatever
that means" (MacCormack 2014, 6). And, for this to take place, our desire
investment has to change. There has to be a movement from the molar to the
molecular, from filiation to alliance and, eventually, ahumanity. But it has to
be a movement of caution; one which retains a minimum of strata, a minimum
of forms and functions, a minimal subject. It comes as no surprise that Lili has
to lie down flat on her stomach at the end of the film, not to resemble Hagen
in any way, but to become part of the pack, to strike an alliance and enter the
relation of movement and rest. As Deleuze and Guattari write:

> Do not imitate a dog, but make your organism enter into composition with
> *something else* in such a way that the particles emitted from the aggregate thus
> composed will be canine as a function of the relation of movement and rest, or
> of molecular proximity, into which they enter. (1987, 274)

Memories of the Anomalous and the Alliance
(Memories of Superdog)

Deleuze and Guattari write that wherever there is a pack multiplicity, "you will also find an exceptional individual, and it is with that individual that an alliance must be made in order to become-animal" (1987, 23). This exceptional (animal) individual—the anomalous—although portrayed by an individual, should neither be thought of as "an individual nor a species" but, instead, as "a phenomenon of bordering" (Deleuze and Guattari 1987, 245). We could thus say that the alliance is extensively illustrated through the relationship between Lili and Hagen in *White God*, and that the phenomenon of bordering—what we might term the *affective field*—can be thought of virtually in terms of movement and intensively as speed. Virtual here does not refer to the cybernetic. Deleuze and Guattari explain reality as consisting of and being in constant flux between the virtual, the intensive, and the actual or extensive. In other words, the virtual, according to them, contains all *real* (but not actual or actualized) existing and emergent properties inherent in diverse multiplicities, along with their immanent singularities and capacities to bifurcate or deterritorialize along lines of flight (DeLanda 2002, 56–61). The intensive, on the other hand, may be said to determine and actualize the virtual, although the intensive is different in kind to actualization. In terms of movement and speed, Deleuze and Guattari do not, in typical fashion, apply the division between these notions consistently in *A Thousand Plateaus* and even equate the two notions to each other at times (Deleuze and Guattari 1987, 280–281). They do, however, offer a distinction in terms of the extensive and the intensive when they state that "movement is extensive; speed is intensive" (Deleuze and Guattari 1987, 381). What I want to argue here is that movement, in terms of the becoming-animal of the human, is still reliant on a subject in that it requires an alliance with an anomalous, whereas speed can be thought of as a "processual *subjectivity-without-a-subject*" (Massumi 2014, 41).

Movement, in the sense of the alliance, remains an integral aspect of the becoming-animal of the human. It also, and importantly, allows for the becoming-superdog of Hagen. Judith Butler might begin such an investigation by framing it in terms of the "social crafting and form" of a body because the "epistemological capacity to apprehend a life is partially dependent on that life being produced according to norms that qualify it as a life or, indeed, as part of life" (2009, 3). In more basic terms we might ask: whose subjectivity is at issue here? Lili's? Hagen's? "This is the point to clarify," write Deleuze and Guattari, "that a becoming lacks a subject distinct from itself" (1987, 238). However, before we get to speed—to the subjectivity-without-a-subject, or what Gerald Raunig calls *asubjective composition*—we need to move through movement; that is, the alliance (2014, 31). But what is the function of the alliance in becoming-animal, or, as Deleuze and Guattari put it in more specific terms, "What exactly is the nature of the anomalous?" (1987, 244). We already know that it is not about a specific individual or species, but about a phenomenon of bordering. This bordering may be described in terms of the *zone of indiscernibility*. "Starting from the forms one has, the subject one is, the organs one has, or the functions one fulfills," write Deleuze and Guattari, "becoming is to extract particles between which one establishes the relations of movement and rest, speed and slowness that are closest to what one is becoming, and through which one becomes" (1987, 272). Thus, the zone of indiscernibility or proximity refers to the movement between the human animal assemblage and the nonhuman animal assemblage in this case, so that both Lili and Hagen can be said to extract common particles from each other in their mutual becoming, which neither Oedipalization nor archetypes can effectively achieve. Hence, Lili extracts canine *tendencies* when she joins the pack by lying flat on the street, whereas Hagen extracts human *tendencies* or *affects* in his leading of the dog insurrection. A proximity—a zone of indiscernibility—is created here through the movement of becoming.

Deleuze and Guattari go on to argue that becoming-animal "implies an initial relation of alliance with a demon" (1987, 247). This demonic aspect, like the Oedipal and mythic (or State, or archetypal) elements of an animal, should be regarded as tendencies or affects rather than concrete substances or physical qualities, properties and attributes in that they "are neither substantive nor quantifiable" (Massumi 2014, 34). In other words, they explain something about the movement in and between assemblages. It is also this demonic tendency that allows Hagen to become-superdog in that the "super" (or demonic) affectivity in underdog narratives involve "an incorporeal nature" (Hall 2015, 10). This is characteristically actualized in a contest.

But what is a superhero? This question may seem to have a self-evident answer, yet when editors Robin S. Rosenberg and Peter Coogan asked the question, they found different answers in each contribution to their book by the same name (2013). They write:

> The superhero genre has moved into the position held by the Western genre for most of the 20th century, when it served as a useful metaphorical way of discussing immigration, Americanization, urbanization, American identity, changing conceptions of race and gender, individualism, capitalism, modernism, and so many other central cultural concerns. (2013, xvii–xviii)

They go on to argue that the present-day popularity of superhero narratives lies in their content which deals with "current, real-world issues"—certainly the case of *White God* which wrestles with the nature and consequences of the human/nonhuman animal divide (Rosenberg and Coogan 2013, xviii). The most basic definition of the superhero is that s/he is "the protagonist of the superhero genre" and what defines her/him, are "the specific conventions— *mission, powers,* and *identity*" (Coogan 2013, 3). Thus, the mission of the superhero is "to fight evil and protect the innocent"; her/his powers (or super-powers) are exaggerated aspects aimed at raising "a person's performance above that of ordinary people"; and her/his identity is composed of two elements, namely "the *code name* (e.g., 'Superman' and 'Spider-Man')" and "the *costume*" (Coogan 2013, 4; 6). The latter two elements are less true for underdog narratives in which the heroes (or underdog-superheroes) typically keep their own names and have no additional gear, although they *do* fight evil and safeguard the innocent, and their natural abilities *are* tested and elevated above that of ordinary people, despite the fact that they compete with fewer resources. The most common thread of underdog-superhero narratives is, arguably, the fight or showdown. We may think, for example, of Sylvester Stallone's *Rocky* (1976), J. K. Rowling's *Harry Potter* (in stages between 1997 and 2011), biblical stories like David and Goliath, J. R. R. Tolkien's *The Lord of the Rings* (in stages between 1937 and 1949), Danny Boyle and Loveleen Tandan's *Slumdog Millionaire* (2008), and so on. Each of these narratives is driven by the underdog-superhero's diminished capacities and moderated probabilities, and the final triumphant moment in which s/he overcomes and succeeds despite the odds. As Will Brooker argues, the "best heroes are those with hidden hurt and secret wounds" (2013, 11). And it is this trauma that could be viewed as the origin of the demonic tendency in the animal underdog-superhero, thus propelling the underdog to move through the Oedipalized and State tendencies and become-superhero. As Deleuze and Guattari state, "there may be no such thing as a lone wolf, but there is a leader of the pack, a master of the pack, or else the old deposed head of the pack now living alone, there is the Loner, and there is the Demon" (1987, 243). Hagen and Lili are precisely that. Hagen the anomalous, swept up in the pack or multiplicity. Lili, the loner at the edge of both the mass multiplicity and the pack multiplicity. Lili now entering into alliance to become-animal, Hagen entering into alliance to become-superhero (Superdog). In other words, there is a co-imbrication, a "logic of mutual inclusion," a modality which accounts for movement or tendencies and affects rather than unified subjects (Massumi 2014, 34). Alliance (subjects)— movement—becoming—affect (asubjective composition)—speed.

Memories of Becoming-Ahuman

I must go back to move forward. I must forget my memories. At any rate, wherever I have "used the word 'memories' in the preceding pages," I was wrong to do so; I "meant to say 'becoming'" (Deleuze and Guattari 1987, 294). I was not recalling memories about Lili and Hagen; I was relating Lily's becoming-animal and Hagen's becoming-superhero, becoming-Superdog. But can this mutual becoming effectuate a subjectivity where the human does not precede the nonhuman in its being? In other words, "is it viable or even possible to ask if we can ever enter entirely posthuman, inhuman, ahuman becomings" (MacCormack 2014, 177–178)? It is not sufficient, MacCormack argues, for the human to claim that we too are animals because to make such an assertion "would erode the histories of violence for which we must be accountable, in whatever ways we negotiate the positive affects of the challenges of bearing witness and responsibility" (2014, 7). Bearing witness surely catalyses—has the *potential* to act as catalyst for—the becoming-animal of the human. *White God* so exquisitely illustrates this, even making space for the nonhuman animal to be central, to become-superhero. Bearing witness could thus also be said to act as catalyst for thinking ethically about animals and the relationality between animals and humans, but such ethicality can never be about anything other than the human. Lili's becoming-animal is not about Hagen or the dog-pack, but solely about her own ethicality. Accordingly, ahuman philosophy must begin, as MacCormack argues, with "the *I will not* which creates the *I am not all* thus *I am not, so the other may be*" (2014, 4). We might begin to wonder here about the extent of Hagen's "superheroness" while Lili is present. Earlier I mentioned the movies *Benji the Hunted* (1987), *Free Willy* (1993), *The Whale Rider* (2002). In each of these, the subjectivities of the animals are tightly woven into those of their human counterparts: Benji the dog and his trainer, Frank Inn; Willy the orca and his rescuer, Jesse; the whale and the twelve-year-year-old Maori girl, Kahu Paikea Aspirana (or Pai). There are naturally many more examples and, of the ones I cited, *The Whale Rider* is by far the most nuanced in that there is a reciprocal becoming which cannot be seen in either of the other two films where the subjects remain fully entrenched in their respective signifying dramatis personae with their clear animal/human split. Such molar systems "need repetition both to maintain their power and to make alterations which would disprove their claimed logic quietly without being perceived as rupturing their own operations" (MacCormack 2014, 180). Hence, although films like *The Whale Rider* and *White God* may be said to deterritorialize so that the molecular emerges, they nevertheless do so without comprehensively disturbing human subjectivity.

In short, media is anything but apolitical and has the capacity to inspire people to move beyond complacency; to shock thought into action. By critically reading the media we can begin to think through new ways to inspire individuals to take collective action in ways that consider the environment and nonhuman others from a non-anthropocentric view. It is, in other words, a question of contingency when we think about the possibility of a subjectivity where the human does not precede the nonhuman in its being, and when we think about the degree of the superheroness of animal subjects. Hagen is our superhero, without a doubt, but so is Lili. Perhaps toward becoming-ahuman we, as an entire human race, might at least learn this: to lie down flat, belly burrowing against the earth, in alliance with the pack and, in so doing, effectuating—through a mutual becoming—an opening to the expressive potential of the superhero-other.

WORKS CITED

Bateson, Gregory. 1972. *Steps to an Ecology of Mind*. Chicago: University of Chicago Press.

Benji the Hunted. Directed by Joe Camp. United States: Buena Vista Pictures, 1987.

Bennett, Jane. 2010. *Vibrant Matter: A Political Ecology of Things*. Durham and London: Duke University Press.

Bignall, Simone. 2013. "Black Swan, Cracked Porcelain and Becoming-Animal." *Culture, Theory and Critique* 54 (1): 121–138.

Blake, Terence. 2010. "Brain Falls: The Power of the Falls" *Cygnos* 26 (1), January 11, http://revel.unice.fr/cycnos/?id=6361

Brighenti, Andrea Mubi. 2010. "Tarde, Canetti and Deleuze on Crowds and Packs." *Journal of Classical Sociology* 10 (4): 291–314.

Brooker, Will. 2013. "We Could Be Heroes." In *What Is a Superhero?*, edited by Robin S. Rosenberg and Peter Coogan, 11–18. London, New York: Oxford University Press.

Butler, Judith. 2009. *Frames of War: When is Life Grievable?* London, New York: Verso.

Canetti, Elias. 1999. *Memoirs: The Play of the Eyes, A Torch in the Ear, The Tongue Set Free*. New York: Farrar, Straus and Giroux.

Coogan, Peter. 2013. "The Hero Defines the Genre, the Genre Defines the Hero." In *What Is a Superhero?*, edited by Robin S. Rosenberg and Peter Coogan, 3–10. London, New York: Oxford University Press.

Dawn of the Planet of the Apes. Directed by Matt Reeves. United States: 20th Century Fox, 2014.

DeLanda, Manuel. 2002. *Intensive Science and Virtual Philosophy*. London, New York: Continuum.

Deleuze, Gilles and Félix Guattari. 1987. *A Thousand Plateaus*. Translated by Brian Massumi, London, Minneapolis: University of Minnesota Press.

Dowd, A. A. 2015. "*White God* is a Mongrel of a Dog Movie, Madly Mixing Genres and Tones." *A.V. Club*, March 26, 2015, accessed August 19, 2016, http://www.avclub.com/review/white-god-mongrel-dog-movie-madly-mixing-genres-an-217094

Free Willy. Directed by Simon Wincer. United States: Warner Bros. Family Entertainment, 1993.

Grosz, Elizabeth. 2008. *Chaos, Territory, Art: Deleuze and the Framing of the Earth.* New York: Columbia University Press.

Grosz, Elizabeth. 2011. *Becoming Undone. Darwinian Reflections on Life, Politics, and Art.* Durham, London: Duke University Press.

Hall, Joshua M. 2015. "Differential–Surface: Deleuze and Superhero Comics." *Transnational Literature* 7 (2): 1–13.

Haraway, Donna. 2008. *When Species Meet.* London, Minneapolis: University of Minnesota Press.

Kropotkin, Peter. 1902[2009]. *Mutual Aid: A Factor of Evolution.* London: Freedom Press.

Lodge, Guy. 2014. "Cannes Film Review: *White God.*" *Variety*, March 18, 2014, accessed 1 September 2016, http://variety.com/2014/film/festivals/cannes-film-review-white-god-1201184899/

MacCormack, Patricia. 2014. *The Animal Catalyst.* London, New York: Bloomsbury.

Maher, John, T. 2014. "Legal Technology Confronts Speciesism, or, *We Have Met the Enemy and He Is Us.*" In *The Animal Catalyst*, edited by Patricia MacCormack, 27–48. London, New York: Bloomsbury.

Margulis, Lynn. 1999. *Symbiotic Plant.* New York: Basic Books.

Massumi, Brian. 2014. *What Animals Teach Us about Politics.* Durham and London: Duke University Press.

Nowak, Martin A. and Roger Highfield. 2011. *Super Cooperators: Altruism, Evolution, and Why We Need Each Other to Succeed.* New York: Free Press.

Raunig (2014) "n-1. Making Multiplicity: A Philosophical Manifesto." In *Art in the Global Present*, edited by Nikos Papastergiadis and Victoria Lynn, 31–44. Sydney, UTS ePress.

Rosenberg, Robin S. and Peter Coogan. 2013. *What Is a Superhero?* London, New York: Oxford University Press.

Sands, Danielle. 2014. "'Beyond' the Singular? Ecology, Subjectivity, Politics." In *The Animal Catalyst*, edited by Patricia MacCormack, 49–65. London, New York: Bloomsbury.

The Whale Rider. Directed by Niki Caro. New Zealand, Germany: Pandora Film, 2002.

War for the Planet of the Apes. Directed by Matt Reeves. United States: 20th Century Fox, 2017.

White God (Fehér isten). Directed by Kornél Mundruczó. Hungary, Germany, Sweden: InterCom, 2014.

Part III

Chapter 8

Bruteness

Gender, Race, and Animality in Buffy the Vampire Slayer

Jeffrey Pannekoek and Karin Anderson

INTRODUCTION

The TV series *Buffy the Vampire Slayer*, directed and produced by Joss Whedon from 1997 to 2003, brought audiences a brand new superhero. The show revolves around the eponymous character, Buffy, who is a vampire slayer. As the narrator explains in the first episode: "In every generation there is a Chosen One. She alone will stand against the vampires, the demons and the forces of darkness. She is the Slayer" ("Welcome to the Hellmouth" 1997). In contrast to this exposition, Buffy does not stand alone. In the fight against evil she is joined by the self-proclaimed Scooby-Gang, named after another group of demon-busting kids and their dog. The primary members of the group are the Slayer herself, shy-teen-turned-witch Willow Rosenberg, sarcastic but ever-reliable Xander Harris, and the Sunnydale High School librarian and Watcher, Rupert Giles. The series pushed the boundaries of feminist discourse on television by taking sexist stereotypes and flipping them on their head. Nearly all strong female characters in television post-1997 can trace their roots back to the vampire-dusting cheerleader from Sunnydale. In other ways, however, the series is less progressive. Attending to these moments is essential in undoing the liberalism that often shrouds radical politics, preventing a more complete call for total liberation. In short, any true liberatory narrative requires an intersectional analysis where the gains of one identity group is not advanced at the cost of another.

While *Buffy the Vampire Slayer* actively works to subvert many of the sexist tropes of its genre, as well as sexist standards in television and society more generally, it is unable to do the same for racial biases. All of the main characters and most of the recurring cast are Hollywood-white, and people of color remain on the sidelines of the narrative. The status of animals as inferior to humans remains unchallenged as well, and within the context of the series, animality is at best considered base and counter to an elevated human nature. At worst, it is considered monstrous. As such, the series largely conforms to mainstream conceptions of animal nature as lesser than or dichotomously opposed to humanity. Moreover, because Blackness and animality are conflated, these prejudices viciously reinforce one another. "Blackness" here refers to the Western social perception of race as it pertains in particular to Black people. In *Habeas Viscus*, Alexander G. Weheliye uses the term to capture the "changing system of unequal power structures that apportion and delimit which humans can lay claim to full human status and which humans cannot" (2014, 3). As such, the term concerns structural forms of oppression that are coextensive with a kind of dehumanization. While there are attempts to subvert this relationship concerning race, the underrepresentation of diversity and the utilization of traditional power paradigms means that the show fails to be intersectionally empowering. And, because no such subverting attempts are made concerning animality, nonhuman animals continue to suffer an unmitigated degraded status as compared to humans in the context of the show. While the series works to elevate the feminine, it ultimately displaces animality onto racial minorities, and fails to be appropriately intersectional, which is a key tenant of Critical Animal Studies.

In order to argue this, we first analyze the conflations of gender, race, and animality, and the ways in which these mutually reinforce each other. Here, we rely primarily on Carol J. Adam's work on the relation between femininity and animality, as well as Simone de Beauvoir's distinction between self and Other. Second, we look at the representation of gender and race within *Buffy the Vampire Slayer*, and discuss its status as a feminist text, as well as its ultimately failed attempts to challenge standard narratives concerning race. Third, we examine the representation of animality in the series, mainly by looking at the character's relationships with and dialogues concerning animals. Finally, we offer an intersectional analysis of *Buffy the Vampire Slayer* that looks at its treatment of gender, race, and animality. We show how the uptake of feminism has displaced the mutual denigration from women and animals onto racial categories, such that insofar as Blackness *is* represented, it is conflated with animality. This interpretation is exemplified in the relationship between Buffy and Sineya, the First Slayer, who is African, prelingual, and presented as brute. Paying attention to these racialized implications is essential to undermining the racism that so often lurks beneath the surface of feminist and animal rights organizations.

OTHERING AND MUTUAL DENIGRATION
OF GENDER, RACE, AND ANIMALITY

In *The Sexual Politics of Meat: A Feminist-Vegetarian Critical Theory*, Carol J. Adams discusses the concept of the absent referent, which is a means of using language to obfuscate certain connections (2010). She explains: "The absent referent is both there and not there. It is there through inference, but its meaningfulness reflects only upon what it refers to because the originating, literal, experience that contributes the meaning is not there. We fail to accord this absent referent its own existence" (Adams 2010, 67). People in consumerist societies engage absent referents all the time. For example, consider purchasing and consuming a caffè latte at your local coffee shop. This seems like a straightforward monetary exchange for a consumable product, but only because we do not think about everything that goes into making the exchange possible. We do not think about the production cycle of the beans, cup, lid, and sleeve, nor do we consider the sourcing of their raw materials and the labor involved in turning those resources into their end-stage products. We often do not even think about the barista's labor in bringing these parts together at our request. All of these elements, from natural resources to human labor, become absent referents in our caffè latte alongside the cows used to produce the milk. They are what makes our purchasing and consuming of the product possible, but their existence is obscured by our physical, psychological, and linguistic distance from its production.

While absent referents are not inherently bad, the way in which they are employed can have devastating consequences. When an object's source and chain of production is obscured, it becomes impossible to take those aspects up in our considerations. Adams exemplifies this in terms of the human use of animals: "Animals are made absent through language that renames dead bodies before consumers participate in eating them" (2010, 66). When we use terms like "meat," "pork," "beef," and "harvesting," instead of "flesh," "pig," "cow," and "murdering," the animal itself is made to disappear from the product that it is turned into. The animal was raised, killed, and processed far away from where it is eaten, and so there is a removal through physical distance. It has also been chopped up into pieces, and so there is a removal in form. And insofar as the animal is renamed from factory farm to plate, there is also a linguistic removal. All of these serve to obfuscate the suffering of animals. Beyond these means of removing the animal from the product, Adams recognizes a metaphorical removal as well, which occurs by employing animal-referents in describing and degrading humans or human experiences (2010, 67). This form is particularly important for the purposes of this chapter. Adams offers the example of victims of sexual violence's describing their experience, explaining that they "felt like a piece of meat" (2010, 67). Here, the term "meat" is used metaphorically, and is meant to signify being perceived and used as a lifeless object. Its use as a metaphor is meant to explicate the experience of a human and erases the animal as a living, feeling subject. In other words, it is not meant to refer to the animal in any way.

When the absent referent is used as a metaphor, it enables the *mutual denigration* of the objects of comparison. Mutual denigration occurs when two categories, such as femininity, African-Americans, immigrants, people with disabilities, or animals, are debased and conflated. Taking two of these categories together and regarding both as inferior, results in the vicious reinforcement of either as lesser. The comparison therefore disparages both of its objects. In "Of Mice and Men: A Feminist Fragment on Animal Rights," Catharine A. MacKinnon discusses the mutual denigration of women and animals when they are co-represented (2004). She notes that, while "a social hierarchy of men over women is often denied," the fact that women are referred to by animal-referents, and animals are considered lesser than humans, entails a hierarchical relationship (MacKinnon 2004, 264). As a result of societal norms that designate both women and animals as lesser, their denigration often involves one another. A clear example of this is cases in which women or female anatomy are referred to in terms of animal-referents. A woman that is considered assertive is called a bitch (a female dog), an attractive younger woman is often referred to as a chick (a baby bird), a woman that is not petite is sometimes called a cow, and a common colloquialism for vagina is beaver (MacKinnon 2004, 266). According to MacKinnon, "Women are called animal names ... to mark their categorically lesser humanity, always drawing on the assumption that animals are lower than humans" (2004, 266). Applying these animal-referents to women is therefore mutually degrading: designating the status of women as lesser than human by emphasizing the status of animals as lesser.

Considering nonhuman animals to be absolutely lesser than humans, merely because they are not part of the biological category of human, is speciesism. From the perspective of a speciesist, to liken women and feminine qualities to animals and animality, is to thereby diminish their humanity and their value. But at the same time this affirms the status of animals as fundamentally lower than that of humans. As Adams notes, there exists "an overlap of cultural images of sexual violence against women and the fragmentation and dismemberment of nature and the body in Western culture" (2010, 65–66). As such, these comparisons, that carry with them value judgments about their subjects, are mutually denigrating. Femininity is traditionally considered to be dichotomously opposed to masculinity. While positively connoted concepts like strength, rationality, and stoicism are connoted by the latter, negative concepts like weakness, intuitions and instinct, and emotions are connoted by the former. However, as Westerners we tend to equally attribute those latter terms to animals, who we generally consider to be non-rational and conquerable.

This process of one group separating itself from another through practice and language is what the French feminist and existentialist philosopher Simone de Beauvoir has called *othering*. According to Beauvoir, this process is a natural result of our limited human psychology. She explains that "The category of the *Other* is as primordial as consciousness itself" (Beauvoir 1989, xxii). Othering in this sense is the process of distinguishing between the categories of self, which is constituted by one's individual self, their characteristics, and their social groups, and that of the Other, which is that which is antithetical to the self. What Adams identifies is an extension of this process, whereby two categories of the Other are linguistically co-identified and denigrated. As Adams argues, "a structure of overlapping but absent referents links violence against women and animals" (2010, 67). Women are dehumanized by being referred to in animal-terms, and this in turn affirms the status of the animal as lesser.

Nevertheless, the mutual denigration that follows from the comparison between the feminine and animality is not necessary. It is built upon preconceived negative conceptions of both objects of the comparison, in this case a combination of sexism and speciesism. Beauvoir notes that while "it might seem that a natural condition is beyond the possibility of change," in fact "the nature of things is no more immutably given, once for all, than is historical reality" (1989, xxv). According to Beauvoir, the Other is able to transform their situation, and even if they cannot eradicate the process of othering in itself, they are at least able to assert themselves as a self (1989). Specifically, in so far as the feminine is turned into an absent referent by her association with animality, she still has the potential to assert her existence and selfhood. Unfortunately, efforts to combat this mutual denigration are often focused on lifting the human subject away from the identification with the animal. This leaves animality behind, compounding our negative conception of animals, but also allowing for the continued disparaging comparison between animals and groups we consider to be Other. A central thesis in feminism is that "women define the human as much as men do" (MacKinnon 2004, 267). Yet, it is generally not taken to be the case that animals define the category of moral concern as much as humans do. Instead, as MacKinnon notes, "animals have to measure up to humans' standards for humanity before their existence counts" (2004, 267). But if we are to take the lesson from feminism seriously, then animals ought to be able to enter into the scope of moral concern on their own grounds.

This mutual denigration does not only exist between the feminine and animality, and in *Bestial Traces: Race, Sexuality, Animality*, Christopher

Peterson examines the social and literary history of comparisons between race and animality (2013). He holds that "the equation of blacks with animals is based on prior negative ideas about nonhuman animals" (Peterson 2013, 2). In fact, he argues that "Speciesism engenders the bestialization of social and political others" (Peterson 2013, 2). In *The Dreaded Comparison*, Marjorie Spiegel supports this view by taking note of the overlap in the definitions of racism and speciesism (1988). The former constitutes "a belief that human races have distinctive characteristics that determine their respective cultures, usually involving the idea that one's own race is superior and has the right to rule others" (Spiegel 1988, 7). The latter constitutes "a belief that different species of animals are significantly different from one another in their capacities to feel pleasure and pain and live an autonomous existence, usually involving the idea that one's own species has the right to rule and use others" (Spiegel 1988, 7). The juxtaposition of these are meant to imply that the structures underlying these kinds of oppression are very similar, if not the very same ones. Delicia Dunham, in "On Being Black and Vegan," recognizes this interaction of oppressive forces, and notes that "Part of the fear that Black women have in caring about the plight of animals that causes them to distance themselves from nonhuman animals is that for so long, Black women have been likened to these beings and thus subjugated as such by speciesist racists" (2010, 45).

Alice Walker, in her preface to *The Dreaded Comparison*, also recognizes the similarity in oppressive structures, writing that "animals of the world exist for their own reasons. They were not made for humans any more than black people were made for whites or women for men" (Walker 1988, 10). And Adams supports this notion of interconnection subjugation as well, noting that "infants, youth, the poor, blacks, Irish, insane people, and women were considered beastlike" (2010, 69). She quotes Keith Thomas: "Once perceived as beasts, people were liable to be treated accordingly. The ethic of human domination removed animals from the sphere of human concern. But it also legitimized the ill treatment of those humans who were in supposedly animal condition" (Adams 2010, 69). Not only does this conflation legitimize the ill treatment of the subjugated groups, it also informs the kinds of treatment to which they were subjected. As Spiegel notes, "When both blacks and animals are viewed as being 'oppressable', the cruelties perpetrated upon them take similar forms" (1988, 25). Recall Beauvoir's point that while othering is a natural psychological pattern, viewing the Other as categorically lesser is not necessary (1989). Furthermore, the identification of the Other with a group we consider categorically lesser entails a relationship that damages the social standing of both groups. Standard efforts to resolve this bias insist on the humanity of Other, but this only reinforces the devaluing of the animal Other. Peterson captures this exact point, stating: "That the human/animal opposition makes the abjection of *human* others possible means that insisting on their humanity as a mode of resistance can only reinscribe the speciesist logic that initiates their exclusion" (2013, 2).

GENDER AND RACE IN *BUFFY THE VAMPIRE SLAYER*

Buffy the Vampire Slayer is frequently hailed as a feminist landmark in television, even being called a "third wave feminist icon" (Pender 2016a). Years of watching horror tropes prompted a desire in Whedon to "see a movie in which a blond wanders into a dark alley, takes care of herself and deploys her powers" (Bellafante 1997). So from the very beginning, the show was meant to challenge sexist stereotypes, both in general and in horror films in particular. In the series, Buffy kicks ass, her relationships with men are important to her but do not define her, and the honest portrayal of the relationship between Willow and her talented witch girlfriend Tara Maclay in all its complexity was groundbreaking. However, in "Reconsidering the Feminism of Joss Whedon," Natasha Simmons challenges the merits of *Buffy the Vampire Slayer*, as a feminist text (2011). She takes note of the fact that the Slayer's power is given to her by men, that the Watchers who preside over each Slayer are predominately male, that Buffy herself is an emotionally weak character when it comes to romantic relationships, and sexually confident women are punished for their promiscuity (Simmons 2011). In light of these objections, it is appropriate to challenge the show's iconic feminist status. Yet, recognizing that the series is not the ideal feminist text does not erase its many (feminist) virtues. While we should not insist on its iconic status where this is not merited, a careful critique of the ways in which the show fails to live up to its progressive reputation should be able to recognize its successes while remaining discerning.

Feminist critics have taken note of several features of the series that undermine its feminist status. One of the features for which the series is sometimes faulted, is the fact that the cast is made up of Hollywood-attractive actors, supporting the traditional Hollywood depiction of women, and fails to challenge the unrealistic standards of beauty that are ubiquitous in the media. Pender, in *I'm Buffy and You're History*, recognizes that Buffy subscribes to and thereby reinscribes "commercial and patriarchal standards of feminine beauty" (2016b). It is difficult the resist the claim that the cast members are attractive, but is should be noted that from its inception, the point of the show was to take the stereotypical blonde cheerleader trope, and overturn it. Rather than see a vampire chase a cheerleader through the gym, trip, and get killed, the (former) cheerleader fights back, and slays the vampire. In this case, the attractive cast seems unavoidable in driving home the satirical point.

One of Simmons' criticisms is that the show repeatedly reinforces the trope that "a woman's sexual actions are dangerous" (2011). She cites a series of examples, including when Buffy's vampire-with-a-soul boyfriend Angel loses his soul after they have sex and he turns back into a villainous demon ("Innocence" 1998). Another example is when Buffy and her college boyfriend Riley almost destroy a house when they get caught up in a magic-fueled sex frenzy ("Where the Wild Things Are" 2000). It is undeniable that sex is represented in complex ways in the show. Given the high school to early college years setting, it might be suggested that this only makes sense since the show is meant to make real and tangible the horrors of adolescence and young adulthood, and this includes the complexities of sex. Yet this response is not entirely satisfying. Simmons takes note of how Angel losing his soul is "explicitly blame[d] on Buffy's sexual agency," and often "strong female characters are sublimated to the weaker, childish males' needs" (2011). While these may mirror real-world problems, the female characters are not allowed to sufficiently redress these chauvinist overtones. *Buffy the Vampire Slayer* nevertheless constitutes an important step forward in how women are represented in popular media. In spite of its serious flaws, it nevertheless stands as a successful feminist challenge to a range of sexist tropes, and is a quintessential case of feminist change in the media.

While the degree to which it accomplishes its feminist objectives should continue to be evaluated and challenged, recognizing its merits allows us to set up the series' treatment of gender over and against its treatment of race and animality. This contextualization brings to light a stark differential treatment. The series can rightfully be critiqued for its racial homogeneity. All of the main characters, and most of the supporting and side characters, are white. The most notable characters of color are Jamaican Slayer Kendra, who appears in only three episodes, Principal Robin Wood and his mother, ex-Slayer Nikki Wood, who are African-American and appear in fourteen and three episodes respectively, as well as Sineya, the First Slayer, who appears to be a prelingual human of African descent and appears in three episodes.

The season four finale, "Restless," follows the Scooby-Gang as they invoke the power of the First Slayer in order to kill the Frankensteinian super-demon Adam, the primary antagonist of the season. In the subsequent episode, Buffy, Giles, Willow, and Xander all spend the night watching a movie at Buffy's house. But they soon fall asleep, and one-by-one we witness their dreams, foreshadowing future storylines and current developments. In Buffy's dream, she, the current Slayer, meets Sineya, the First Slayer. Buffy and Sineya are posited as the self and Other. This is illustrated well toward the end of her dream, when Buffy walks into the desert and she comes face to face with the First Slayer. Tara is also there, as she has to interpret for Sineya, who is referred to in the script as the Primitive:

BUFFY (to the Primitive): Why do you follow me?
TARA: I don't.
BUFFY: Where are my friends?
TARA: You're asking the wrong questions.
BUFFY (calm anger): Make her speak.
TARA: I have no speech. No name. I live in the action of death. The blood-cry, the penetrating wound. I am destruction. Absolute. Alone.
BUFFY (realizing) The Slayer.
TARA: The first.
BUFFY: I'm not alone.
TARA: The slayer doesn't walk in the world.
BUFFY: I walk. I talk. I shop, I sneeze, I'm gonna be a fireman when the floods roll back. There's trees in the desert since you moved out, and I don't sleep on a bed of bones. Now give me back my friends.
PRIMITIVE: No ... friends ... just the kill ... we are ... alone.
BUFFY: That's it. I'm waking up.
("Restless" 2000)

Buffy asks why the First Slayer is following her, but she is not. Her presence in the dream merely points to her presence in Buffy. She, who seems fundamentally Other, being without language and Black, posited as the absolute opposite of Buffy, who is social and white. Buffy resists the notion that a Slayer is merely an agent of death: the previously empty life of the Slayer (the desert) has others in it now (trees), and there is more to her existence than death (bed of bones). The First Slayer is pushing Buffy to conform to the demands of her origins. She needs to leave behind the social, the rational, even the human, so she can fully walk the path of destruction.

In "Journey Toward Compassionate Choice," Tara Sophia Bahna-James describes this as what Carol Gilligan has called the "point of initiation" (2010, 161). This is the point that "girls typically encounter when they first receive cues to discard and discount their own experience in order to enter into society and uphold the hierarchy of authority" (Bahna-James 2010, 161). Similarly, Beauvoir takes note of the historical conditions of the oppressed, for both women in patriarchal cultures and Black people in the United States, who found themselves in a situation wherein "the caprice of others determined whether they were to be changed into objects; their subjectivity no longer had means of concrete expression, being only a secondary phenomenon" (1989, 331). Buffy rejects this objectification and asserts herself as a self. This need not be an explicit rejection of the racial Other, and can instead be interpreted as a rejection of the demonic source of the Slayer's power. Nevertheless it reinforces the traditional power structure, because Buffy as a white person has the ability to choose her identity, while Sineya as a Black person is stuck with the one that has been forced upon her.

There are attempts to reverse this relationship. For instance in Giles' dream when Buffy ends up with a gray-blue mud on her face. The mud, which in our view is not a nod to blackface, covers up Buffy's social identity, leaving the slayer aspect. This causes Giles to recognize the First Slayer in her ("Restless" 2000). Buffy also spreads this mud on her face in her own dream, signaling this same identification. In contrast, when we see Sineya, her face is largely painted white. While the style is undoubtedly meant to be tribal, the contrast with Buffy's change in appearance is notable. But the reversal is ultimately unsuccessful. At the very end of the episode, Buffy remarks: "the First Slayer. I never really thought about it. (Sighs) It was intense" ("Restless" 2000). This is precisely the nature of the relationships between self and Other. For the self, this relationship of disenfranchisement and oppression is obscured by their position of privilege. In effect, Sineya is the absent referent in Buffy. Buffy's existence as the Slayer is only possible because of the First Slayer, but her status as a social and rational person obfuscates this connection. Subsequently, the existence of the First Slayer sinks back to the background and is not really taken up by Buffy. Sineya's status as absent is maintained, at least until the end of the series.

ANIMALITY AND *BUFFY THE VAMPIRE SLAYER*

Unlike the dialogue surrounding feminism and racial issues, the issue of speciesism is not at all present. Within the narrative, the human-animal relationships is never complicated or challenged, which means that animals suffer a degraded moral standing in comparison to humans. This is evident first and foremost in the way the moral status of animal in the show reflects the general disregard for animals that our society has. The characters display all of the ordinary ways in which humans tend to actualize their speciesism, by consuming dead animals or by the use of animals for the purpose of entertainment. They eat meat, go to the zoo, wear leather, have pets, and never consider the harm these acts entail for the animals involved. Any potential exceptions to the human-animal hierarchy and the general disregard of animal sentience also follows societal constraints.

The human-pet relationships is exemplified in the appearance of Miss Kitty Fantastico. In "New Moon Rising," Tara discusses her desire to get a pet, making sure that Willow is comfortable with cats, since she wants her dorm room to be "Willow-friendly" ("New Moon Rising" 2000). In the next episode, "The Yoko Factor," the audience is introduced to the dorm-crashing cat. Willow and Tara are hanging out together in Tara's room and discuss Miss Fantastico's cuteness ("The Yoko Factor" 2000). Aside from Miss

Fantastico's brief appearance in Willow's dream-sequence in "Restless," she is only seen once more a few episodes later, in "Family" (2000), and is subsequently not seen or heard of again, until her absence is explained in the final season, when Xander and Buffy's monk-made little sister are searching through Xander's car:

DAWN: Xander, my crossbow is not out here. I told you, I don't leave crossbows around all willy-nilly. (pauses guiltily) Not since that time with Miss Kitty Fantastico. ("End of Days" 2003)

The clear implication is that Miss Fantastico was killed in a crossbow incident. The reveal is obviously meant to be a moment of comic relief in an otherwise very tense episode. It is apparent from the narrative treatment of Miss Fantastico that she does not really serve a purpose. Her death is merely a punchline. She appears in a total of three episodes, is just there to be referenced when convenient, and can be eliminated without second thought, only to have her death explained in a moment of entertainment. This reflects the status of domesticated animals in our society as objects that we can legally own.

There are instances in which animals or animal-like creatures are given moral consideration. But these hardly serve to challenge the prevailing paradigm, since these are cases in which it is not the animal that is valued as such, but their underlying humanity. Examples of these include the concern for Amy the rat, the fellow Sunnydale High School student and witch who turned into a rat to escape Salemesque prosecution ("Gingerbread" 1999; "Triangle" 2001), the treatment of Hyena-possessed Xander ("The Pack" 1997), and the moral concern for werewolves. The latter is illustrated when Buffy and Giles are searching for a werewolf they think has been killing animals and might murder people in the future, and they run into Cain, a werewolf hunter:

GILES: Y-you hunt werewolves f-for sport
CAIN: No, no, I'm in it purely for the money
BUFFY: And it doesn't bother you that a werewolf is a person twenty-eight days out of the month
CAIN: That's why I only hunt 'em the other three. ("Phases" 1988)

Here, the source of moral considerability is made explicit by Buffy's comment. The question of whether it is wrong to kill werewolves hinges on their underlying humanity, not the part of their nature that is wolf. According to Buffy and Giles, the mistake that Cain makes is a failure to recognize the persistent human-value in the werewolf. The fact that in killing a werewolf Cain would be killing a fellow human is expressed, perhaps incidentally, in his name and its biblical referent. Cain clearly captures the sentientist attitude, by emphasizing the absolute degree to which nonhuman bodies are exploitable and disposable.

Another way the status of animals is demonstrated is by the conflation of monstrosity and animality. Indeed, throughout the show, animal-referents are used to describe monsters and demons. While cases like this abound, a few examples in particular are worth mentioning here. For instance, after the Scooby-Gang finds out about Angel's identity as a vampire, they discuss his rise to infamy in centuries past. Xander asks "a hundred years or so before he came to our shores, what was he like then?" And Giles replies "Uh, like all of them. Uh, a vicious, violent animal" ("Angel" 1997). Similarly, when Kendra describes Angel, who she recognized to be a vampire, she says, "He looked to me just like anodder [*sic*] animal" ("What's My Line, Part 2" 1997). And finally, while Buffy is training potential future Slayers in the final season, she explains "A vampire is an animal. Sometimes they run in packs, sometimes alone" ("Potential" 2003). These are specific cases that point to a pattern of describing the status of monsters and demons by describing them as animals. This denigrates animals to a status of soulless and valueless, very much dispensable in the way that monsters and demons are as well. The only exceptions to this are, once again, when a demon regains their humanity as is the case with Angel and, in later seasons, Spike, that is, vampires with a soul ("Sleeper" 2002).

The "Doublemeat Palace" storyline, where Buffy out of financial necessity picks up a job at a quintessentially American fast-food company, potentially represents a departure from this devaluing of animals at various points. Early on, when some of the Gang visit Buffy at her job, she gets Xander a burger:

BUFFY: There you go, and I double-sized it for ya.
XANDER: Oh, thank you.
(Xander unwraps the burger and takes a big bite)
BUFFY: And cut way back on the cat.
XANDER: (mouth full) Cat?
BUFFY: Just kidding. (Xander gives a sarcastic laugh) Probably.
("Doublemeat Palace" 2000)

Xander's disgust at the thought of eating cat offers an opportunity for the narrative to move to a more critical position on animal consumption. But the point is never pursued, and the irony in being disgusted at the thought of eating cat, but not at eating a cow or chicken (or a doublemeat combination thereof) is never made explicit. The concern with eating cat can therefore be explicated purely in terms of their arbitrarily elevated status as pets when compared to other non-domestic animals. Of course, this status is elevated only relative to other animals.

Later, Buffy finds a human finger in the meat-grinder. She takes a burger to the Gang for investigation and relays the suspicion that the burger's "secret ingredient" is in fact people. Xander, having already started in on the burger that was meant to be examined, overhears this:

XANDER: What?
(Buffy and Dawn turn to look at him. The empty burger wrapper is on the table beside him)
XANDER: (swallows) People.
BUFFY: Xander, you ate the burger?
XANDER: (stands up, yells) Well, first you say it's cat, then you come in and hand me a burger, blah blah blah, five minutes later 'oh and by the way, it happens to be hot delicious human flesh.'
("Doublemeat Palace" 2000)

Note that while human meat is spoken of in terms of flesh, animal meat is not, and so the animal remains an absent referent. And, while it follows from the exchange that eating a cat might be considered somewhat bad, the fact that the doublemeat burger contains both cow and chicken is never considered to have any ethical implications.

In the end, it turns out that the doublemeat burger is made from vegetables, or more specifically "a formed and texturized vegetable based meat-like product, suitable for grinding" ("Doublemeat Palace" 2000). While the fact of a securely vegetarian fast-food conglomerate would be of note, this potential is undone when it is revealed that the vegetable mixture is "blended with large amounts of rendered beef fat for flavor" ("Doublemeat Palace" 2000). Buffy poignantly asks, "Wait, the secret ingredient in the beef is ... beef" ("Doublemeat Palace" 2000)? In the end, the episode is more an indictment of fast-food consumer culture, suggesting that these conglomerates will even sully their meat with vegetables to achieve greater profits, rather than of the animal industrial complex and its inherent cruelty. This is emphasized by Xander's disgust at having possibly consumed human flesh, but the uninvestigated irony of eating animal flesh as common place. After analyzing human/animal relationships in the Buffyverse, it is evident that animality is generally considered a sign of monstrosity, and the only animals that are treated well experience this benevolence due to their underlying humanity, such as in the cases of werewolves and Amy the rat.

AN INTERSECTIONAL ANALYSIS OF GENDER, RACE, AND ANIMALITY IN *BUFFY THE VAMPIRE SLAYER*

One way in which *Buffy the Vampire Slayer* maintains its feminist status is by rejecting the conflation between the feminine and animality. This is captured particularly well in Buffy's concern with her humanity, her ability to love, and her relationships. In season five, in the throes of a season-long conflict with a hell god, Buffy seeks further guidance. She and Giles venture into the desert where she encounters the Guide in the form of the First Slayer:

GUIDE: You're afraid that being the Slayer means losing your humanity.
BUFFY: Does it?
("Intervention" 2001)

But the guide ensures her that she is full of love, and that love will bring her to her gift. When Buffy asks for clarification, the Guide explains that "Death is your gift" ("Intervention" 2001). But Buffy rejects this. She is very much concerned with her life and humanity, rejecting anything that might make her more animal-like.

The displacement of animality from a whitened version of femininity to Blackness is exemplified in the relationship between Buffy and Sineya, the First Slayer. Sineya is prelingual, and this reflects the structure of power to which she is subject. Adams recognizes the importance of language, and considers how being mute "connotes issues of language and power" (2010, 107). She cites Elaine Showalter, who states that "muted groups must mediate their beliefs through the allowable forms of dominant structures" (Adams 2010, 107). This status is clearly reflected in Sineya's muteness, and her limited ability to communicate, being forced to be mediated by Tara and in dreams ("Restless" 2000; and "Get It Done" 2003). Sineya is denied her own voice, and she is only allowed to speak through bodies and minds of sophisticated, rational, white characters. This is also considered to be the primary means of communications for animals, that is, they are taken to be unable to communicate for themselves, and need people to defend their interests. It is, however, important to note that in "Feminism and the Treatment of Animals," Josephine Donovan challenges this notion, arguing that while animals frequently communicate their objections to ill treatment, humans ignore their plight (2008, 49).

In "Restless," Sineya is presented as a kind of proto-human. She is primitive, in fact, as we noted earlier, the episode's shooting script refers to her as "the Primitive" ("Restless" 2000, shooting script). She does not have language, she growls and crouches, walks around on all fours, she is violent (a trait repeatedly characterized as animal-like within the context of the series, as illustrated in the previous section), and behaves in a predatory manner. Various descriptions in the shooting script underwrite this interpretation of the character. In Willow's dream, when she looks out the window into the desert landscape, the description reads: "Something moves, briefly, out of focus. A human shape, in grey and dirty rags, moving like an animal" ("Restless" 2000, shooting script). In Xander's dream, "the Primitive is just coming around the corner, walking on her knuckles like an ape" ("Restless" 2000, shooting script). Sineya's description is very much on the line between human and animal. Her form is human, but her predator-like behavior is animal. This follows the standard narrative of the comparison between the racial Other and animals, where their superficial similarity with humans is recognized, but their nature is likened to that of the lesser animals.

It is notable that toward the end of Giles' dream, when he has already had an inkling as to who is after them, he instructs Willow to "look through *The Chronicles* for some reference to a warrior beast" ("Restless" 2000). Where "beast" has connotations of an animal-like monster. Moments later, when he finally figures out it is the First Slayer pursuing them and that they are attacked by her, he says "I know who you are. And I can defeat you … with my intellect. I … can cripple you with my thoughts" ("Restless" 2000). It is clear that Giles juxtaposes himself over and against Sineya by referencing his superior human rationality. He cannot countenance her having power over him, and must assert his selfhood by pushing back against hers.

The question of Buffy's nature comes up again in the final season of the series. In one of the central narrative episodes of the season, "Get It Done," Buffy meets the creators of the First Slayer and the Slayer lineage, the Shadow Men. The scenario emphasizes the violence involved in the creation of the Slayer. Shortly after Buffy meets the Shadow Men, one of them knocks her out ("Get It Done" 2003). She awakens chained down, and the men present her with a box that contains the source of the slayer's strength: "Black smoke comes out of the box in long tentacles; it seems sentient as it dances around the circle. The men keep tapping their staves rhythmically" ("Get It Done" 2003). The Shadow Men insist that the smoke, the essence of the demon, must become one with Buffy, as this will make her "ready for the fight" ("Get It Done" 2003). "By making me less human?" Buffy asks ("Get It Done" 2003). The action in this scene is initially driven by patriarchal power, and the violence is acutely akin to sexual assault in terms of the loss of power, the physical constraint, and the bodily violation. The language in the script makes this explicit: "Buffy struggles … as the black smoke … enter[s] her body" ("Get It Done" 2003). In case the sexual-imagery is lost on the audience, Buffy asks: "You think I came all this way to get knocked up by some demon dust?" ("Get It Done" 2003). And in response to the Shadow Men's attempt to explain the necessity of what they are forcing up on her,

Buffy explains: "You violated that girl, made her kill for you because you're weak, you're pathetic" ("Get It Done" 2003). After Buffy fights and defeats the Shadow Men, she breaks their staff causing the smoke to disappear, and driving home the phallic-metaphor, saying: "I knew it. It's always the staff" ("Get It Done" 2003).

The imagery of sexual assault affirms the dehumanizing violence committed against Sineya. This is emphasized in the way that this sexual violence mirrors certain kinds of violence perpetrated against animals. When humans want to use animals for their purposes, continued use generally requires reproductive success. Adams recognizes this analogy between sexual violence against women and our treatment of animals, taking note of the use of "rape racks," which "enable the insemination of animals against their will" (2010, 82). This is strikingly similar to the imagery from the scene above. For both humans and animals, to be treated like a piece of meat, "is to be treated like an inert object when one is (or was) in fact a living, feeling being" (Adams 2010, 82). This is reflected in the way the Shadow Men treated Sineya, and are now treating Buffy, that is, without any regard for their bodily autonomy, their dignity, and their own feelings and desires.

Buffy resisting the Shadow Men is a clear demonstration of her feminist resistance of the patriarchy. But Buffy's rejection of the patriarchy's power over her is connected to her rejection of animality as part of her nature. In her attempt to reject the reduction of the Slayer to the animal, she exerts her human equality, her strength, her rationality; that is, the features of humanity that have traditionally been considered masculine and stand opposed to animality. Sineya was of course not free in her fate. It was forced upon her. In this sense the origins of her perceived bruteness reflects the imposition of animality onto Blackness in the Western world. And this offers an opportunity for critical thought concerning our perceptions of race and animality. Nevertheless, in the greater context of the show, this interpretation is never given any weight. Buffy recognizes after the dream encounter in "Restless" that "she never really thought about it" (2000). The "it" here constituting a complex reference to the ontological source of her power, the First Slayer, and her status. But this confrontation is brief and the implications never come to explicit realization in the show. In the process of asserting her own humanity, Buffy leaves behind animality as lesser. In her rejection of the "power" that she is offered, she at the same time refuses to occupy the space of the Other. And in so doing, she leaves behind Sineya, who is stuck with her animality that is by implication tied up in her race. Spiegel recognizes this as a broader mechanism of oppression, holding that "as long as humans feel they are forced to defend their own rights and worth by placing someone beneath them, oppression will not end. This approach, at the very best, results only in an individual or group of people climbing up the ladder by pushing others down" (1988, 16). And this is precisely the mechanism that Adams (2010) exposed in the oppression of women and animals, that Peterson (2013) identified in our social consciousness, as well as Wehelive (2014) in relation to the flesh, Blackness and animality. Mutual denigration is rarely resolved through mutual or intersectional gains. Instead the oppression of one denigrated class is too often fought against by demonstrating their equality to their mutual oppressor, at the expense of other denigrated classes. In turn, this declaration of equality is reinforced by maintaining the disenfranchisement of the other denigrated class. For instance, the mutual degeneration suffered between women and animals is overcome by insisting that women are morally equal to men. And in order to reinforce this conception of equality, it is further insisted upon that women and men are both superior to animals. And so, animals and those understood as nonhuman are left behind in the movement for moral recognition.

CONCLUSION

Within the narrative of *Buffy the Vampire Slayer* there is some struggle with the representation of race, although it remains minimal. It certainly never actualizes into a full critique, and in fact in the end it falls back into standard social conceptions, without posing a threat to the dominant ideology. The status of animals in the show remains entirely unchallenged. As Spiegel notes, "with regard to the animals themselves, most still feel that it is acceptable to treat them ... as we say, 'like animals.' That is, society has decided that treatment which is wholly unacceptable when received by a human being is in fact the *proper* manner in which to treat a non-human animal" (1988, 17). While the series is able to escape the frequent conflation of femininity and animality, the uptake of feminism has displaced the mutual denigration from women and animals onto the racial. And the representation of Sineya as brute is exemplary of this shift. The show's inability to successfully challenge the standard representations of race and animals results in the mutual denigration of Blackness and animality, where they are ultimately understood as brute and lesser than human. Ultimately, having awareness over how media matters can help reshape culture in order to promote a more radical form of scholarship and activism that can produce successful methods for praxis.

WORKS CITED

Adams, Carol J. 2010. *The Sexual Politics of Meat: A Feminist-Vegetarian Critical Theory*. Twentieth Anniversary Edition. New York: Bloomsbury Academic, An Imprint of Bloomsbury Publishing Plc.

Bahna-James, Tara Sophia. 2010. "Journey Toward Compassionate Choice: Integrating Vegan and Sistah Experience." In *Sistah Vegan: Black Female Vegans Speak on Food, Identity, Health, and Society*, edited by A. Breeze Harper, 155–168. New York: Lantern Books.

Beauvoir, Simone de. [1952] 1989. *The Second Sex*, translated and edited by H. M. Parshley. New York: Vintage Books.

Bellafante, Ginia. 1997. "Bewitching Teen Heroines: They're all Over the Dial, Speaking Out, Cracking Wise and Casting Spells." *Time* 149(18).

Buffy the Vampire Slayer. "Angel." 1997.1.7. Directed by Scott Brazil. Written by Joss Whedon and David Greenwalt. The WB Television Network.

BuffyWikia. 2016. Buffyverse Wiki, a Fandom TV Community. http://www.buffy.wikia.com/wiki/Buffy_the_Vampire_Slayer_and_Angel

BuffyWorld. N.d. A Complete Guide to all of the "Buffy the Vampire Slayer" and "Angel" Episodes. http://www.buffyworld.com

———."Doublemeat Palace." 2000. 6.12. Directed by Nick Marck. Written by Joss Whedon and Jane Espenson. The WB Television Network.

———."Family." 2000. 5.6. Directed by Joss Whedon. Written by Joss Whedon. The WB Television Network.

———."End of Days." 2003. 7.21. Directed by Marita Grabiak. Written by Joss Whedon and Douglas Petrie. United Paramount Network.

———."Get It Done." 2003. 7.15. Directed by Douglas Petrie. Written by Joss Whedon and Douglas Petrie. United Paramount Network.

———."Gingerbread." 1999. 3.11. Directed by James Whitmore. Written by Joss Whedon and Jane Espenson. The WB Television Network.

———."Innocence." 1998. 2.14. Directed by Joss Whedon. Written by Joss Whedon. The WB Television Network.

———."Intervention." 2001. 5.18. Directed by Michael Gershman. Written by Joss Whedon and Jane Espenson. The WB Television Network.

———."New Moon Rising." 2000. 4.19. Directed by James A. Contner. Written by Joss Whedon and Marti Noxon. The WB Television Network.

———."Phases." 1998. 2.15. Directed by Bruce Seth Green. Written by Joss Whedon and Rob DesHotel. The WB Television Network.

———."Potential." 2003. 7.12. Directed by James A. Contner. Written by Joss Whedon and Rebecca Sinclair. United Paramount Network.

———."Primeval." 2000. 4.21. Directed by James A. Contner. Written by Joss Whedon and David Fury. The WB Television Network.

———."Restless." 2000. 4.22. Directed by Joss Whedon. Written by Joss Whedon. The WB Television Network.

———."Sleeper." 2002. 7.8. Directed by Alan J. Levi. Written by Joss Whedon and David Fury. United Paramount Network.

———."The Pack." 1997. 1.6. Directed by Bruce Seth Green. Written by Joss Whedon and Matt Kiene. The WB Television Network.

———."The Yoko Factor." 2000. 4.20. Directed by David Grossman. Written by Joss Whedon and Douglas Petrie. The WB Television Network.

———."Triangle." 2001. 5.11. Directed by Christopher Hibler. Written by Joss Whedon and Jane Espenson. The WB Television Network.

————."Welcome to the Hellmouth." 1997. 1.1. Directed by Charles Martin Smith and Joss Whedon. Written by Joss Whedon. The WB Television Network.

————."What's My Line?: Part 2." 1997. 2.10. Directed by David Semel. Written by Joss Whedon and Marti Noxon. The WB Television Network.

————."Where the Wild Things Are." 2000. 4.18. Directed by David Solomon. Written by Joss Whedon and Tracy Forbed. The WB Television Network.

————."Restless" shootings script. 2000. A Complete Guide to all of the "Buffy the Vampire Slayer" and "Angel" Episodes. http://www.buffyworld.com/buffy/scripts/078_scri.html

Donovan, Josephine. 2008. "Feminism and the Treatment of Animals: From Care to Dialogue." In *The Animal Ethics Reader*, edited by Susan J. Armstrong and Richard G. Botzler, 47–54. New York: Routledge.

Dunham, Delicia. 2010. "On Being Black and Vegan." In *Sistah Vegan: Black Female Vegans Speak on Food, Identity, Health, and Society*, edited by A. Breeze Harper, 42–46. New York: Lantern Books.

IMDb. "Buffy the Vampire Slayer." 2016. The International Movie Database. http://www.imdb.com/title/tt0118276/?ref_=tt_ov_inf

MacKinnon, Catharine A. 2004. "Of Mice and Men: A Feminist Fragment of Animal Rights." In *Animal Rights: Current Debates and New Directions*, edited by Cass R. Sunstein and Martha C. Nussbaum, 263–276. New York: Oxford University Press.

Pender, Patricia. 2016a. "Buffy Summers: Third-Wave Feminist Icon." *The Atlantic*. https://www.theatlantic.com/entertainment/archive/2016/07/how-buffy-became-a-third-wave-feminist-icon/493154/

Pender, Patricia. 2016b. *I'm Buffy and You're History: Buffy the Vampire Slayer and Contemporary Feminism*. New York: I. B. Tauris.

Peterson, Christopher. 2013. *Bestial Traces: Race, Sexuality, Animality*. New York: Fordham University Press.

Showalter, Elaine. 1985. "Feminist Criticism in the Wilderness." In *The New Feminist Criticism: Essays on Women, Literature, and Theory*, edited by Elaine Showalter. New York: Pantheon Books.

Simmons, Natasha. 2011. "Reconsidering the Feminism of Joss Whedon." themarysue.com. http://www.themarysue.com/reconsidering-the-feminism-of-joss-whedon/

Spiegel, Marjorie. 1988. *The Dreaded Comparison: Human and Animal Slavery*. Philadelphia: New Society Publishers.

Thomas, Keith. 1983. *Man and the Natural World: A History of the Modern Sensibility*. New York: Pantheon.

Walker, Alice. 1988. Introduction to *The Dreaded Comparison: Human and Animal Slavery*, by Marjorie Spiegel Philadelphia: New Society Publishers.

Weheliye, Alexander G. 2014. *Habeas Viscus*. Durham: Duke University Press.

Chapter 9

Cyborgs, Companion Species, and the General Will

The Deeply Constitutive Relationship Between Bats and Batman

Matt Evans

What is the relationship between bats and Batman? A human-centric reading might suggest that Batman represents a wealthy orphan's effort to overcome a childhood fear of bats by transforming it into an anti-crime deterrent and tool for justice. In turn, it transforms a dreadful nocturnal symbol to haunt criminals, scare them straight, and bring the city back to good people of Gotham. While plausible, this does not tell the full story of the central meaning of bats within this superhero epic in relation to Critical Animal Studies (CAS) or give much agency beyond nonhuman objects and animals to define the past, present, and future. As a result, I seek to present a feminist-inspired CAS reading that looks to the "strange otherness" of the "superbody" (Taylor 2007, 347). My hope is to undermine the atomism of the vigilante (Dittmer 2007; Locke 2005). I believe this is best accomplished by highlighting the "false binaries" between human and nonhuman animals, creator and created, cause and effect, subject and object, and agent and system (Best 2009, 14). In short, my reading offers an interpretation of Donna Haraway's companion species and cyborgs to explain the interdependence of technosciences, animals, voice, and morality in Batman. Cyborgs and companion species can be brought together into a single theoretical architecture to read Christopher Nolan's Dark Knight trilogy of *Batman Begins*, *The Dark Knight* and *The Dark Knight Rises* as a singular fault-line text "where cultural hegemony can be met with resistant readings" (Russell 2016, 173). I demonstrate how Batman exists as a cyborg improving his body with technology, while bats are not only the companion species that possess agency to drive the plot forward but also help advance the transformation of Bruce Wayne into Batman.

Both Batman and bats are intimately involved in the construction of general will. By this, I mean a type of morality that makes a singular political identity for a community possible in creating political subjects (Rousseau

1978). Batman and bats establish their connection to the community with their voices. The dark knight aloofly supports capitalism, even benefiting from the destructive impact of capitalism on Gotham. Villains like Bane and the Joker challenge capital in a way that reinforces the system itself. By paying attention to these cultural artifacts we can better learn how discourse operates within society in order to challenge the most oppressive configurations. Looking toward Batman and the villains he fights makes it easier to critically interrogate how power operates socially throughout civil society.

Put differently, bats operate as a companion species to the cyborg of Batman. Companion species are "fleshy semiotic presences in body of technosciences" (Haraway 2003, 5). They are "vulnerable on the ground work that" brings "together nonharmonious agencies and ways of living that are accountable both to their disparate inherited agencies and their barely possible joint futures" (Haraway 2003, 7). Cyborgs function as border territory fiction and lived experience, imagination and material reality, machine and organism, mind and body, self developed and externally designed (Haraway 1991, 150). Companion species are related to cyborgs because the latter acts "as junior species in the much larger queer family of companion species" (Haraway 2003, 15). In my reading, the ecology of these two beings does not suggest a simple hierarchy, but a complicated interplay of causes and outcomes that play out with material existence and human meaning. To this end, for Bruce Wayne bats are more than just totems because he must look to them to become Batman. His formative experience is deeply entangled with an engagement with bats—whether falling into a cave, seeing his parents' death, or completing his ninja training through the League of Shadows. Bats make Batman, perhaps more than anything else, even though they are in some representations of Batman just a totem representation for the nonhuman animal itself. *Batman Begins* is a story of the growth of a cyborg and companion species. This is a process that unfolds as Bruce Wayne develops emotionally, cognitively, and physically in his growth and aging (Winterhalter 2015).

The stages of his growth at important moments draw upon bats. Like a dog making their human companion happy after a trying day at work, these animals become important emotional resources that can transform Bruce Wayne into Batman. Bats help transform a sheltered young boy into an angry young man. The former happens through his brush with bats at the bottom of the well and his parent's death. The latter comes through the formative process of exile ending in the final graduation scene where Wayne must beat Ducard, along with a group of ninjas from the League of Shadows, while overcoming the hallucinations of bats. Bats through their shrieking and flight perform a pedagogically transformative role for a junior species of Bruce Wayne. The companion species sweep Bruce away from his childhood and his self-exile from Gotham. They assist his cyborg transformation by helping him take on a savior complex and gain an impossible set of good ninja skills as Gotham's richest son.

Through Lucius Fox, Batman progressively applies technology to improve his body, and thus becomes a cyborg. Fox and bats play a role in transforming Bruce Wayne's body into the cyborg of Batman through the body armor, mask, cape, utility belt, and weapons. As a cyborg, the question emerges about how much efficacy the technology possesses, and how much the physical body or wealth of the individual deploying the tech possesses. Within the story the cyborg shifts away from an unknowable origin progressing toward an "apocalyptic telos" never quite achieved. Such a movement aims toward "an escalating domination of abstract individuation, an ultimate self untied at last from all dependency, a man in space," but clutches more tightly to the surrounding objects (Haraway 1991, 192). Batman gets better over time as he employs more and more technology upon his own body and others. He draws on more types of species as human companions like Fox and Jim Gordon and other types of technology like antidotes and mass production.

At the same time, Wayne never loses sight of his relation with bats. At formative moments, he brings bats into the scene. After picking off mob boss Carmine Falcone and his henchmen, the audience sees a thrashed Falcone tied to a spotlight to resemble a bat. When Scarecrow captures Rachel and holds her in a drug-induced hallucinating fever in Arkum Asylum, Batman rescues her and flees from the police with the assistance of bats. To flee the asylum and escape the police, Batman draws upon his cyborg tech, using a subsonic noise emitter to attract bats and provide cover from the melee of individuals who might do him and Rachel harm. As a film, *Batman Begins* (2005) centralizes the role of bats. These animals play a significant role in the genesis, constitution, and regeneration of Batman beyond the totem representation of bats in other depictions of the character.

In contrast to the significance of bats of *Batman Begins* (2005), the film *The Dark Knight Rises* (2012) possesses few scenes with bats. They do present themselves at formative moments: in a flashback of his father raising him out of the well at Wayne manner, at a decisive moment in an escape attempt from Bane's prison, and in a scene with Blake shining a light in the middle of the bat cave much as Bruce had done at the beginning of Batman. While the beginning of the film sets the stage for the absence of Batman within Gotham and his vilification as the "murderer" of Harvey Dent, the movie sets the stage for the absence of bats with what seems like a crack of ice around a bat symbol in the beginning sequences. In fact, bats are largely absent in this scene and others. When Bruce Wayne returns to the bat cave within Wayne Manor, there are no bats. When Batman winds through the sewers of Gotham slowing picking off the League of Shadows ninjas and unsuccessfully fighting Bane, there are no bats. Their absence from the sewers proves extremely curious. A wet, dark, enclosed place underground seems like the closest thing to caves that bats might find in a large city like Gotham—and thus a place where one would expect to find them.

Bats are mostly absent within this movie because of the de-naturalizing of the body of the cyborg escaping a relationship with companion species. Instead, Batman surrounds himself in vaunted mansion ceilings blocking out everybody except Alfred. This isolation makes him weak and without the full powers of his body or his companion species to confront Bane. Instead, Wayne draws on a particular privilege deriving from his wealth and company. He demonstrates a type of eco-abilism to employ his "enabling desires" to direct "the relationship between" himself and his environment by regenerating his body with a mechanical exoskeleton knee and other devices (Wolbring 2012, 80). This augmentation, though, proves insufficient in beating the cyborg Bane who possesses a different relation to his technology than Wayne. Technology holds the frailty of Bane's body intact in a way that makes it less aged and precarious than Wayne.

Furthermore, Batman draws increasingly on technology but forgets its deep constitution with the natural world of things like bats. When Bane says that he was born in the dark and Batman merely adopted it, he is asserting the absence of the natural world and companion species. The bats left Batman in the process of turning the physical and social body into the artificial through the use of Wayne enterprise defense products. Bane beats Batman not because of his youthful strength, but because he possesses a better grasp on the ecology of companion species. He understands that Batman's effort to ethically relate to bats has failed because of its instrumental foundations. The original basis of such control was a "sado-humanist and techno-capitalist projects which have jointly normalized the exploitative instrumentalization (and commodification) of nonhumans"; in its current form, the animal manipulation seeks "(the fantasy of) our ingenuity and omnipotence reflected back to us through their 'improved' bodies" (Weisberg 2009, 30). Bane's critique remains pointed at the instrumental rationality Batman imposes upon his companion creatures in turning them into merely a means to an end. This ultimately creates an "anthropocentric logic of mastery over nonhuman human others by naturalizing unequal instrumental relations between species—that is, relations in which humans are the users and nonhumans are the used" (Weisberg 2009, 28). From Bane's perspective, Batman is ultimately an anthropocentric narcissist.

Bane deploys this narcissistic critique against Bruce Wayne's leisure. By making the claim about adopting the dark, Bane is also accusing the superhero of taking up the hobby of the dark, not placing it at the center of his being, but utilizing economic institutions to advance space for his own leisure while denying it to others that spend their time working (Veblen 2005). Batman can shift into his alter ego of a millionaire playboy on a whim, whenever he decides it works to his benefit or desire. For unrequited love, Wayne never fully embraces the role of the playboy in *The Dark Knight Rises* (2012). Batman, though, can transform into Bruce Wayne. Bane can never shift into an alter ego or another way of being. He resents the social and economic fluidity of Wayne—a cyborg that can adapt to the environment—and challenges it by refusing to stand on pretexts of calling Bruce Wayne by his superhero name. In addition, anti-capitalism appears throughout various actions Bane takes against other wealthy elites (Schimmelpfennig 2017). When Daggett expresses his frustration with Bane's schemes to help him capture control of the Wayne Enterprises Board of Directors and implies that the money spent on all of Bane's evil schemes have been wasted, Bane reminds the businessman that his money possesses no power over him. His point is that the function of wage slavery—where the worker has sold their labor for access to life sustaining resources that the capitalist possesses—has never existed for him (Marx 1990, 769). He does not have to sell his labor to Daggett for sustenance, as the wage has no power over him, nor do the physical threats of capitalists like Daggett. Furthermore, when Bane speaks to the people of Gotham, he highlights their growing economic disparity and asks the working class to free the prisoners at Blackgate prison held without trial (Russell 2016, 176).

This form of anti-capitalism operates much more explicitly than with the villain in *The Dark Knight* (2008). Throughout the film, the Joker demonstrates the core of his psyche untouched by the profit motive. When Gotham's mobsters present him with a giant stack of cash for seemingly killing Batman, he sets the pile on fire. In trying to make sense of the Joker, Batman consults his butler. Alfred must tell him about a bandit in the forests of Burma. The bandit stole the gems only to give them away to poor children, showing that while some people commit destruction for its own sake others pursue some rational goal. The Joker, in this sense, uses chaos "to undermine any faith in the system, its rules, or its heroes" (Lewis 2009). He reinforces this chaos by suggesting the interdependence between good and evil: Joker's evil must be placed against Batman's good because he believes that the former must find its purpose against the latter. In this way, the Joker challenges the existence of capitalism but ultimately wants to transcend it through a greater, more timeless struggle. Bane, on the other hand, wants to mobilize anti-capitalism to support the revenge scheme of a companion species hidden from the audience's view (Fradley 2013, 19). Prior to being a cyborg, he was the protector species of a small girl in the same way a child might possess a guard dog to protect the house from intruders. After becoming a cyborg, he advances the clandestine revenge scheme of helping Talia al Ghul to destroy Gotham and kill Batman. His anti-capitalist rhetoric, in this sense, is only a facade. Bane does not want to advance the freedom of the working class, but the chaos that would ultimately culminate in the city's destruction. The city, as does capital, avoids being destroyed by Bane.

Capital in its formal and informal forms lurches on in spite of evil. The informal economy means the growth of the household as the logic for economics, "whereby jobs are being redefined as female and feminized," and "factory, home, and market exist on a new scale" (Haraway 1991, 166). While the formal economy retracts, corporations turn away from their Fordist economic ideology of social safety nets, public education, and safe working conditions (Hirsch 1991). Corporations turn toward networks of subcontractors to efficiently maximize profits (Haraway 1991, 169). Subcontracting of work means that the workplace shifts into the home and a larger number of smaller workplaces, leaving few places for concentrations of workers (Jessop 1992). Externalization means that a range of costs, once covered by corporations, are pushed out into the public and/or the government (Mies 1998, 110). This disorganization requires corporations to engage in networking of social organizations and resources, and "high tech repressive apparatuses ranging from entertainment to survival and disappearance" to hold together their profitability (Haraway 1991, 169). Disappearance requires the concentration of a large security apparatus of police, military, weapons manufacturing, intelligence gathering—a very formal and violent aspect of the economy—part of the government and sublimated to private corporations (Steinmetz 2003, 338). This concentration is a military industrial complex, a "military metaphysics" that comprises an "intricate and vast web of political, bureaucratic, social and international, as well as economic, institutions and processes" across "corporate profit-driven industries, research institutions and domestic systems of employment, production and consumption" (Salter 2015, 14). This institutional web advances the development and profitability of military weapons, the valorization of the military, and the largess of capitalism (Mills 2000). This draws on cheaper, less regulated, sites of unregulated labor and nonhuman bodies through the prison industrial complex and the animal industrial complex (McDonald 2015; Nocella, Salter, and Bentley 2013).

The informal economy envelops the cyborg. The kennel, similarly, houses the companion species in physical space and materialist economic practices. It is the site of domestication and training of humans and their animals as well as death, domination, abuse, and emotional management (Taylor 2010). Domestication is an "emergent process of cohabitating involving agencies of many sorts and stories that don't lend themselves to stories of the fall" (Haraway 2003, 30). These agencies come through people, social structures, economic practices, physical environment, and animals. The process of domestication ties animals and humans together that projects an outcome without preconceived ends that can be ugly, bestial, beautiful, or a combination of all three. It also exists within a complex web of material economic relations that shift and drag the construction of subjects, agents, and social structures throughout different epochs—creating differential animal-human relations under different time periods. In other words, because the informal economy depends on taking elements of the private sphere and making them prevalent throughout the public sector engaging in "housewification," Batman depends on publicizing private material conditions of bats for the public (Mies 1998, 100–110). Gotham must be turned into series of caves that bats and Batman may operate within to maximize their comfort. Batman's success of defeating criminals large and small depends on creating the space upon which he can master and affirm the precariousness of other's existence within a set of spatial logics. Gotham operates as a home for this cyborg known as Batman. Gotham remains Batman's kennel. As Bruce Wayne and Batman remain shaped by bats and their habitats, they must recreate the physical presence of darkness and moistness—an urban space that blurs the boundaries between open and closed at the point of a dark horizon.

One of Batman's central talents is the ability to direct physical space and fear against injustice. The darkness and dampness of the cage must feel at home for Bruce Wayne, as well as the capitalist social relations. As a dark cave and an open space in pitch black might possess analogous logic, the creation of bat habitat that Batman can control autonomously suggests the seeming quandary of agency. Wayne's position in the economy grants him great freedom to purchase and travel in relative proportion to others, but there are some limits that Wayne and Batman must possess in their roles as capitalist and vigilante. This limit seemingly reveals itself in *The Dark Knight Rises*: In losing the fight to Bane in *The Dark Knight Rises* (2012) Wayne travels to a physical space—of some prison in an older part of the world—that seems to offer a great space for Batman's or Wayne's powers. This space, a cave at the bottom of the well, parallels the well scene in *Batman Begins* (2005). He cannot buy or fight his way out of this situation, but then he does find himself figuring out how to master this particular cave and granting the prisoners an escape rope. Like any successful capitalist, he possesses the rare agency to manipulate and redirect physical space (Lefebvre 1991).

Like Haraway's kennel where dogs and their owners can compete with each other to become more doggish, Wayne tries to structure much of the space around him, but his actions do not fall fully under his own control or intentions. As one creates social institutions, the very space starts to shape and cultivate the individual with unintended consequences that blur the line of cause and effect. Wayne is like a bat evolving the capacity to properly manipulate his environment like an effective patriarch that micro-manages the technical and natural worlds (Schimmelpfennig 2017). At the same time, the capitalist relations juxtapose the opulence of wealth and the destitution of poverty within Gotham. The power of one man's decision to mothball the largest research and development project at Wayne Enterprises implies the slow receding of jobs and other corporate benefits like charity and profit. One can only imagine the economic devices that Gothamites are left to in the decline of the economy and the difficulty of responding efficiently and efficaciously to these larger structures. Thus, *The Dark Knight Rises* (2012) introduces us to the orphan-turned-cop Blake and other orphans that come into being because of economic circumstances. At a certain age, their existence depends on working in an informal, illegal economy in the sewers for Bane, which renders their lives precarious and sometimes nonexistent. Sewers are human-made caves that exceed the violent talent of Batman who can easily defeat minor henchmen but not the arch villain Bane in this space.

While Bane may claim that Batman has only adopted the dark, the films reveal how deeply entrenched darkness and caves are for Batman. The series of bat caves—at Wayne Manor and the dark streets of Gotham—are thoroughly capitalists and paternalistic, but not entirely atomistic. The rhetoric and belief of individuals within Gotham come off as atomistic because people believe that corporate charitable giving by a single wealthy individual or a vigilante can save Gotham if sufficiently willed so (Dittmer 2007; Locke 2005). Even Batman's teacher Ra's al Ghul, manifesting himself as his alter ego Ducard, must beat into him the lesson that "the will is everything" regardless of training, ability, or means. This ideology mystifies the material economic conditions that make possible Batman, Bruce Wayne, the Wayne family, Wayne Enterprises, the city of Gotham, and the endless construction of bat caves possible—the formation of an informal economy that makes some individuals economically and physically precarious, while others become seemingly economically and physically invincible. Bane confronts this precariousness when he takes over the city and disrupts capitalist relations by repossessing property, cutting off the city from the rest of the world, and allowing an anti-capitalist court. The people's court has already determined the injustice of capitalism and is merely dishing out punishments accordingly (as Dr. Jonathan Crane reminds us in his role as a judge). Batman loses a few fights, but eventually triumphs. Wayne goes bankrupt, but he gets to keep his house and his social status and eventually gets to live a completely different cosmopolitan life in Europe with his girlfriend Selina.

The trilogy's ending not only suggests an important role of producing bat cave habitat, but also placing that capability into a few elites within the social structure. While Wayne as a successful capitalist may believe he is a completely autonomous being, a career of creating bat caves takes its toll on Wayne who can never fully divorce himself from it. As Alfred tells him in *The Dark Knight Rises* (2012), the death of Wayne's one true love and childhood friend Rachel turned him into a recluse. As such, he no longer takes on the role of Batman and defers crime-fighting to the police department that he financially supports as wealthy patron, but remains unresponsive to the police's indifference to civil rights of accused criminals and its deleterious impacts. The caves define him, but demonstrate a certain agency of capitalist relations to entrap their subjects. Wayne can leave the confines of bat caves but then spends his nights recreating their physical space. He can take his family company out of the logic of the profit motive, but he cannot escape the brutal efficiency of capitalism, just as the worker cannot escape the brutal logic of the capitalist's decisions imposed in the workplace and upon the economy.

The military industrial complex plays an important role in these films (Christensen 2002; Toh 2010). Wayne Enterprises produces dangerous weapons—that if they fell into the "wrong" hands might greatly harm the world. The theme of proper possession plays out with the villains Bane and Ra's al Ghul seizing dangerous weapons created by Wayne Enterprises. The microwave gun plays a central role in the scheme to tear apart Gotham through hallucinogenic gas in *Batman Begins* (2005). The ability for the League of Shadows to maintain military control over Gotham depends on their seizure of the corporate arsenal consolidated by Fox in *The Dark Knight Rises* (2012). Both films demonstrate a similar theme that reinforces the utility of weapons systems in the right hands—the state—and their danger in the wrong hands—non-state violent actors (or terrorists). The military industrial complex becomes more ubiquitous when one considers the larger schemes of Wayne Enterprise CEO William Earle to focus the company on military contracts in *Batman Begins* (2005). Seemingly a pivot to the military industrial complex, this only demonstrates its ubiquity. Fox's innovations were not created for Batman, but to make a profit in advancing the military capacities of the nation-state. Batman, in this sense, celebrates the "hard body" and the military industrial complex by turning it into a cause of superhero technology (Toh 2010, 137).

Faced with a parallel situation, Bane's schemes depend on Daggett's money, and thus the business of domestic construction and illegal arms trade and resource extraction. Daggett, as the villain, has his business focused on mass destruction and death vilified, unlike Wayne Enterprises. The exact nature of Daggett's customers and competitors eludes us. We know that the business draws upon the illicit arms trade. In trying to create an asymmetrical advantage, other states start to feel insecure and buildup their arms, eliciting an arms race where no one feels more secure in demonstrating the tragic logic of the security dilemma (Jervis 1978). States may feel less secure with more arms, but corporations and other actors within the military industrial complex will be enriched and invigorated. On another note, the technological developments of Bane's body reveal a larger set of social institutions. *The Dark Knight Rises* (2012) reveals that the prison doctor produced the apparatus that

Bane employs to manage his pain—deriving from being assaulted in prison. The doctor's abilities point toward a thriving set of profit-driven institutions, a prison industrial complex, that advances the growth of prisons as a solution to social problems and creates a permanent underclass of workers paid below subsistence wages (McDonald 2015). The labor that inmates perform illicitly and legally, to displace free laborers, remains out of view.

The illicit economy of prostitutes, operating as a feminist constitutive other to the masculine war machine, is less elusive than prison labor (Enloe 2014). The audience learns of these economic activities through the petty thievery of Selina Kyle and her friend Jen. The latter reveals the blurred boundaries between thievery and prostitution, utilizing the illusion of the latter to engage in the former. Kyle reveals how workers can seamlessly circulate through both the formal economy as waiters and the informal economy as thieves. The formal and informal depend on the creation of wealth created by the military industrial complex and the prison industrial complex. The Wayne Foundation feeds money from his industry back into the police and prisons. The cyborgs possess different consciousness of these circulations: Batman seems somewhat oblivious except in his general distrust of all people other than Alfred that allows him to catch Kyle stealing his mother's pearl neck-lace, Bane utilizes this circulation to draw in the working class to serve the League of Shadows. Except for Kyle, the type of workers Bane employs in his illicit economy are male.

The most visible and highly valorized aspect of the community, though, remains the general will. It creates a common and equal moral standing, identity, and agency for all beings within the community. This allows people to come together to rationally deliberate on and ultimately decide laws for all members of the community, Rousseau opens the door for animal community members through animal cruelty. Animal violence acts as a symptom for other types of violence and inequalities that might exist within society among humans (Wolloch 2008). A non-hierarchical community is much less likely to lash violently against those outside of its boundaries. In this consideration for animal cruelty, Rousseau opens up the space for moral consideration that animals should be treated in a particular way and should be considered within the broader notion of community (Schill 2014). In Rousseau's separation between natural and artificial inequalities—whereby the latter are produced socially and are thus unjustified—provides space of interspecies communi-ties in a type of "zoopolis" where "animals are recognized not just as sentient individuals, but as members of political communities" (Kymlicka and Don-aldson 2014, 132). There are inequalities between humans and animals in the way they speak, but both species possess a sociality and can relate to each other, a type of enabling space that creates "participatory structures" (Lloro-Bidart 2015, 100). The agency comes through the pedagogical function of companion species to advance particular points of view through more primal human perceptions and associations. This makes the formation of general laws—that composite the general will and require that all citizens come together—into a difficult act, but an ontologically possible one. As cyborgs are part of a queer family of species, they might also possess moral standing and agency.

At a deeper level, though, Batman utilizes his cyborg body and bat companion species to advance the possibility of community. The speech presented by Batman to the community—to help create and constitute it, as well as to fill it with general laws that apply to all—seems greatly divorced from voice and words. His actions of delivering criminals to justice and ending their physical and mental terror upon the city of Gotham address the community. Batman, like bats, engages in a type of propaganda by deed, whereby the action sends a message counter to and in confrontation with the hegemonic ideology of the era. It comes not with an explanation, but speaks for itself as a type of intervention in the feedback loop of capitalism, akin to how people can listen to animals through the signals that pollution offers to the polity about their conditions and desires (Dryzek 1995). If people will not listen to the socio-economic signals of the decay of social institutions and depravity of human bodies, then heroic acts will be brought forth. Batman's violence speaks against the breakdown of the community and for the construction of a general will to bind the entire community. Much as anarchist violence against the state spoke against the brutal oppression of capitalism and opened the space for another notion of social relations and political being (Linse 1982). Batman's violence speaks against depravity and oppression in Gotham to help form a general will. His efforts are unsuccessful because of the destruction of capitalism that has enabled and produced these conditions. The existence of the informal capitalist economy reduces the likelihood of forming the general will because of the economic deprivations upon Gotham that reduce the ability for citizens to fully consider their role in the community because work overtakes their time and cognitive capacities. The general will never quite materializes, but Batman still aims for a fragile semblance of a community.

This defense becomes apparent in a scene that brings together the logic of companion species and cyborgs. Bats utilize sonar to map their environment. Cyborgs utilize the singularity of computer code to collapse differential physical manifestations throughout the world into singularity (Nehaniv 1997). To defeat the Joker in *The Dark Knight* (2008), Batman up-scales the cell phone mapping technology developed by Fox for a singular device that helps him catch the money-laundering Hong Kong accountant. Fox is shocked by this clear violation of the public's privacy, and Batman promises that after capturing the Joker he will destroy the device. This particular trick turns all of the residents within Gotham into cyborg companion species that blurs the line between themselves and their phones, humans and bats.

The action remains an involuntary and clandestine imposition upon the public for their benefit, as much as it remains a short suspension of liberal regime of rights in order to save it and a type of statecraft from below whereby citizens enact the violence of and suspend the juridical order of the state (Schmitt 1985; Doty 2003). After capturing the Joker, Batman suspends his community of cyborg companion species with only two people knowing. In this sense, his sonar technique is not a type of propaganda by deed, as the public remains ignorant of the existence of this language. His trick, though, shows how bodies can circulate through and out of the military industrial complex without even knowing. At its roots, creating this city-level sonar remains a trick of coding. All of the cell phones in the city must transmit information back to a computer that can interpret it as a single language in contrast to the range of different people and landscapes that it maps. All of the code transforms everything in the city into information to be manipulated by Batman, and thus reveals his asymmetrical relation to the military industrial complex. Batman objectifies the people of Gotham, and takes away their agency. This should not make Batman a nemesis of community, but demonstrate the difficulty of constructing a meaningful community morality.

What, then, is the moral of this story about cyborgs and companion species in the Dark Knight movie series? My point is that Batman exists as a cyborg improving his body with technology, while bats are the companion species that possess agency to drive the plot forward but also help advance the growth of Bruce Wayne into Batman. Bats play a pedagogical role for Wayne and a moral role for the community. Wayne tries to recreate the bat cave throughout Gotham. The space of Gotham also brutally enforces the logic of the informal economy, the habitat of the cyborg, and places Batman in a structural economic advantage over others, who are prey to his economic whims as the head of Wayne Enterprises. The habitat of caves and the informal economy shape Batman and Bruce Wayne through techniques that are beyond his control. While Wayne wills Batman into existence to bring justice to Gotham and improve conditions of the city, he ultimately fails in creating the general will within Gotham because of the continuing economic disparities. This situation is not so dissimilar from reality and is precisely why cultural studies are so important in presenting alternative possibilities to how our world operates today.

My reading of Batman operates as a type of metaplasm, a "change in word by adding, omitting, inverting, or transposing its letter" (Haraway 2003, 20). It is also a "myth system waiting to become a political language to ground one way of looking at science and technology" and a blasphemy against orthodoxy of feminism (Haraway 1991, 181; 149). Haraway's reading heuristic may undermine her authorial intent of these concepts by inviting non-orthodox and non-literal readings. As such, we may re-assemble her framework in a way that addresses concerns about technological optimism and anthropocentrism at the center of her work to become the heretic at the site of inter-theoretical translations between CAS and her own notion of feminism. In this essay, Haraway moves away from "the side of the victors in the sado-humanist project of domination" (Weisberg 2009, 60). This causes a shift toward the side of tricksters that display their "charisma and intelligence" that bring about ambivalent responses (Pacini-Ketchabaw and Nxumalo 2015, 164). Her conceptual architecture, then, may "openly avow its explicit ethical and practical commitment to the freedom of well-being of all animals and to a flourishing planet" (Best 2009, 12).

WORKS CITED

Best, Steven. 2009. "The rise of Critical Animal Studies: Putting theory into action and animal liberation into higher education." *Journal for Critical Animal Studies* 7(1): 9–52.

Bordoloi, Mridul. 2012. "Re-packaging Disaster Post 9/11 and Christopher Nolan's: The Dark Knight Trilogy." *Journal of Creative Communications* 7(1–2): 87–100.

Braidotti, Rosi. 2006. "Posthuman, all too human: Towards a new process ontology." *Theory, culture & society* 23(7–8): 197–208.

Chagani, Fayaz. 2014. "Critical political ecology and the seductions of posthumanism." *Journal of Political Ecology* 21: 424–436.

Christensen, Jerome. 2002. "The Time Warner Conspiracy: JFK, Batman, and the Manager Theory of Hollywood Film." *Critical Inquiry* 28(3): 591–617.

D'Arcy, Stephen. 2007. "Deliberative democracy, direct action, and animal advocacy." *Journal for Critical Animal Studies* 5(2): 1–16.

Dittmer, Jason. 2007. "The tyranny of the serial: Popular geopolitics, the nation, and comic book discourse." *Antipode* 39(2): 247–268.

Dryzek, John S. 1995. "Political and ecological communication." *Environmental Politics* 4(4): 13–30.

Enloe, Cynthia. 2014. *Bananas, Beaches and Bases: Making Feminist Sense of International Politics.* Berkeley, CA: University of California Press.

Fradley, Martin. 2013. "What do you Believe In? Film scholarship and the Cultural politics of the dark Knight Franchise." *Film Quarterly* 66(3): 15–27.

Haraway, Donna. 1991. "Cyborg Manifesto: Science, Technology, and Socialist-Feminism in the Late Twentieth Century." In *Simians, Cyborgs and women: The reinvention of nature,* 149–181. New York: Routledge.

———. 2003. *The companion species manifesto: Dogs, people, and significant otherness. Vol. 1.* Chicago, IL: Prickly Paradigm Press.

Hassler-Forest, Dan. 2015. "Of Iron Men and Green Monsters: Superheroes and Posthumanism." In *The Palgrave Handbook of Posthumanism in Film and Television,* edited by Michael Hauskeller, Curtis D. Carbonell, Thomas D. Philbeck. 66–76. London, UK: Palgrave Macmillan UK.

Havercroft, Jonathan. 2011. *Captives of Sovereignty*. Cambridge, UK: Cambridge University Press.

Hirsch, Joachim. 1991. "From the Fordist to the post-Fordist state." In *The Politics of Flexibility: Restructuring State and Industry in Britain, Germany and Scandinavia*, edited by Bob Jessop and Hans Kastendiek. Cheltenham, UK: Edward Elgar Pub.

Jervis, Robert. 1978. "Cooperation under the security dilemma." *World Politics* 30(2): 167–214.

Jessop, Bob. 1992. "Post-Fordism and Flexible Specialisation: Incommensurable, contradictory, complementary, or just plain different perspectives?" In *Regional Development and Contemporary Industrial Response: Extending Flexible Specialisation*, edited by H. Ernste H. and Meier V. John Wiley. Redfern, Australia Australia Ltd.

Kymlicka, Will, and Sue Donaldson. 2014. "Animal Rights, Multiculturalism, and the Left." *Journal of Social Philosophy* 45(1): 116–135.

Lefebvre, Henri. 1991. *The Production of Space. Vol. 142*. Oxford, UK: Blackwell.

Lewis, Randolph. 2009. "The dark knight of American empire." *Jump Cut 51*.

Lloro-Bidart, Teresa. 2015. "Culture as Ability: Organizing Enabling Educative Spaces for Humans and Animals." *Canadian Journal of Environmental Education* 20: 92–107.

Locke, Simon. 2005. "Fantastically reasonable: Ambivalence in the representation of science and technology in super-hero comics." *Public Understanding of Science* 14(1): 25–46.

Marx, Karl. 1990. *Capital, Volume I*. Translator Ben Fowkes. New York: Penguin Classics.

McDonald, CeCe. 2015 *Captive Genders: Trans Embodiment and the Prison Industrial Complex*. Oakland, CA: AK Press.

Mies, Maria. 1998. *Patriarchy and Accumulation on a World Scale: Women in the International Division of Labour*. New York: Palgrave Macmillan.

Mills, C. Wright. 2000. *The Power Elite. Vol. 20*. Oxford, UK: Oxford University Press.

Nehaniv, C. Lev. 1997. "Algebraic models for understanding: coordinate systems and cognitive empowerment.'" In *Cognitive Technology: Humanizing the Information Age*. Second International Conference, 147–162. Los Alamitos, CA: Institute of Electrical and Electronic Engineering (IEEE) Computer Society Press, 1997.

Nibert, David. 2013. *Animal Oppression and Human Violence: Domesecration, Capitalism, and Global Conflict*. New York: Columbia University Press.

Nocella II, Anthony J., Colin Salter, and Judy KC Bentley. 2013. *Animals and War: Confronting the Military-Animal Industrial Complex*. New York: Lexington Books.

Pacini-Ketchabaw, Veronica and Fikile Nxumalo. 2015. "Unruly raccoons and troubled educators: Nature/culture divides in a childcare centre." *Environmental Humanities* 7(1): 151–168.

Pedersen, Helena, and Vasile Stanescu. 2014. "Future directions of Critical Animal Studies." In *The Rise of Critical Animal Studies, from the margins to the center*, editors Nik Taylor and Richard Twine, 262–275. New York: Routledge.

Rousseau, Jean Jacques. *On the Social Contract: With Geneva Manuscript and Political Economy*. New York: Macmillan, 1978.

———. "Discourse on this Question: Which Is the Virtue Most Necessary for a Hero and Which Are the Heroes Who Lack This Virtue?" *Collected Writings of Rousseau Volume 4*, edited by Roger D. Masters and Christopher Kelly. Hanover, New Hampshire: Dartmouth College Press, 1994.

Russell, Patrick Kent. 2016. "Christopher Nolan's The Dark Knight Trilogy as a Noir View of American Social Tensions." *Interdisciplinary Humanities* 33(1): 171–186.

Salter, Colin. 2015. "Animals and War: Anthropocentrism and Technoscience." *NanoEthics* 9(1): 11.

Schill, Parker. 2015. "Animals within the Rousseauian Republic." *The Journal for Critical Animal Studies* 13(1): 6–32.

Schimmelpfennig, Annette. 2017. "Capitalism and Schizophrenia in Gotham City-The Fragile Masculinities of Christopher Nolan's *The Dark Knight* Trilogy." *Gender Forum* 62: 3–20.

Schmitt, Carl. 1985. *Political Theology: Four Chapters on the Concept of Sovereignty*. Chicago, IL: University of Chicago Press.

Smith, Adam. 2010. *The Theory of Moral Sentiments*. London: Penguin.

Steinmetz, George. 2003. "The state of emergency and the revival of American imperialism: Toward an authoritarian post-Fordism." *Public Culture* 15(2): 323–345.

Taylor, Aaron. 2007. "'He's Gotta Be Strong, and He's Gotta Be Fast, and He's Gotta Be Larger than Life:' Investigating the Engendered Superhero Body." *The Journal of Popular Culture* 40(2): 344–360.

Toh, Justine. 2010. "The Tools and Toys of (the) War (on Terror): consumer Desire, military Fetish, and regime change in Batman Begins." *Reframing* 9(11): 127–139.

Veblen, Thorstein. 2005. *The Theory of the Leisure Class; An Economic Study of Institutions*. Delhi, India: Aakar Books.

Wanzo, Rebecca. 2009. "The superhero: Meditations on surveillance, salvation, and desire." *Communication and Critical/Cultural Studies* 6(1): 93–97.

Weisberg, Zipporah. 2009. "The broken promises of monsters: Haraway, animals and the humanist legacy." *Journal for Critical Animal Studies* 7(2): 22–62.

Winterhalter, Benjamin. 2015. "The Politics of the Inner: Why the Dark Knight Rises is Not a Conservative Allegory." *The Journal of Popular Culture* 48(5): 1030–1047.

Wolbring, Gregor. 2012. "Expanding ableism: Taking down the ghettoization of impact of disability studies scholars." *Societies* 2(3): 75–83.

Wolloch, Nathaniel. 2008. "Rousseau and the Love of Animals." *Philosophy and Literature* 32(2): 293–302.

Chapter 10

Ain't No Thing Like Me, Except Me

Rocket Raccoon, Cyborg Queerness, and Toxic Masculinity

Sean Parson

"Ain't no thing like me, except me!" said the smiling and smug CGI raccoon in the surprising 2014 hit *Guardians of the Galaxy*. Rocket, a cyborg raccoon voiced by Bradley Cooper, is a cyborg raccoon that was pieced together through medical and scientific experiments. "Well, I didn't ask to get made! I didn't ask to be torn apart and put back together over and over and turned into some little monster!" cries the reluctant hero, drunken, in an intergalactic bar later in the film. The character is much more complex than is often discussed and pieces together a range of different topics and themes that are central to a Critical Animal Studies (CAS) analysis of superheroes and culture. Rocket ties together vivisection, toughness, vulnerability, toxic masculinity, interspecies relationships, and technology.

The film, which tells the origin of a group of galactic anti-heroes fighting to save the universe from a deranged religious zealot has earned nearly 800 million dollars globally, while the sequel, *Guardians of the Galaxy 2* (2017), has outperformed the original in the box office (Box Office Mojo 2014; 2017). Both films have also been critical successes; with the first *Guardians* film rated at 91% on Rottentomatoes.com and the sequel at 81% (Rotten Tomatoes 2014; 2017). While critics and audiences alike have enjoyed the film, there has been little in-depth analysis into the political and social dimensions of the film. In this chapter, I centralize critical animal studies, cyborg feminism, and toxic masculinity in my analysis. I argue, following the work in cyborg and critical animal studies, that Rocket Raccoon is at core a deeply queer figure—queering the lines between natural/artificial, able/disabled, human/nonhuman—but is not depicted or understood as a queer figure because of the use of toxic masculine tropes. Toxic masculinity, as I use it in this chapter is a form of masculinity that aggressively reacts to any perceived threat to itself and that uses misogyny and homophobia as a defense mechanism. In the case of Rocket Raccoon toxic masculinity is used as a way of projecting and defending against charges of queerness.

SUPERHERO FILMS AND SOCIAL COMMENTARY

Much like any cultural product in a society, films provide valuable insight into the inner workings of a political culture, and in an era in which mass culture was married by the fear of terrorism, the superhero has protected the cultural conscious. Stuart Hall in his short piece "encoding and decoding" argued that cultural productions—film, television, and music—are expressions of different political and cultural entities attempting to forge a hegemonic order (Hall 2007, 94–95). This means that the text of the film is encoded, and embedded with political and social meaning. This meaning can, according to Hall, be decoded in a way that allows scholars to explore the symbolic meaning encoded within the culture (2007, 93–95). Similarly Fredric Jameson argues that text and stories have symbolic and deep-seated psycho-political meaning that are part of the project of culture—stories, movies, and the like are not just entertainment but an attempt to structure and develop a specific narrative about how the world works, or ought to work (1994, 2007). In both Hall and Jameson, and the field of cultural studies as a whole, these encoded meanings provide political insight into the dominant social institutions of society.

Within comic studies Matthew Costello's *Secret Identity Crises* particularly and Jason Dittmer's book *Captain American and the Nationalist Superheroes* both decode comics and explore the way that they reproduce aspects of the American hegemonic order (2009; 2013). In Costello's case, comics in the 1960s provided a defense of the "cold war consensus" that emerged between liberals and conservatives, within the United States, around anti-communism (2009). Characters like Iron Man, Captain America, and Nick Fury all were used to contrast the good (United States) against the evil (Soviet) threat, portraying the enemy as weak, unhappy, and morally debased (Costello 2009). Similarly, Dittmer argues that comics reinforce a liberal conception of international relations by having a nationalist superhero representing nearly every country on earth (2013). A figure like Captain America, who uses a shield as his primary weapon, also represents how Americans view their own foreign policy. The United States is a reluctant hero, defending through offense (Dittmer 2013).

Alaniz takes a different approach in *Death, Disability, and the Superhero* and uses superhero narratives to engage with cultural anxieties and tensions around ability and disability (2014). Exploring the ways in which figures, such as the Thing and Daredevil, for instance, engage with aspects of disability and disfigurement, Alaniz provides a lens to explore the themes that emerge from blindness and disfigurement in society (2014). Similar to Alaniz, Fawaz in *The New Mutants* looks to the ways that comics have not only reinforced social norms but also opened up spaces for counter-narratives and stories of inclusion and democracy (2016). Peppered throughout the book Fawaz argues that the mutant's in the X-Men world serve as a metaphor for social outcasts and oppressed people (2016). As such the X-Men comics have historically played with issues related to the marginalized and have thus provided a space for non-white, queer, and female readers to find a cultural home in American society as well as a place to engage and develop a democratic counter public (Fawaz 2016). The stories and tensions that arise in X-Men are therefore about tensions that exist within our dominant society between civil rights, gay rights, feminist concerns and struggles against the status-quo and the politics of hatred (Fawaz 2016).

Superheroes are embedded within a complex web of meanings, and different characters tap into different aspects of that web, depending on the context and political usage (Nama 2011; Cocca 2016; Stevens 2015). They are also ways for us to engage with, and explore, our own anxieties and fears (Rogin 1988). The villain of comics often represents things our culture fears, and the struggle between heroes and villains becomes part of a collective and cultural solution to vexing problems (Deis 2013). Since 9/11 terrorism has been the primary fear expressed by the superhero genre. For instance, the first *Avengers* (2012) film has an alien race flying their UFO war machines into New York City buildings, as an overt node to 9/11. In both *Batman Begins* (2005) and *Batman: The Dark Knight* (2008) the main villains—Ra's al Ghul and the Joker respectively—terrorize Gotham via elaborate plots to break down social order. In addition, *Iron Man 3* (2013) focuses the entire story around a global network of terrorists organized by the Mandarin, which threatens the political stability of the entire planet. But terrorism is not the only concern that superhero stories and films can explore with our cultural anxiety around.

DECODING GUARDIANS OF THE GALAXY

Martin Barker in describing the neglect of academic research on comics contends that the public often views comics as both escapist fun and socially dangerous, for what social and cultural influence they have. In describing this he writes that "we might summarize these standard claims as follows: comics ought to be harmless fun, but aren't" (Barker 1989). By viewing comics as "low culture" it has often meant that cultural critics have ignored the genre and, without this in-depth analysis and critique, the ideological underpinning of the superhero genre is not decoded and there is no space for critical engagement with the medium. Decoding and deconstructing a film opens up space for the audience and the readers to critically engage with the concepts and ideas embedded within the cultural production. A film like *Guardians of the Galaxy* (2014) especially needs to be deconstructed since the politics of the film are often ignored or unstated.

That said, the few analyses have often noted the overall conservative and sexist aspects of the film. Most notably, the main villain—Ronan—can be read as a Muslim terrorist, opening up a range of conservative and reactionary readings of the film. Lee Pace, the actor who plays the main villain Ronan, in an interview said that to him the character was "like Osama bin Laden—he's like a religious fanatic" and that he attempted to model his acting for the character on the "former terrorist leader" (Comicbookmovies. com 2014). Linking this terrorist trope to a broader political perspective, one blogger noted:

> It doesn't take much unpacking to read this as an allegory for American exceptionalism and the War on Terror, especially since the film's primary bad guy— Ronan—is designed to sound like a Muslim radical. In his opening scene, he lays out his motivations: the universe has been corrupted by bad morals, and the only way to save the sinners is to destroy them. Sounds like an argument against the West by Al Qaeda or ISIS to me. (Gittell 2014)

By making the main villain a religious zealot and terrorist, who plans to destroy the planet by flying his aircraft into the capital city, the makers of the film clearly intended to link the film to 9/11, thereby justifying the ensuing "war on terror" as a legit approach to save lives form barbarous monsters.

The clear connection between Ronan and the Muslim terrorist trope was not lost on conservative columnists either. Mythos Holt, writing for the conservative *The Daily Caller* claimed that the film symbolizes the struggle between Israel and Palestine. In making this argument Holt writes, "Despite Pace's likening of his character to Osama bin Laden, a far more plausible (and topical) comparison presents itself—namely, that Ronan the Accuser is one of the great satiric representations of the terrorist organization Hamas ever put on film" (Holt 2014). In Holt's reading, Ronan represents Islamic extremism, more specifically the Palestinian Islamic political organization Hamas. Xandar a peaceful and liberal world stands in for the nation of Israeli. Lastly, the Guardians—led by the American Peter Quill—function as the American-led international world working to stop a potential genocide from Ronan. From this reading *Guardians of the Galaxy* (2014) reinforces and defends the American foreign policy position around the "war on terror" in much the same way that early Iron Man and Captain America comics worked to legitimate the "cold war consensus" of anti-communism in the 1960s (Costello 2009).

The film has also been analyzed for its gender politics. Critics have noted that James Gunn, the director, has a history of posting and publishing sexist blog content, including one titled "50 Superheroes you want to have sex with," where he wrote, "For the second year in a row, Princess Diana is the big winner. It seems like many guys out there are hoping she'll lasso their penises and make them tell the truth—which is that they want to be inside of Princess Diana!" Gunn sexualized a host of female characters in the blog post—including a racist commentary about Storm and a mocking of statutory rape and pedophilia in a post about X-23, a fifteen-year-old clone of Wolverine (Shaw-Williams 2012). Feminist comic critics and fans have argued that his history of sexualizing characters impacts the *Guardians of the Galaxy* (2014) as most of female characters in the film are disposable (Baker-Whitelaw 2014). Further still, Gamora's character is nearly always filmed using the male gaze—a film technique that turns female characters bodies into sexual objects for male voyeurism—focusing on her butt, legs, and tight clothing (Ross 2014). That said *Guardians of the Galaxy* (2014) is one of the few superhero films to pass the Bechtel test and was generally popular with female moviegoers as around 44% of moviegoers were women—a number that is significantly higher than other Marvel films (Adewunmi 2014).

While it is clear that *Guardians of the Galaxy* (2014) embraces a conservative politics around foreign policy, and has problems associated with the ways it uses gender, a thorough deconstruction of the film also shows that it has a complicated relationship with masculinity and animality as well.

"RACCOON? WHAT'S A RACCOON?" ROCKET RACCOON, QUEERNESS AND TOXIC MASCULINITY

The character Rocket Raccoon is a victim of years of horrific medical and scientific experiments. These experiments turned him from a normal earth raccoon into a super soldier and bounty hunter. While being processed for prison, Corpsman Day describes Rocket for the audience saying: "Subject 89P13 calls itself rocket. The result of illegal genetic and cybernetic experiments on a lower life form." The cybernetics provided Rocket with super intelligence, making him an expert scientist and tactician. It also gave him the ability to speak, learn, and train his skills. In the years of training Rocket has turned himself into a living weapon—he is a skilled marksman, martial artist, and an accomplished pilot. While the references to animal experimentation are few in the film, mostly used to engender sympathy for the character, it is unsurprising that the film ignores the moral and ethical dimensions of the practice. Vivisection, the practice of conducting medical and scientific experiments on living animals, has been under criticism from activists and scholars for decades—as the practice is scientifically questionable and ethically dubious. The process, which uses living, sentient, beings as objects to be broken apart and dissected for human usage goes against any ethical concern allowing beings to live free from torture and death and the usage of nonhumans for the benefit of humans has been criticized for its anthropocentrism—or human-centered—utilitarian value (Perlo 2007). While animal testing is often associated with pharmaceutics and cosmetics, animal testing is regularly used in the field of "cybernetics." One of the most well-known cybernetic vivisectors, Nikos Logothetis, under activist pressure, recently started using rats in place of the primates he was using for his studies on neural networks (Vogel 2015).

Overall, the use of vivisection as the basis of Rocket's unique abilities does two things. First, it hides the real violence of vivisection that exists. Every year over 100 million animals are ripped open and killed in the name of scientific progress and human advancement (PETA 2017). Rocket is a stand-in for their experiences, but his survival makes it seem that nonhumans have the potential to survive the process of medical experimentation. Secondly, Rocket is depicted as a success for vivisection because it was only through his experimentation that he gained human traits—from the ability to speak, to build complex machinery, and develop military strategy. Of course, Raccoons are, already, sentient and intelligent beings but the audience is brought to believe that Rocket's uniqueness only occurred due to the success of medial experimentation on him. The film seems to argue that while it is sad what he experienced, without the torture he endured he would not be the superhero he is today. By centering human intelligence as the marker, Rocket follows others anthropomorphized nonhumans in films and actively discounts the already-existing intelligence of nonhuman animal. The linking of intelligence to his ability to use weapons and engage in military strategy works to naturalize the worst of human social behavior—war and violence—marking it a product of human intelligence rather than a result of human political and social structures (Parson 2016).

The process of vivisection is also used in the film to blur the boundaries in which Rocket exists—queering the character. Feminism, queer theory, decolonial thought and many other theoretical approaches have, since the post-structural turn in the late 1960s, provided powerful critiques of the dominant dualistic thinking of western society (Merchant 1989; Butler 2006; Byrd 2011). According to Val Plumwood the structure of binary thinking is central to the western world's assault on the natural world (2003). She argues that the nature/artificial dualism—which to her links to and is connected to male/female dualism—has been one of the primary means through which western philosophy has forced a separation between humans and the natural world. This separation has allowed a legitimization of violence and barbarity toward the world and the nonhumans who inhabit the world with us. She writes that "the connection of the dualisms with the perspective of the master appears plainly in many ancient sources which make clear the role of domination in shaping the relationship between 'superior' and 'inferior' sides in instrumental terms" (Plumwood 2003). In this account, the dualism of western society is rooted in structures of inequality and hierarchy. As such, in the nature/human divide that emerges within the west, nature is denigrate and humanity is elevated. When a figure, group, or symbol threatens this dualism it also threatens the entire structure that the dualism is built upon. This is why Greeta Gaard noted that European colonizers feared the supposed queerness of the native people as a threat to their own heterosexist order (1997). They saw effeminate men, sexual openness, and overall queer action and, instead of questioning their own rigid social categories, used their fear of native genders and sexualities as an excuse for colonial and genocidal violence.

In her widely read and influential article "A Cyborg Manifesto" Donna Haraway explores the complex ways in which gender, sexuality, technology, and capitalism intersect (2013). In her analysis modern technological production requires a rethinking of cultural binaries and a shift in, especially, feminist and Marxist politics. She writes that "by the late twentieth century, our time, a mythic time, we are all chimeras, theorized and fabricated hybrids of machine and organism; in short, we are cyborgs" (Haraway 2013). At its core the cyborg manifesto served as an argument for expanding and complicating the socialist feminist discussions around technology, nature, and labor. Developing a more complex theory of interconnectedness allows Haraway, and other cyborg feminists, to engage in a complex assemblage theory—before such theories were as popular as they are today. For instance, most of us are linked together into a complex and long web of interconnected technological relationships that break down the binary of natural/artificial (Bogost 2012). As Tristan Harris, a former Google employee has argued, our smart phones are designed to be addictive, using research in psychology, neural pathways, and genetics to make us more connected to our phones, all in order to maximize profits (Bosker 2016). Simply put, the goal of cyborg theories is to show the extreme complexity that exists within current technological life and the ways in which this complexity breaks down and shatters conventionally and culturally held social categories.

For many cyborg theorists, like Haraway, the scope of the complexity means that the overly critical stance against technology promoted by radical environmentalist and animal rights activists is wrong. In *When Species Meet* Haraway argues that there is a much more complex ethical and moral relationship between the scientist and the nonhuman animals that are experimented on (2008). In what she calls "Sharing suffering" she looks to develop an animal-testing process that allows for care, compassion, and shared emotional vulnerability (Haraway 2008, 86–93). In her analysis she argues for an ethics of complexity, "I think feminism outside the logic of sacrifice has to figure out how to honor the entangled labor of humans and animals together in science and in many other domains" (Haraway 2008, 80). Her argument is that we need to complicate our understanding of vivisection and focus not on violence and torture but around the labor and care that both humans and nonhumans provide. Her analysis, and the danger of cyborg theory in general even beyond Haraway's conceptions of it, is that complexity replaces politics and allows for dynamics of power to be erased, or complicated to the point of erasure. The result is that a system of extreme suffering and exploitation is maintained because of the nonhuman bodies that are used as metaphorical stand-ins. Her unwillingness to incorporate and explore political and power dimension around nonhuman animals and technology provides insight into her failure to understand that there would be cultural fear around boundary crossing.

Rocket stands within the liminal space of many-contested dualisms throughout the film. Early on Rocket's cyborgness is made central to his character. After being introduced to the audience, Rocket's scarred up and technologically infused back is shown to the audience as he cowers, soaking wet and naked, after being cleaned before accessing the prison. In this scene the scars are a reminder to the audience that Rocket is not fully natural (or as natural as a talking fighting CGI raccoon could ever be). Rocket Raccoon as the cyborg in the crew is also the most technologically sophisticated, as he is the go-to character to deal with technological problems—from his complex scheme to escape the prison to his construction of new weapons. His gift with technology and engineering is because he is a cyborg.

In addition to blurring the line between natural and artificial Rocket queers the boundaries between human and nonhuman. In the history of comics and animation there have been a large number of anthropomorphized animal characters—from Bugs Bunny to the Teenage Mutant Ninja Turtles—and audiences are willing to accept talking and human-like nonhuman characters. While audiences often root for the nonhuman anthropomorphized animal in film, comics, and animation it is clear that these characters blur socially constructed boundaries in much the same way as cyborgs do. For this reason, issues of sexuality is regularly ignored for both cyborg and nonhuman characters and when that is not the case the characters' sexuality often becomes an object of fear, like we see in the film *Ex-Machina* (2014). Or it can be seen as a source of confusion for the other characters in the film. Think of the scene in *Wayne's World* (1992) when Garth asks Wayne: "Did you ever find Bugs Bunny attractive when he put on a dress and played a girl bunny?" The scene, which after a few seconds of awkward silence responds with both of them nervously saying "no." As Amber George argues, comics and cartoons anthropomorphize characters to make it easier for audiences to connect with and empathize with them, and as such the reality of the nonhuman animal is distorted for the benefit of comforting human concerns—often with detrimental effects (2016). Similarly, the critic and audience panned film *Howard The Duck* (1986), which Rottentomatoes.com included in its list of films that pushed the boundaries on sexuality, for the sexual tension that existed between the two main characters, Howard the Duck and a human named Beverly (2017). At the same time, there is definitely a sexual appeal, for some, to anthropomorphized nonhuman animals, as shown by the fury fetish community, but also by sexualization of some female cartoon animals, such as Lola in *Space Jam* (1996). There is also a well-known trope that links animality, race, and sexuality within the comic book narrative—as characters like Vixen, and Catwoman are linked to animal sexuality (Brown 2013). This is largely because the blurring of boundaries between human and nonhuman, like that between natural and artificial, queer the character. In western society queer females are sexualized, and treated as objects for the male gaze, while queer males are a threat to hetero-patriarchy.

Carmon Dell'Aversano argues that in western society those that express or show love and compassion for nonhuman animals are often feminized and queered in a way to undermine their claims for political change (2010). This is similar to the ways in which the linking of women to nature was used as a means to demonize and undermine both feminist and environmental struggles. Dell'Aversano states that

> human love for animals is ridiculed, marginalized, despised and repressed with a violence that easily escalates to murder even more than same-sex love between humans in the most homophobic societies. Modes of political consciousness which question the legitimacy of the routine and murderous oppression of other species by our own are delegitimized as political positions and denied hearing in the political arena. (Dell'Aversano 2010)

The queering of the animal lover, is a common trope in film and broader politics more generally—as can be seen about jokes on tofu as being "unmasculine" while meat is often sexualized as masculine (Adams 2015).

In *Guardians of the Galaxy* (2014) the two non-humanoid characters— Rocket Raccoon and Groot—are both desexualized. Peter Quill and Gamora are clearly sexualized and Draxx's primary motivation is to revenge his murdered wife and children. The above analysis argues that should this be the case, as a queer figure, Rocket's sexuality would be uncomforting as a male anthropomorphized figure. As such there are few, if any moments in which anything even closely resembling sexuality or an emotional relationship emerges for Rocket. When they do occur, they could be read as being related to other concerns—and therefore not sexual. But, these brief moments can also be read as Freudian slips in which the queer nature of the character—for just a second—is revealed to the audience. In the film, the Freudian innuendos occur during Rocket's time in prison—a cultural space that is coded as both hyper-masculine and queer. Most notably, while in prison a large alien sexually harasses Peter Quill, by making a fleeting reference to rape, before Groot intervenes to protect him. While the large sexual predator lies on the ground Rocket, in a loud booming voice says to the prison "Let's get something clear! This one here [Peter Quill] is our booty. You wanna get to him, you go through us ... or, more accurately, we go through you!" While the phrase booty can be understood as an expression of the fact that, as bounty hunters, they are claiming their prize, in the context of a prison sex dynamic the booty has a more sexual connotation. In another homoerotic prison scene, Rocket, Peter Quill, and the other men in the prison have created a "cuddle pile" in which all the men are sleeping and holding one another. While these are only two minor moments, this is to be expected, because Rocket's sexuality is cloaked by toxic masculinity.

According to salon writer Amanda Marcotte, toxic masculinity "is a specific model of manhood, geared towards dominance and control. It's a manhood that views women and LGBT people as inferior, sees sex as an act not of affection but domination, and which valorizes violence as the way to prove one's self to the world" (2016). This understanding of masculinity is deeply tied to psychological concerns and fears. What is increasingly being accepted is that practices such as toxic masculinity have emerged as an overcompensation for threats some men feel to gender, sexual, and racial erosions of straight white male system of privilege in the United States and Europe. In a recent psychological study, researchers found that the willingness of male participants to find gay and women jokes funny was directly linked to how much they perceive their masculinity as threatened (O'Connor, Ford, and Banos 2017). Likewise many studies have found that that homophobes tend to have higher rates of latent and closeted homosexual behavior (Bryner 2012). When psychologists think of toxic masculinity, they are describing defense mechanisms used to protect a specific hyper-masculine value of the self from internal and external threats—be it latent homosexual feelings or fear that their social position, as straight men, is being threatened by women and queer rights.

Wendy Brown in *Walled States, Wanning Sovereignty* provides one of the most comprehensive and clear overviews of the Freudian concept of "theory of defense" (2014). The concept emerged from Sigmund Freud's "The Neuro-Pscyhosis of Defense" (2001). It was later expanded upon by Anna Freud's *Ego and the Mechanism of Defense* which concerns the psychological ways in which individuals put up mental protections against unwanted, or confusing, sexual desires and impulses (1993). Brown, in explaining how this process works writes, "So Freud identifies two possibilities for the ego's response to unacceptable desires. There is either complete conversion to another idea (defense), which, while producing periodic hysterical outbursts, wholly suppresses the original anxiety, or there is conversation of the unacceptable desire's energy into an obsession of phobia" (W. Brown 2014). In effect, Sigmund and Anna Freud both argue that when someone with a fragile ego has their sense of self confronted via something that forces them to question themselves, like homosexuality, the person will respond through psychological defense mechanisms. Most commonly the individual will either repress their internal desire and act out violently or they will aggressively react to the source of the anxiety and turn their internal desire into a phobia—homophobia, for instance. In both cases, the expressed phobia or aversion is an attempt to defend from a perceived threat in a way that reifies their "masculinity" via violence, political hatred, vile jokes, or the like.

Rocket Raccoon, as a queered subject, can be analyzed as using forms of toxic masculinity to protect himself, and the audience, from having to accept his queerness. Rocket commonly turns to jokes that mock people—women, older men, and the disabled—which serves as a means to deflect from his own perceived shortcomings. This creates the impression that Rocket is emotionally distant and tough, while in reality this toughness is a form of psychic defense meant to protect the fragile ego of the character. From the beginning, the character expresses toxic masculine traits, as with our first introduction to Rocket, where he and Groot are scanning the people in Xandar looking for a bounty to collect. He says, spying on a small child walking with his parents, "Look at this thing. It thinks it's so cool. It's not cool to ask for help! Walk by yourself, you little gargoyle!" before moving his attention to a metrosexual looking man. "Can you believe they call us criminals when he's assaulting us with that haircut?" Finally he witnesses an old man, played by famous comic creator Stan Lee, hitting on a younger woman, where he says, "Where's your wife, you old codger?" In all three instances, Rocket mocks people that he feels superior to: children, queer men, and old people—people who are socially cast as weak.

This type of mocking of marginalized figures continues, as when explaining his plan to escape rocket says:

ROCKET RACCOON: If we're gonna get outta here, we gonna need to get into that watch tower, and to do that, I'm gonna need a few things. The guards wear security bands to control their ins and outs. I need one … . That dude there. I need his prosthetic leg.
STARLORD: His leg?
ROCKET RACCOON: Yeah. God knows I don't need the rest of him. Look at him. He's useless.

After the plan is executed we learn that Rocket never needed the leg. He "was just kidding about the leg. I just need these two things. ... No, I thought it'd be funny! Was it funny? No, wait, what'd he look like hopping around?" The basis of the joke, which is repeated, again in the original and the sequel shows Rocket mocking and laughing at disabilities. This form of mocking is an example of toxic masculinities attempt to defend against his own shortcoming by mocking the physical appearance and supposed weakness of those society tells us are inferior. The claim, "God knows I don't need the rest of him. Look at him. He's useless," maintains a commonly used ablest joke that those with disabilities are monstrous and useless. Sunaura Taylor in *Beasts of Burden* explores the ways in which overlapping analytical frames constrain and define both the differently abled and nonhuman animals as dependent (2017). In the case of nonhuman animals, they are depicted as dependent on humans for survival—even though they are actually being the exploited, murdered, and used by humans—while the disabled are culturally perceived as burdens, or dependent on others (Taylor 2017). In addition, during the prison escape plan Rocket also makes fun of Gamora. He says, after being asked how they are going to get all the items they need to escape:

ROCKET RACCOON: Well, supposedly, these bald bodies find you attractive, so maybe you could work out some sort of trade.
GAMORA: You must be joking.
ROCKET RACCOON: No, I really heard they find you attractive.

Again, similar to the joke mocking the disabled, here Rocket denigrates Gamora by debasing her appearance while also objectifying her as an object to be exchange for what he needs. It also reminds her of her place within the patriarchal order and establishes himself as her superior within this system. Overall, Rocket's comedic styles can be described as punching down, a process in which those with social power use their power to tear down those who are marginalized instead of focusing that energy on undermining oppressive structures (Koul 2016).

Beyond mocking the marginalized figures, Rocket regularly engages in statements and actions that are meant to show that he lacks basic empathy and concern for those around him, while secretly caring about them. The practice of refusing to show vulnerability is part of the process of toxic masculinity and is a form of defense mechanism designed to protect the ego from emotional closeness with others. There are a handful of scenes in which Rocket is aggressively hostile to attempts by others to bring him close, most notably after Ronan defeats the Guardians on planet Knowhere. In a short back and forth with Draxx, whose actions almost got everyone on the team killed and allowed Ronin to get the infinity stone, Rocket says, "Aww, boo-hoo.

My wife and child are dead. I don't care if it's mean. Everybody's got dead people! But it makes no excuse to letting everyone else around get killed along the way!" In addition, after Peter Quill provides his, suicidal plan to stop Ronin, Rocket is the last in the group to stand up to offer his support. In standing up, he shrugs and says "Aww, what the hell, I don't got that long a lifespan anyway," and then looking around, to break the tension of vulnerability and connection at the moment says, "Well now I'm standing. Happy? We're all standing now. Bunch of jackasses, standing in a circle."

These moments of emotional toughness are another aspect of toxic masculinity because it provides ways for Rocket to avoid being close with anyone. It allows him to maintain a sense of separation from others and a sense of toughness that is often prized by contemporary masculinity. But of course this is an attempt used to cover actual emotional vulnerability and distract from the queer nature of the character. One of the few moments of vulnerability occurs when Rocket Raccoon, while drunk:

ROCKET RACCOON: Well, I didn't ask to get made! I didn't ask to be torn apart and put back together over and over and turned into some little monster!
PETER QUILL: Rocket, no one's calling you a monster ...
ROCKET RACCOON: He called me vermin! She called me rodent! Let's see if you can laugh after five or six good shots in your freakin' face!

In this scene, he drunkenly, expresses his anger and frustration about his own existence but also about the mean and aggressive things people say about him. While normally he would diffuse this anxiety with a joke or an insult, in this moment his defenses are weaker and he expressed the actual pain he feels.

The most emotionally charged relationship in the film is between Rocket and Groot. The two have a close relationship, an intimate bond in which the two of them show genuine love and care for each other. Toward the end of the film, after their plan to stop Ronan fails and the Guardians are crashing, most likely to their death, Groot extends the plant material of his body and covers the entire crew, becoming a wooden humanoid shield. In this moment, Rocket realizes that Groot is planning on sacrificing himself for the rest of the crew and cries: "No, Groot! You'll die! Why are you doing this? Why?" Groot replies, "WE ARE GROOT," for the first time saying something other than "I AM GROOT." After this crash the camera pans to Rocket, crying on the ground grasping and holding the left over twigs of his former best friend.

Rocket's vulnerability and emotional defense mechanisms opens up a space to theorize a more open and engaging form of queer theorizing. Following J. Halberstam, who in the *Queer Art of Failure*, offers a critique of the purity and perfection often demanded queer subjects and argues instead for a more nuanced queer politics that openly embraces failure as a queer political act (2011). Looking to film, television, art, and music Halberstam argues that failure has value, even beyond what we learn from failing, and works to undermine the linear logic of neoliberal political subjectivity. They write:

> discover our inner dweeb, to be underachievers, to fall short, to get distracted, to take a detour, to find a limit, to lose our way, to forget, to avoid mastery, and, with Walter Benjamin, to recognize that "empathy with the victor invariably benefits the rulers" (Benjamin, 1969: 256). All losers are the heirs of those who lost before them. Failure loves company. (Halberstam 2011, 121)

Learning to fail not only means creating space to learn and grow, it also means a non-judgmental acceptance of others as they are. Becoinge who you really are, means embracing failure, and that might even apply to the failure in figuring out who you actually are.

In the case of Rocket, thus means understanding his character as going through a difficult process of coming to terms with his own sexuality and social position. While not discounting the sexist and ableist aspects of his character, it is important to understand the source of this anger and frustration, and to contextualize his actions within this large psychic space. Rocket is a monstrous figure—a cyborg and a queer body—that is afraid of more than his own shadow. Toxic masculinity is his mask, is part of his larger attempt to reject and hide his monstrous qualities from himself and the world around him. Rocket is taught to hate and fear himself, but in reality, his freedom and liberation exists in the acceptance of who he is: a queer, cyborg, monster.

CONCLUSION

A cultural studies analysis of film offers critical theorists a unique lens and space to engage with the anxieties, fears, and desires of contemporary society. In our culture, it has increasingly over time, become unacceptable to be an overt bigot. But this does not mean that bigotry, hatred, and racial bias do not exist. It clearly does. Instead of looking to public opinion, focus groups, or policy analysis, cultural studies attempts to decode the symbolic and psychological meaning of our societies' cultural products. Films create drama and tension by linking into widely accepted fears, anxieties, or desires and as such, decoding the meaning of these films help us delve into the collective unconscious of contemporary American society.

A critical reading and decoding of Rocket Raccoon helps to explore the collective cultural values around masculinity and our hetero-patriarchal fears around queering the species and technological boundaries. Rocket represents a form of American masculinity that perceives itself as threatened and it responds by creating defense mechanisms to protect itself from both outside fears and internal anxieties. He is, following Halberstam, a queer monster in disguise. He mocks those marginalized by society, distances himself emotionally from all around him, and he is unwilling to be openly vulnerable, except when drunk and his mask falls off.

As radical scholars committed to total liberation—the liberation of human, nonhuman, and the earth's ecosystems collectively—it is essential that we engage with cultural productions to understand the ideological apparatus currently in place. An understanding of current narratives around masculinity are essential for anyone interested in dismantling the dominant social institutions and reconstruct the world around egalitarian and nonviolent values. New narratives of masculinity need to be written, narratives that accept the fluidity of species, sexuality, and the like and that reveals and enjoys the queer space of contemporary life.

WORKS CITED

Adams, Carol J. 2015. *The Sexual Politics of Meat: A Feminist-Vegetarian Critical Theory.* Bloomsbury revelations edition. Bloomsbury Revelations Series. New York: Bloomsbury Academic, An imprint of Bloomsbury Publishing Inc.

Adewunmi, Bim. 2014. "Why Do Women Love Guardians of the Galaxy? | Film | The Guardian." August 15. https://www.theguardian.com/film/shortcuts/2014/aug/05/women-love-guardians-galaxy-marvel-half-audience

Alaniz, José. 2014. *Death, Disability, and the Superhero: The Silver Age and beyond.* Jackson: University Press of Mississippi.

Baker-Whitelaw, Gavia. 2014. "'Guardians of the Galaxy' Passes the Bechdel Test—but It Fails Women | The Daily Dot." August 4. https://www.dailydot.com/via/guardians-of-the-galaxy-fails-women/

Barker, Martin. 1989. *Comics: Ideology, Power, and the Critics.* Cultural Politics. Manchester [England] ; New York : Manchester University Press ; Distributed in the USA and Canada by St. Martin's Press.

Bogost, Ian. 2012. *Alien Phenomenology, Or, What It's like to Be a Thing.* Posthumanities 20. Minneapolis: University of Minnesota Press.

Bosker, Bianca. 2016. "Addicted to Your iPhone? You're Not Alone—The Atlantic." https://www.theatlantic.com/magazine/archive/2016/11/the-binge-breaker/501122/

Box Office Mojo. 2017. "Guardians of the Galaxy Vol. 2." http://www.boxofficemojo.com/movies/?id=marvel17a.htm

Brown, Jeffery A. 2013. "Panthers and Vixens: Black Superheroes, Sexuality, and Stereotypes in Contemporary Comic Books." In *Black Comics: Politics of Race and Representation,* edited by Sheena C. Howard and Ronald L. Jackson. London ; New York: Bloomsbury Academic, an imprint of Bloomsbury Publishing Plc.

Brown, Wendy. 2014. *Walled States, Waning Sovereignty*. First Paperback Edition. New York: Zone Books.

Bryner, Jeane. 2012. "Homophobes Might Be Hidden Homosexuals—Scientific American." April 10. https://www.scientificamerican.com/article/homophobes-might-be-hidden-homosexuals/

Butler, Judith. 2006. *Gender Trouble: Feminism and the Subversion of Identity*. Routledge Classics. New York: Routledge.

Byrd, Jodi A. 2011. *The Transit of Empire: Indigenous Critiques of Colonialism*. First Peoples : New Directions Indigenous. Minneapolis: University of Minnesota Press.

Cocca, Carolyn. 2016. *Superwomen: Gender, Power, and Representation*. New York: Bloomsbury Academic, an imprint of Bloomsbury Publishing Inc.

Comicbookmovies.com. 2014. "Lee Pace Says 'Ronan the Accuser' Is Less Relatable, More Evil In GUARDIANS OF THE GALAXY." Comicbookmovie.com. https://www.comicbookmovie.com/guardians_of_the_galaxy/lee-pace-says-ronan-the-accuser-is-less-relatable-more-evil-in-guardians-of-the-galaxy-a101428

Costello, Matthew J. 2009. *Secret Identity Crisis: Comic Books and the Unmasking of Cold War America*. New York: Continuum.

Deis, Chris. 2013. "The Subjective Politics of the Supervillain." In *What Is a Superhero?*, edited by Robin S. Rosenberg and Peter M. Coogan, 95–100. New York: Oxford University Press.

Dell'Aversano. 2010. "The Love Whose Name Cannot Be Spoken: Queering the Human-Animal Bond." *Journal of Critical Animal Studies* 8 (2): 73–125.

Dittmer, Jason. 2013. *Captain America and the Nationalist Superhero: Metaphors, Narratives, and Geopolitics*. Philadelphia: Temple University Press.

"Experiments on Animals." 2017. *PETA*. Accessed July 3. https://www.peta.org/issues/animals-used-for-experimentation/animals-used-experimentation-factsheets/animal-experiments-overview/

Fawaz, Ramzi. 2016. *The New Mutants: Superheroes and the Radical Imagination of American Comics*. Postmillennial Pop. New York ; London: New York University Press.

Freud, Anna. 1993. *The Ego and the Mechanisms of Defence*. London: Karnac Books. http://karnacbooks.igpublish.com/Book.nsp?cid_BOOKCODE=DEMOKARNACB0000299&cid_BOOKPAGE=1

Freud, Sigmund, James Strachey, and Sigmund Freud. 2001. *Early Psycho-Analytic Publications: (1893–1899)*. The Standard Edition of the Complete Psychological Works of Sigmund Freud, transl. from the German under the general editorship of James Strachey ; Vol. 3. London: Vintage.

George, Amber E. 2016. "Would Bugs Bunny Have Diabetes?: The Realistic Consequences of Cartoons for Non/Human Animals." In *Screening the Nonhuman: Representations of Animal Others in the Media*, edited by Amber E. George and J. L. Schatz. Critical Animal Studies and Theory. Lanham, Maryland: Lexington Books.

Gittell, Noah. 2014. "The Conservative Politics of 'Guardians of the Galaxy.'" *Reel Change*. August 6. https://reelchange.net/2014/08/06/the-conservative-politics-of-guardians-of-the-galaxy/

Halberstam, Judith. 2011. *The Queer Art of Failure*. Durham: Duke University Press.

Hall, Stuart. 2007. "Encoding, Decoding." In *The Cultural Studies Reader*, edited by Simon During, 3. ed, 90–103. London: Routledge.

Haraway, Donna. 2013. *Simians, Cyborgs, and Women: The Reinvention of Nature.* https://nls.ldls.org.uk/welcome.html?ark:/81055/vdc_100025667684.0x000001

Haraway, Donna Jeanne. 2008. *When Species Meet*. Posthumanities 3. Minneapolis: University of Minnesota Press.

Holt, Mythos. 2014. "'Guardians Of The Galaxy' Is Weirdly Analogous to Gaza." *Thedailycaller.com.* http://dailycaller.com/2014/08/07/guardians-of-the-galaxy-is-weirdly-analogous-to-gaza/

Jameson, Fredric. 1994. *The Political Unconscious: Narrative as a Socially Symbolic Act*. 7. print. Ithaca, NY: Cornell Univ. Press.

———. 2007. *Archaeologies of the Future: The Desire Called Utopia and Other Science Fictions*. London: Verso.

Koul, Scaachi. 2016. "Why Punching Down Will Never Be Funny." *Buzzfeed. com.* https://www.buzzfeed.com/scaachikoul/why-punching-down-will-never-be-funny?utm_term=.rspylqBYg#.lfKqd9LAV

Marcotte, Amanda. 2016. "Overcompensation Nation: It's Time to Admit That Toxic Masculinity Drives Gun Violence—Salon.com." *Salon.com.* http://www.salon.com/2016/06/13/overcompensation_nation_its_time_to_admit_that_toxic_masculinity_drives_gun_violence/

Merchant, Carolyn. 1989. *The Death of Nature: Women, Ecology, and the Scientific Revolution*. New York: Harper & Row.

Nama, Adilifu. 2011. *Super Black: American Pop Culture and Black Superheroes*. 1st ed. Austin: University of Texas Press.

O'Connor, Emma C., Thomas E. Ford, and Noely C. Banos. 2017. "Restoring Threatened Masculinity: The Appeal of Sexist and Anti-Gay Humor." *Sex Roles*, April. doi:10.1007/s11199–017–0761-z.

Parson, Sean. 2016. "Ape Anxiety: Intelligence, Human Supremacy, and Dawn and Rise of the Planet of the Apes." In *Screening the Nonhuman: Representations of Animal Others in the Media*, edited by Amber E. George and J. L. Schatz, 91–100. Critical Animal Studies and Theory. Lanham, Maryland: Lexington Books.

Perlo, Katherine. 2007. "Should Anti-Vivisectionists Boycott Animal-Tested Medicines?" *Journal of Critical Animal Studies* VOLUME 5, (ISSUE).

Plumwood, Val. 2003. *Feminism and the Mastery of Nature*. Reprinted 1997. Transferred to digital print 2003. Feminism for Today. London: Routledge.

Rogin, Michael Paul. 1988. *Ronald Reagan, the Movie: And Other Episodes in Political Demonology*. 1. paperback printing. Berkeley, CL: Univ. of California Press.

Ross, Julianne. 2014. "'Guardians of the Galaxy' Finally Gives Us the Female Hero We Deserve." August 1. https://mic.com/articles/95430/guardians-of-the-galaxy-finally-gives-us-the-female-hero-we-deserve#.HR1cau2Qy

Rotten Tomatoes. 2014. "Guardians of the Galaxy." https://www.rottentomatoes.com/m/guardians_of_the_galaxy/

———. 2015. "15 Boundary-Pushing Movies That Broke Sexual Taboos." https://editorial.rottentomatoes.com/article/15-boundary-pushing-movies-that-broke-sexual-taboos/

————. 2017. "Guardians of the Galaxy Vol. 2." https://www.rottentomatoes.com/m/guardians_of_the_galaxy_vol_2/

Shaw-Williams, Hannah. 2012. "James Gunn's Tasteless History Resurfaces As He Preps To Write And Direct Guardians Of The Galaxy—Bleeding Cool News And Rumors." November 29. https://www.bleedingcool.com/2012/11/29/james-gunn-prepares-fao/

Stevens, J. Richard. 2015. *Captain America, Masculinity, and Violence: The Evolution of a National Icon*. First Edition. Television and Popular Culture. Syracuse, New York: Syracuse University Press.

Taylor, Sunaura. 2017. *Beasts of Burden: Animal and Disability Liberation*. New York: New Press.

Vogel, Gretchen. 2015. "Embattled Max Planck Neuroscientist Quits Primate Research." *Sciencemag.org*. http://www.sciencemag.org/news/2015/05/embattled-max-planck-neuroscientist-quits-primate-research

Index

About the Contributors

José Alaniz is an associate professor in the Department of Slavic Languages and Literatures and the Department of Comparative Literature at the University of Washington, Seattle. He has published two books, *Komiks: Comic Art in Russia* and *Death, Disability and the Superhero: The Silver Age and Beyond*. His articles have appeared in the *International Journal of Comic Art, The Comics Journal, Ulbandus, Studies in Russian and Soviet Cinema, The Slavic and East European Journal, Comics Forum* and *Kinokultura*. He has written chapters in the anthologies *Disability in Comic Books and Graphic Narratives, The Ages of The Avengers: Essays on the Earth's Mightiest Heroes in Changing Times* and *Russian Children's Literature and Culture*. Since 2011 he has served as chair of the Executive Committee of the International Comic Arts Forum (ICAF). In 2014 he assumed the directorship of the University of Washington's Disability Studies Program.

Karin Anderson is a professor of english and literature at Utah Valley University, in Orem, Utah, where she has served as department chair and head of creative writing. She holds a PhD in creative writing and literary theory from the University of Utah. She has published in *American Literary Review, Saranac Review, Western Humanities Review, Quarter After Eight, Fiddleblack, Sunstone, Dialogue,* and other venues. Her academic and creative work focus on depictions of family, genders, and materiality and landscape, particularly in relation to the Great Basin. Her fictionalized memoir, *breach,* published by Fiddleblack, depicts some inherent paradoxes of heterosexual marital relations within contemporary Mormon "family values" in the seat of the religion's defining geography. Her current research turns toward localized Native American—Anglo relations in nineteenth-century Utah and Idaho; female impersonation, queerness, occultism, and suicidality in the historic rural west; and legacies of bituminous coal mining in arid central Utah. She is a long-term fan of *Buffy the Vampire Slayer* and *Angel*, as are her offspring.

Matheus da Cruz e Zica is a professor in the sciences of religions department at the Federal University of Paraíba (Brazil) where he has been a faculty member since 2012. He is his department's associate chair for supervised internship and also the coordinator of the master's program in sciences of religions at that institution. In addition, he collaborates in the master's program in history of the Federal University of Campina Grande (Brazil). He completed his PhD in education at Federal University of Minas Gerais and his undergraduate studies in history at the same university. His research interests lie in the areas of cultural studies and history of education. Furthermore, he researched the problem of slaves' non-formal process of education in Brazilian nineteenth century, during his post-doctoral residence. In recent years, he has focused on analyzing the role of spirituality in the process of teaching/learning East Asian martial arts in Brazil.

Allison Dushane received her PhD in English from Duke University in 2008 and is currently an assistant professor in the Department of English and Modern Languages at Angelo State University. Her research and teaching interests include eighteenth- and nineteenth-century literature, aesthetic theory, science studies, and posthumanism. She has published articles on Erasmus Darwin, Samuel Taylor Coleridge, William Wordsworth, Jean-Jacques Rousseau, and the relevance of Romantic-era aesthetics to contemporary environmental concerns. She is coeditor, with Adam Komisaruk, of a scholarly edition of Erasmus Darwin's *The Botanic Garden* (Routledge 2017).

Matt Evans works as professor of political science at Northwest Arkansas Community College in Bentonville, AR. He received his PhD in political science from Northern Arizona University in 2015. As a political theorist, his research addresses power and agency in the following relations: embodiment and power, state violence and soldiers, popular media and state power, Israeli anti-militarism and social movements, animals and the military industrial complex, and green anarchism and feminism.

Chantelle Gray van Heerden is currently employed as a senior researcher at the Institute for Gender Studies at the University of South Africa (UNISA). Her research centres on the philosophical collaboration between Gilles Deleuze and Félix Guattari and she is one of the organizers of the Deleuze and Guattari Studies conferences in South Africa (http://deleuzeguattari. co.za/). Chantelle has been an avid supporter of animal liberation for many years and has presented on the subject at the local ICAS (Institute for Critical Animal Studies) conference. She is also a member of the editorial board of *Gender Questions*, a peer-reviewed research journal.

John Lupinacci is an assistant professor at Washington State University where he researches and teaches in the Cultural Studies and Social Thought in Education (CSSTE) program using an approach that advocates for the development of scholar-activist educators. Dr Lupinacci's research focuses on how people—specifically educators, educational leaders, and educational researchers—learn to both identify and examine destructive habits of Western industrial human culture and how those habits are taught and learned in schools. He is a co-author of *EcoJustice Education: Toward Diverse, Democratic, and Sustainable Communities* and his experiences as a K-12 classroom teacher, an outdoor environmental educator, and a community activist-artist-scholar all contribute to his research, teaching, and development of projects open to the possibilities of how people can learn to live together in diverse, democratic, and sustainable communities.

Jeffrey Pannekoek is currently working on his PhD in philosophy at the University of Tennessee, in Knoxville, TN. His areas of interest are embodied cognition, agency, philosophy of action (in particular free will), ethics, animal ethics, and popular culture. He has written on a broad range of animal ethics related issues, including the importance of empathy in animal ethics, animal cognition and embodiment, and animal activism in relation to terrorism. He is a fan of all things Joss Whedon, and interested in the philosophical implications of the Whedonverse. In 2014, he presented a paper at the *Life the Universe and Everything* conference entitled "Facing Our Demons: The Deconstruction of Self & Other in Joss Whedon's *Buffy the Vampire Slayer*." This essay analyzed the race and gender relation between Buffy and Sineya, the First Slayer. It also served as a starting point for the chapter in this volume.

Sean Parson is an assistant professor in the Departments of Politics and International Affairs and the master's program in sustainable communities at Northern Arizona University. In addition to co-editing this book, he is currently working on two more edited books that relate to issues of critical animal studies. His forthcoming book *Cooking up a revolution: Food Not Bombs, Homes Not Jails, and Resistance to Gentrification* should be released in early 2019. He is currently working on a book length project on horror, climate change, and nihilism. When not writing and grading he mostly spends times hiking the mountains with his four-legged best friend Diego.

Márcio dos Santos Rodrigues is a Brazilian comic book researcher graduated in history from the Federal University of Minas Gerais (2007), master's degree in history from the Federal University of Minas Gerais (2011). Researcher in the comic books and graphic novels as historical sources. He is currently developing a PhD thesis on the representation of the Amazonia in comic books from the 1970s to the present day. He is part of the postgraduate program in social history of the Federal University of Pará, in Brazil. He is the technical-scientific director of a collection of a Brazilian publisher, Prismas, and the objective of the collection *Estudos das Histórias em Quadrinhos* (Comic book Studies) is to publish theoretical studies on comics. In addition to the interest in the study of comics and graphic novels, he conducts research in the field of history teaching, political history, history of political ideas and environmental history. In the latter area, he has devoted his attention to socially constructed relations between men and nature in the comics and graphic novels and activism in defense of animal rights.

J. L. Schatz is the director of debate at Binghamton University where he serves as a lecturer and teaches courses on Media & Politics out of the English department. He has published book chapters on representations of apocalypse in the *Terminator* films, the construction of disability in the *Resident Evil* films, and ecological security in the TV show *Lost*. Dr Schatz has also published peer-reviewed journal articles on apocalypse and the environment as well as subjectivity in relation to teaching pedagogy in debate. Beyond his own publications he has co-edited a special issue for the *Journal of Critical Animal Studies*, a book titled *Screening the Nonhuman*, and has been in charge of organizing several conferences, including the thirteenth and fourteenth annual North America Institute for Critical Animal Studies and the first and second annual Eco-Ability Conference.

Kent Worcester is a professor of political science at Marymount Manhattan College. He is the author, editor, or coeditor of ten books, including *C.L.R. James: A Political Biography* (1996), *A Comics Studies Reader* (2008), and *The Superhero Reader* (2013). His latest book is *Silent Agitators: Cartoon Art From the Pages of New Politics* (2016).

CPSIA information can be obtained
at www.ICGtesting.com
Printed in the USA
BVOW08*0554021217
501697BV00001B/2/P

9 781498 549264